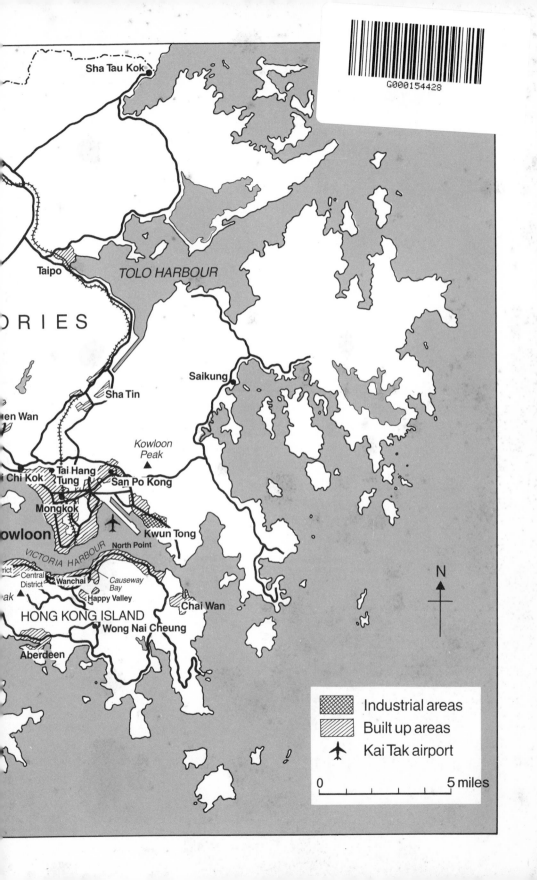

Sha Tau Kok

Taipo

TOLO HARBOUR

ᴓRIES

Saikung

Sha Tin

en Wan

Kowloon
Peak

Chi Kok   Tai Hang
Tung   San Po Kong

Mongkok

ᴓwloon   Kwun Tong

VICTORIA HARBOUR   North Point

rict
Central
District   Wanchai   Causeway
Bay   Chai Wan
ak   Happy Valley

HONG KONG ISLAND

Wong Nai Cheung

Aberdeen

N

Industrial areas

Built up areas

Kai Tak airport

0   5 miles

Mouldering Pearl .

MOULDERING PEARL

Hong Kong at the Crossroads

Felix Patrikeeff

GEORGE
PHILIP

The extracts from *Chinese Crackers* by
the Honourable Edward Ward,
published by John Lane The Bodley
Head in 1947, are included by kind
permission of David Higham Associates.

British Library Cataloguing in Publication Data

Patrikeeff, Felix
  Mouldering pearl: Hong Kong at the
  crossroads
  1. Hong Kong
  I. Title
  951'.2505

  ISBN 0-540-01188-6

© Felix Patrikeeff 1989
Map © George Philip Limited 1989
First published by George Philip Limited,
59 Grosvenor Street, London W1X 9DA.

Printed in Great Britain by Butler and Tanner,
Frome, Somerset

Contents

To the memory of Ezekiel Abraham

Preface

The fate of Hong Kong, Britain's last important colony, was formally sealed on 30 June 1985, when the Sino-British Joint Declaration officially came into force. The document states that the colony will revert to Chinese hands on 1 July 1997, when it will become a 'Hong Kong Special Administrative Region' of the Chinese People's Republic and, from that date, will use the name 'Hong Kong, China'. The Joint Declaration guarantees the people of Hong Kong that their social and economic systems will remain unchanged, as will their lifestyle, for fifty years beyond the handover date. During that time the Hong Kong SAR will remain a free port and a separate customs entity, will continue to allow the free flow of foreign exchange, and will have independent finances and its own system of taxation. The systems of law and government are to remain the same. The government is to be made up of Hong Kong people, with a chief executive (replacing the Governor) being appointed by Beijing 'on the basis of the results of elections or consultations to be held locally'. The maintenance of public order will be the responsibility of the SAR government. In place of the Letters Patent and Royal Instructions, which bind Hong Kong to the British Constitution, will be a Basic Law, which is to serve as the SAR's own constitution and link the territory with the constitutional framework of the People's Republic.

Three supplementary clauses are appended to the main declaration: one is an elaboration by the Chinese Government of its intentions towards Hong Kong, another outlines the creation of a Joint Liaison Group to oversee the transitional period, and a third deals with the question of land leases. Finally, tagged on to the end of the agreement are two memoranda stating Britain's and China's positions on the issue of nationality.

The enactment of this document should have been important, perhaps even momentous. Yet my most vivid memory of the years of uncertainty over Hong Kong's future has little to do with the agreement itself. As I sat down to breakfast one Sunday morning in late January 1984 I picked up a copy of the *Sunday Times*. On the front page was the stark headline: 'Thatcher hands Hong Kong to China'. After months of prevarication and, it seemed, hard bargaining, Britain had quietly, in mid December, relinquished both sovereignty and any intention of maintaining an administrative presence in Hong Kong after 1997. The news came as a profound shock. It was the end of a world as I had known it for 29 years. At that moment the formal agreement and any details of guarantees were unimportant.

Even though I had cut my connection with Hong Kong three years earlier and had come to regard Britain as home, that morning brought home to me how deep my roots in Hong Kong were. For the first time in my life I knew what it was to be a refugee. Distant, hazy memories of my parents' arrival in Hong Kong as refugees from China now seemed to be a dress rehearsal for this day. I was engulfed by a profound feeling of loneliness and of separation. Such was my parting with my past and with the shelter of the 'barren rock'.

The effect on the people of Hong Kong can be compared to what a loyalist in Belfast would feel if he were to awake to read that the British Government had unilaterally acceded to Unionist demands. Or the City to suddenly find that its handover to Soviet Russia was a *fait accompli*. Fanciful parallels? No more drastic, I think, than handing over five and a half million good, loyal capitalists to a Communist regime, no matter how benign it may seem at the moment. The majority of people in Hong Kong were either born into *laissez-faire* capitalism, or escaped to it. Is it realistic to consider that they will – or should – feel more open-minded than the Northern Irish Protestants or the financiers of the Square Mile to a 'bold experiment' which involves a merger with their virtual antitheses? As any serious student of socialist politics and economics will confirm: coexistence and cohabitation are not quite the same thing.

This book is a view from the inside of the processes leading to this merger, largely written by the people who wake each morning to find themselves a step closer to whatever awaits them on 1 July 1997. I would therefore like to offer my heartfelt thanks to my many friends and acquaintances in Hong Kong for their patience and willingness to share their thoughts with me. Whatever qualities this book has are largely due to them. Glaring errors of omission and commission are, however, attributable solely to the author. One set of omissions should be explained. Many of those who spoke to me agreed to do so on an informal basis or requested that their identities remain undisclosed. Rather than providing aliases or elaborately disguising my sources of information, I have chosen to refer to my respondents by their more general titles. I hope this will not detract from the reader's enjoyment of the book. A word of thanks should also go to the members of the Hong Kong Government Office in London and the Government Information Services in Hong Kong with whom I have had dealings over the past five years. Their frequent assistance, often at short notice, is much appreciated.

I can be more forthcoming about those who have helped me with the process of writing. Lydia Greeves bore my sometimes near-fatal optimism, and the resulting delays and erratic prose, with patience and greatly appreciated good humour. She and Jane Edmonds have done much to make the book as readable as it has become. Robert Skidelsky, with whom I spent long, enjoyable days in London and Cambridge reasoning out the Hong Kong situation for our series of articles in *The Times*, encouraged me to write this book. Harry and Barbara Shukman, too, have been most supportive of my work. In addition, they have read the manuscript, provided many useful suggestions and, most important of all, a greatly cherished friendship. Sue Johnson has been my most critical reader and a long-suffering source of love and inspiration. My greatest debt, however, is to my mother, Nina Patrikeeff, who arrived in Hong Kong with no English, no Cantonese, two American dollars in her purse and a child under her arm. With courage, wisdom and charm she single-handedly built up a new life for herself and for me. The following essay is really her story too.

Felix Patrikeeff
Oxfordshire, 1988

CHAPTER ONE

From Stepping-Stone to First World

Hong Kong covers an area of only 370 square miles – a little larger than the Orkney Islands – and an energetic explorer can survey all its nooks and crannies in a year. Apart from a few intrepid walkers, few do: most of the land mass is hilly and barren, as are the 235 small islands that dot Hong Kong waters so spectacularly.

Tiny though its area is, Hong Kong is a place of great physical contrasts, many of which are rooted in the territory's history as a British colony. The bulk of the population lives on about 80 square miles, or 10 per cent of the total area, largely confined within the boundaries laid down by Britain's first two treaties with China in 1842 and 1860, i.e. in the city of Victoria on Hong Kong Island and on the southern tip of Kowloon peninsula a mile across the harbour to the north. The area known as the New Territories – the surrounding islands (with the exception of Stonecutters' Island, which was included in the 1860 treaty) and the mainland to the north, leased to Britain for 99 years in 1898 – is much less densely settled.

Boundary Street marking the 1860 extent of Kowloon City runs parallel to a more obvious boundary: that of the Kowloon Hills. Together with the higher peaks overlooking Victoria on Hong Kong Island itself, this range shelters the heart of the colony and also acts as a spectacular backdrop to everyday life. The urban area lies in a natural cradle which both cocoons and confines it.

The city itself has undergone a process of almost constant and at times dramatic change since the colony was first founded. Roads

11

appear and disappear, buildings are continually being torn down to make way for some yet more modern construction. Indeed, the very coastline bulges to accommodate new structures. On the corridor of habitable land that runs along the harbour on Hong Kong Island, life seems to have been squeezed in with a shoehorn. A sea of rooftops, roof dwellings, washing lines and poles is broken by clusters of jagged, glittering skyscrapers. In the middle of this corridor, below the middle-class Mid-levels, is Central District. Bright new tower blocks are gradually edging out the tired, dirty concrete faces of the buildings of the fifties and sixties. Just occasionally there is a squat three- or four-storey relic of the thirties and forties, encrusted in grime. At Wanchai to the east the corridor widens into what is known as Happy Valley, site of the island's race course, some sports clubs and the older colonial cemeteries.

Everywhere there are contrasts between old and new, rich and poor. Tin, plywood and corrugated-iron huts cling like scabs to hillsides only a few hundred yards from multi-million dollar apartment buildings. Contrasts on the street are just as vivid. A street sleeper's plank and cardboard bedsit, its sparse contents lovingly set out to create travesties of a kitchen (a tray with pans, cutlery and bottles of soya sauce) and a bathroom (an enamel basin), will be set up within the green glow of a high-tech 7-Eleven, an all-night store offering the latest in American-style convenience.

A path round the peaks above Victoria leads to a vista of the southern side of the island, its crumpled contours concealing a thousand beaches and bays. One of the larger inlets shelters the ancient port of Aberdeen, known as Hong Kong before the coming of the British, when its name gradually came to refer to the entire colony. A tide of sea-going junks moves in and out of the small harbour, while sampans ferry tourists to floating restaurants.

Some of the most densely populated areas are not on Hong Kong Island but on the Kowloon peninsula across the harbour, fringing the grand artery known as Nathan Road which runs up the centre of the peninsula. To their south is a Chinese district, a warren of narrow backstreets and small shops. To their north a sharp turn right leads to an oasis of middle-class life, with streets named after British counties and cities: Cornwall Street and Somerset Road, York Road and Cambridge Road. High walls hide old two- and three-storey houses set in tranquil gardens, preserved from development by the need to maintain a corridor to Kai Tak airport to the east. Beyond the airport is the industrial concentration of Kwun Tong, mirrored by that of Tsuen Wan on the other side of Kowloon.

The hamlets and villages in remote parts of the mainland and on outlying islands are also little changed, many of them accessible only by slow-moving ferries that plough their way from one small concrete pier to another. Rough-walled houses with gloomy, dimly-lit interiors entered through wooden slatted gates rather than doors might have been plucked from photographs of the turn of the century or earlier if it were not for the ubiquitous television aerials fixed precariously to the tiled roofs. Life in these settlements revolves around small vegetable plots, chicken, duck and fish farms, and fruit growing. Villagers will rarely stray from their immediate locality or have experience of anything other than traditional lifestyles. Foreigners are still regarded with curiosity and visits to the city, only 15 miles away even in the most distant places, are regarded with great trepidation.

Only a decade ago, it was easy to draw the line dividing rural and urban Hong Kong: city life ended at the foot of the Kowloon Hills. Today the distinction is not so clear. Sleepy market towns in the New Territories have mushroomed into mini-cities, drawing in the human overflow from the urban heart of the colony. Multi-lane motorways have sliced across narrow winding country roads and the spread of quiet, high-speed electric trains has gradually trans-formed day-trip territory into commuter belt.

Other elements of traditional life are also in retreat. The boat people, whose floating homes were crowded together in harbour after harbour along the coast, have been encouraged to find their land legs. The traditional servants known as *amahs*, dressed in tunics and wide trousers and with their sleek black hair pulled back severely, are being replaced by Filipina maids. Illiterate coolies (labourers) in black baggy suits are also disappearing, their places taken by moderately educated younger people in jeans, 'T' shirts and track shoes. Rickshaws have been guided into planned obsoles-cence. The few remaining rickshawmen are allowed to continue to ply their trade until they retire or die, but no more licences will be issued.

The planned destruction of the Walled City, a tiny, congested area in Kowloon, will sever another link with the past. Originally an island of Chinese sovereignty within British Kowloon, it became the object of a long-running tug-of-war between Britain and China.

Today the wall has long since disappeared, and only an unusually high density of buildings marks the area of the city, packed with unregistered doctors, dentists, drug dealers, gambling dens and cabaret joints. In February 1987 the Hong Kong Government announced the Walled City would be demolished and replaced with a park.

The Mandarin Hotel, said to be among the ten best in the world, is a direct contrast to the squalor of the Walled City. A few minutes spent in quiet observation from one of the overstuffed leather armchairs liberally scattered about the lobby here will reveal one facet of Hong Kong's success story. Amongst the giant oxblood vases and the gilded temple carvings sits a middle-aged American speaking discreetly into a wireless telephone, barely disturbed by the soft murmur of conversation from the veranda-like Clipper Lounge above. Beside him is his Chinese secretary, scribbling information he passes on from his conversation into her file. Neither is a guest, but it does not seem to bother anyone that they should use the lobby as an office-on-the-hop. A few steps away an Australian, his business meetings completed, gathers his family for the day's sightseeing. They plan to 'do the mainland'. An Englishman rises from another of the armchairs to greet a Chinese man. After exchanging stiff pleasantries, they walk away discussing a business meeting they are about to attend (an increasingly rare occurrence with the shrinkage of the British commercial presence here). As they cross the polished marble floor to the glass doors leading out to Connaught Road, a doorman in an immaculate red uniform and starched white gloves opens the door of a hotel limousine in the narrow covered driveway a few steps below. A new set of guests emerges with their slim leather briefcases and Louis Vuitton bags. In the late afternoon, during the rush hour, a queue of tired, well-heeled workers from nearby office buildings converge on the hotel to avail themselves of the doorman's services in hailing a taxi. A two-dollar tip saves them an endless wait at the taxi rank a street away. The doorman skilfully shuttles between incoming and departing guests and the lucrative evening sideline. His manner oozes civility.

With a few adjustments, this scene is one that has long characterized Hong Kong. The Mandarin stands in Central District, the hub of the territory's business centre and birthplace of the city. Ice House Street, a narrow thoroughfare which runs past the hotel, was the location of Lot One (purchased by Gribble, Hughes & Co. for £80) of the initial fifty plots of marine frontage put up for auction in the summer of 1841. A week before he initiated the auction, Captain Charles Elliot RN, Superintendent of Trade and the architect of the new British outpost, had proclaimed the island a free port and invited merchants to trade from there. From the start the new government, chosen from army and navy officers, tapped its one precious resource: land. The auction was to have sold two hundred plots of waterfront and urban land but the total was reduced to fifty and finally thirty-four after some were reserved or withdrawn altogether. Prices, the merchants' representatives complained to Elliot, were artificially high. And if Elliot was not popular with the merchants, nor was he with the British Government. The Superintendent had conceded too much of the advantage gained by British forces in the First Anglo-Chinese War (the so-called Opium War) to secure an island of less than 30 square miles for the Crown. British residents in Guangzhou joined in the chorus, mocking the folly of such an acquisition. In late August 1841, Elliot was on his way home, replaced by Sir Henry Pottinger as plenipotentiary in China.

Despite the criticisms that were heaped upon Elliot, his vision had been true. The Anglo-Chinese War was fought ostensibly over opium. The real motive, however, was the regularization and broadening of trade with China. In this the merchants and the British Government were as one. Until then trade had been conducted through Guangzhou and erratically controlled by Chinese authorities. The trading season lasted only three to four months each year; for the remainder of the time British merchants languished in the nearby Portuguese colony of Macau. The process was akin to buying and selling from a loose doorstep. The need to break this constriction of trade was made all the more urgent by the introduction of the lucrative commodity of opium. But the British Government had only a nebulous conception of how matters could be improved. Force, it felt, was sufficient to transform the cramped conditions under which its merchants worked. The war had to be a punitive exercise which would lead to the opening up of additional trading points farther north. Elliot reasoned in a different way. British trading interests would remain vulnerable until a stable commercial environment had been established; the events leading up to the Sino-British conflict had amply demonstrated this. Such an environment could not be achieved until 'Her Majesty's flag flies on these coasts in a secure position' he concluded, even before the outbreak of hostilities in 1839.

Hong Kong and its deep natural harbour had been noticed by Elliot's predecessors, Lord Napier and Sir George Robinson, as a potential resting place for merchants and their ships. Indeed, Robinson had suggested as early as January 1836 that British interests would be best served by occupying one of the islands in the vicinity, thereby stepping away from the difficult situation at Guangzhou. In April he named Hong Kong as such an island and in a November dispatch announced that he was moving his office there. A measure of the disapproval associated with such a policy can be gauged from the fact that, upon receipt of his January communication, London had decided to do away with Robinson's post and directed him to hand over his files to Elliot. Indeed, the British Government's opposition to the assumption of sovereignty over Hong Kong persisted for more than two years after the territory was handed over. Final acceptance was as a result of a *fait accompli*: the new plenipotentiary Sir Henry Pottinger – initially, like Elliot before him, the Administrator of the colony, but from the summer of 1843 its first Governor – had simply accepted the treaty that his predecessor had hammered out with his Chinese counterpart. In London, the Foreign Secretary Lord Aberdeen was, like Palmerston before him, pressing for the opening up of four or five treaty ports instead. But it was not only the government's representative in Hong Kong who sensed the value of the island. By 1838 sizeable numbers of foreign ships were already using its harbour and in the same year Jardine Matheson built a bullion repository there to store the returns from their opium sales – having failed to secure payment in silks instead. Such behaviour helped to ensure that the new British colony of Hong Kong would be a foregone conclusion.

Neither Elliot, nor Robinson before him, was much in favour of the opium trade. They saw the import of the drug to China as an increasing source of friction with the Chinese Government, but could do little to bring the problem under control in the face of traffickers' mounting enthusiasm, the corrupt practices associated with the trade and Britain's refusal to stem the flow of opium at its source in India. Elliot would have been gratified by the present-day image of Hong Kong, for it is the product of the modest imperialism he sought to promote from the start. Setting aside the moral taints associated with the drug, Elliot's position was clear: a single commodity – no matter how profitable it was in the short term – was not worth the sacrifice of a sound basis for long-term trading relations. It is a simple principle that Hong Kong has subsequently adhered to with great success. All the more unfortunate, then, that Hong Kong's amoral mercantilism should have found its earliest form through treaties ending a bitter scrap over the immoral trade in opium.

In late 1980, two years before the issue of Hong Kong's future entered the public domain, I was in a classroom of a school in Kowloon, teaching Asian history to the Upper Sixth. We were discussing the Anglo-Chinese Wars when one of my pupils raised his hand: 'Who was at fault, sir?' he asked. The question has remained with me ever since.

In China the conflict marks the beginning of modern history, an era symbolized by the class of 'unequal treaties': one-sided documents granting foreigners unreciprocated rights in China. The Treaty of Nanjing in 1842, which finally ended the First Anglo-Chinese War, established five treaty ports on China's seaboard and ushered in new principles of economic relations. At first limited to terms and locations of foreign trade with China, some fifty years later these were broadened to a full-scale scramble for financial involvement throughout the country in railway construction, mines, industry and commerce. Forcibly and from time to time violently educated in foreign ways, affronted by the naked inequity of extraterritoriality (by which foreign nationals were all but immune to Chinese law, while Chinese nationals did not have similar privileges abroad), weakened by growing economic indebtedness, the Chinese empire staggered into the twentieth century, nationhood and the decades of revolutionary foment and civil war that followed. Only with the final triumph of the Chinese Communist Party in 1949, and the gradual squeezing out of overt foreign presence from the country and its economy, did China gain a temporary respite from this brutal process of modernization. Nor will the Chinese state be allowed easily to forget its painful heritage. This historical watershed also gave birth to Hong Kong.

In one sense the development of the colony is a stark reminder to all Chinese, including the teenager who posed the question to me, of the injustices China had to endure in its modern development. Against this is Hong Kong's long-standing role as a magnet for a vast number of Chinese and as a shelter from the political and fiscal storms buffeting China during the same period. Was it possible to condemn the one strand while leaving the other intact? The question I had been posed could never be answered satisfactorily.

The population of Hong Kong is another, and the most important, reason for its success. The popular idea of a society of able workers and shrewd entrepreneurs tends, however, to obscure a significant point. It is not so much the skills that have been developed in the colony, many of which, particularly during the early stages of its industrial development, were imported, so much as the actual flow of people through its portals that has stimulated growth. How large this flow has been can be judged from the very earliest figures. When the British formally took charge of Hong Kong, the population was a little over 5000. If the Tanka boat people, who spent most of their lives afloat, were added to this figure, the total would have been about 7000. By mid 1844 the population had already trebled. Ten years later it had trebled again. Following the cession of the Kowloon Peninsula in 1860, the figure rose to just under 120,000. In 1901 the total was 301,000 and in 1919 it had risen to a little over 598,000.

Large numbers were absorbed. Some of them became employees of the foreign trading houses that had moved to Hong Kong from Guangzhou, but the bulk of those who stayed found employment in the construction business, which adopted a frenetic form almost from the start, and in the gradual expansion of a sound indigenous economic base. The latter occurred in parallel with the foreign trading activities and not, as the British might have liked to think, as a result of direct stimulus from a new government. After the New Territories were added as a leasehold in 1898, the traditional activities of agriculture, fishing and quarrying practised on the island were supplemented by a variety of commercial crops cultivated on the mainland, including fruit, sugar-cane and peanuts.

Larger numbers still passed through Hong Kong. The beginnings of the Taiping movement in China in 1853 brought a sharp rise in the population of the colony. The movement was of an elemental nature, combining the reaction of poor peasants plagued by inequalities with the anti-Manchu and pro-modernization sentiments emerging in other sectors of Chinese society. The rebellion raged for almost ten years, causing severe dislocation over a remarkably large area of the country. Hong Kong became a temporary haven for tens of thousands and took on the guise of a stepping-stone to the outside world for the first time; a role that it has never been able to shed.

Particularly after 1857, the colony became a transit camp for coolies on their way to the 'gold mountains' of America and Australia, or Jamaica and British Guiana. And a profitable transit camp it proved to be. With trade reduced by the effects of civil strife in China, the handling of this human commodity helped to compensate for losses in more conventional areas of commerce. At the turn of the century, when South Africa was in need of labour for its diamond and gold mines, an attempt was made to formalize the channelling of indented labourers to that country, employing specially constructed camps at Lai Chi Kok, in western Kowloon, and government officers to oversee their occupants. Although it never fully got off the ground, the scheme did help to fuel the debate over 'Chinese slavery' initiated by liberals in Britain. During World War I the use of Hong Kong as a front for the recruitment of indentured labour from China cropped up again. Once again, the political embarrassment that this caused the government of the day* prevented the formal scheme from going beyond the discussion stage. However, more discreet forms of recruitment for the Western Front were eventually employed, bringing thousands of Chinese to Hong Kong: some, because they had become local residents, were hired as 'British-Chinese'; others were contracted in the interior of China by the French, who used the British colony as a transhipment centre. The camps that had been built for the abortive South African scheme served a function after all.

In the early years the flow of people led to a curious phenomenon. A variety of buildings devoted to cheap temporary accommodation sprang up on the waterfront. These dingy and crowded structures housed the transitory residents of Hong Kong on their way to new lands, as well as providing a more permanent residence for coolies working in the colony itself. Almost all the transitory residents were male: single men who would return to seek brides in their native provinces once they had established themselves abroad; or married men who had left their wives and families behind while they sought the wherewithal to bring them to a new home. Because of this, and the reluctance of the more well-to-do Chinese to expose their womenfolk to the unseemly character of the new colony, Hong Kong society

---

* As it happened, the government was formed by the Liberal Party, which had been primarily responsible for the defeat of the South African plan.

was predominantly male. Little wonder, then, that *The Times* of 15 March 1859 described Hong Kong as 'a noisy, bustling, quarrelsome, discontented and insalubrious little island'.

The newspaper should have added that this represented the results of over a decade of creative chaos. The colony had been thriving and was constantly threatening to burst its seams. With the growth of the population and the need for essential services, especially the provision of a steady water supply, the government was obliged to consider how to broaden its sources of revenue. This led to the controversial tax on opium sales, together with more general and stable forms of municipal taxes.

The administration was also being forced to grasp the nettle of how to steer a course between the interests of Hong Kong's tiny foreign community, which has consistently been less than two per cent of the total population, and its Chinese population. An early directive by Elliot that Chinese residents of Hong Kong should be bound by Chinese law and custom, while foreigners were to be governed by British legal principles, was already thought to be impracticable, even under Pottinger's governorship (1841-4). Had a unified system of colonial law not been introduced, an interesting variant of the practice of extraterritoriality might have been allowed to develop. Chinese residents would technically live on British soil, but answer in the main – felonies, under the British definition, were excluded – to the Chinese code of justice!

As it was, the main changes under the next Governor, John Francis Davis (1844-8), were a transition to a civilian civil service, and the creation of Legislative and Executive Councils (which have come to be known as Legco and Exco respectively, and serve as the territory's quasi-parliament). The Councils, which were to act in a purely advisory capacity, were made up of Official Members (from the colonial administration) and Unofficial Members (co-opted from society at large). Legislation was brought in to begin to break the back of the anarchic, freewheeling society and to cast it in a formal colonial mould. This proved to be a difficult task. Registration was introduced for residents, a measure that proved immensely unpopular with the Chinese population and resulted in the colony's first general strike. Legislation prohibiting public gambling (1844) and the creation of a police rate (1845) also proved to be unpopular. When these measures were introduced, many people voted with their feet, leading to the population falling by a fifth in 1846. Nor were the British merchants a particularly happy group, as Davis's administration produced measure after measure to shift the financial burden of governing Hong Kong from Britain to the colony itself. The Governor's efforts brought about a financial system that is still in existence today.

Under Davis, the city began to assume a colonial appearance. There were the first proposals for a cricket ground and a racecourse. The construction of a cathedral and government offices was initiated. Before either of these buildings was finished, and a full six years before a start was made on an official residence for the Governor, the Hong Kong Club had already opened its doors. It is, on reflection, an appropriate sequence of priorities. The Club, as it is known in Hong Kong, has long been described – one suspects only in half-jest – as the seat of real power in the colony. Here, the Governor and senior civil servants would sit in regular, informal sessions, usually over breakfast or lunch, with members of the commercial élite.

The Club has undergone two metamorphoses, the most recent being the product of an Australian architect who, from the reactions of its more conservative members, has unwittingly wreaked the colonial's revenge on this sacrosanct institution. Spurred by sharply rising land prices in the late seventies, club members succumbed to an offer too good to refuse for the redevelopment of the site. The dignified if somewhat sombre Victorian building was levelled and for a time its human contents were transferred to temporary lodgings a few yards from where the 'Old Club' had stood. The new building, which is a combination of office block, shopping complex and – for the first few storeys – club, would not look out of place in the fashionable glitter of New York or the airy classlessness of Sydney.

Subsequent Governors gradually structured the colonial edifice along the lines laid down by Davis. An important reinforcement of this process was ensuring that Hong Kong remained aloof from the politics of China proper. This sleight of hand, which has been the key element in Hong Kong's survival till now, was produced in two ways. First of all, Sir Samuel George Bonham (1848–54), who replaced Davis, set a crucial precedent by maintaining the colony's firm neutrality during the Taiping Rebellion. Second, the Governor's role was divided into two distinct sections. Up until Sir John Bowring's tenure as Governor (1854–9), the office combined the posts of Superintendent of Trade in China and Governor. For some time it seemed that this combination of posts would continue and that Hong Kong would be the formal nerve-centre of all British activities in China as a whole. Had such a situation been allowed to persist, there seems little doubt that Hong Kong would soon, and probably fatally, have been drawn into the turbulence of the Chinese body politic. Under Davis the stature of Hong Kong as a centre for British authority in China was diluted through the distribution of a certain amount of power to the British consuls at the treaty ports. Under Bowring, however, the role of Superintendent Governor was split. The superintendency became the responsibility of the Foreign Secretary, while the gubernatorial function of the post was left to the command of the Colonial Office alone. In time, the latter duties took precedence and the Governor of Hong Kong ceased to involve himself directly in Chinese affairs.

The evolution of Hong Kong's political and fiscal policies was accompanied by the increasing imposition of a colonial order on the Chinese populace. Bowring, and Sir Hercules George Robert Robinson (1859–65) after him, presided over a period troubled by anti-colonial feeling, particularly at the time of the Second Anglo-Chinese War in 1856, and by Chinese resistance to regulatory legislation. Their response was to err on the side of severity.

Only with the arrival of Sir John Pope Hennessy in April 1877 was there a serious attempt to correct the political and social imbalance that had developed between the Europeans and the Chinese. Although his principal brief from London was to introduce some Chinese representation in the administration of the colony, Hennessy, prompted by his own beliefs, tackled a catalogue of injustices that he found had been foisted upon a powerless Chinese population. In a city where even the princely hong* of Jardine Matheson could only manage to scrape in at the very bottom of the top twenty landholders (all the others being Chinese), the Chinese had by convention been barred from holding property in the prestigious area of Central. Pope Hennessy reversed this situation, even though strongly opposed by local Europeans. Foreigners were further incensed by Hennessy's plans to abolish the barbaric practices of public flogging and the branding of those to be banished from the

*A term that derives from Cohong, a small group of Chinese merchants who dealt with and supervised foreign traders; it has subsequently become a label for the old foreign trading companies themselves.

colony. These reforms, it was felt, would lead to a serious disruption in the quality of life enjoyed by Europeans and cause lawlessness in the society as a whole. Members of the Legislative Council organized a public meeting on the subject of corporal punishment, and later petitioned London, but to no avail.

It is interesting to reflect that, of the early group of administrators and governors of Hong Kong, those who contributed most to the formation and furtherance of the colony seem to have had least public recognition. Hong Kong is festooned with thoroughfares and geographical and man-made landmarks commemorating its founding fathers. There is a Pottinger Peak, a Bonham Road and Strand (and Building), a Bowrington Road and Robinson Crest. Only Captain Charles Elliot has no memorial. (There was, briefly, an Elliot's Vale, but this was later changed to Glenealy.) Davis has a mountain named after him, but one that is tucked away on the lonely western point of Hong Kong Island. Hennessy was eventually relegated to a road in the less than salubrious district of Wanchai. Neither Davis nor Hennessy were eulogized by the foreign community on the passing of their governorship. They are the only Governors to have left without this vote of thanks from their European charges.

And what of the Chinese views on the men who ruled their lives? It has become the custom for the last Governor to have been the 'greatest, most productive and best loved ever'. That way the need for an overt, and true, value judgement can be avoided and the person on the street can discreetly express his or her hope that the next Governor will be as good or even better: in other words, that he should not make a botched job of it! The truth is that even the most radical Governor leaves very little lasting impression on the common person in Hong Kong. The office of Governor, even with the 'common touch' and walkabouts in open-necked shirts that have entered into its *modus operandi* in recent years, is far removed from the lives of most of the population. This was sadly reflected in the reaction to the tragic death of Sir Edward Youde in Beijing in December 1986, the only Governor to have died while in office. He was a man who, through his humble manner and diligence, did more than any of his predecessors to bring the post closer to the Chinese character. Even die-hard cynics expressed surprise at the sight of a hundreds-long queue snaking its way along Garden and Upper Albert Roads to sign the condolence book in Government House. This, they said, was evidence that a Governor had at last found his way into the hearts of the common people. And, indeed, in many cases he had. Nonetheless, one Chinese businessman, having passed the queue on his way to work, could not resist sending his secretary to ask each person in it their reasons for being there. The majority replied that this was their first opportunity to see inside Government House. The next most prevalent reason was to show respect to a Governor who had dressed and behaved in a modest way.

The attitude of the predominantly Cantonese population to its European masters has from the beginning been somewhat tellingly represented in the translation of their names into Chinese. These can be openly scathing, as in the case of Lord Napier, the first Superintendent of Trade in China, whose name became 'Laboriously Vile'. Often European names would be transformed into representations of character by Chinese appointed to teach newly-arrived cadets the rudiments of Cantonese. It was years before one burly police officer discovered that his teacher had rechristened him Attila the Hun! The most recent victim of such embarrassment was the present Governor, Sir David Wilson, a man who has built up a considerable reputation as a Chinese scholar and linguist, and who received his first intensive course in Chinese at the University of Hong Kong in 1960. Shortly after his appointment it came to light that his Chinese name (pronounced Ngai Tak-ngai in Cantonese) concealed the description 'twin ghosts come a-knocking'; a title in keeping, it must be said, with Sir David's distant glance and pallor.

But there was a more serious side to this seemingly playful punning. To a superstitious society deeply concerned with its future, Wilson's name was a bad omen. He completed a triumvirate (the other members being the British Ambassador to China, Sir Richard Evans, and the late Governor Youde) that was prominent in the 1983–4 negotiations with China on the colony's fate. Neither of the Chinese names for the other two were particularly auspicious. Some intellectuals who were suspicious of Youde's seeming readiness to accommodate Beijing against Hong Kong's own interests altered his name to 'Yau Tak' (loosely translated as 'also possible'). Shortly after his death a black joke began to circulate: 'Yau Tak, Yau Tak . . . M-tak!' 'also possible, also possible . . . no longer possible!' Of the three, however, it was Wilson's name that had a distinctly ominous connotation to it, and it was he who had been chosen to lead Hong Kong through a difficult transitional period, having already taken an important part in the engineering of what many still see as a British sellout. In spite of a disclaimer that 'in Chinese you can have great fun with anyone's name', Wilson quickly adopted a less ill-boding Chinese name.

The gulf between Chinese and foreigner in Hong Kong has been partly disguised by the relative absence of the kind of overt and violent waves of anti-foreignism that characterized the early twentieth century in China itself. Glimpses of this gulf are, however, readily visible even today: they range from examples of crude racism to a simple acceptance of irreconcilable 'differentness'. Differences are unavoidable. Generation after generation of foreigners has arrived to take up positions of superiority. Often the changes in professional and social standing that the incoming foreigner experiences are intoxicating, as one man pointed out some years ago, soon after he had made the transition from a working-class district in Lancashire. There he had, in his own words, been climbing telephone poles for the Post Office. In Hong Kong he was in charge of hundreds of workmen, enjoyed seductive evenings and weekends at a club, on the tennis courts and beside the swimming pool. Such a transform-ation, he said, was simply unthinkable in Britain. Rarely are such Cinderellas willing, or able, to alter their attitudes to the people and culture that have provided the opportunity for their metamorphosis. Little of their language is learned, aside from the curious, broken forms of pidgin English (and Cantonese); little of the culture is absorbed.

Sources of friction between the races are many. The Chinese have had to patiently endure inequities of salary and opportunity (although now, with senior posts in government and businesses being increasingly occupied by Chinese, it is more often the expatriates who unthinkingly speak of their resentment!). Aggravation at the office, the shop and public recreation spots results from the lack of an adequate medium of communication and blatant – although not necessarily intentional – expressions of superiority are frequently uttered by European mouths. New generations are perpetuating the divisions that have existed for a hundred years: European children leading a cloistered existence on the Peak and Mid-levels can be heard to say that they don't know the traditional Chinese area of Kowloon at all. Or youngsters will loudly proclaim that Hong Kong Chinese cinema, television and music have nothing but curiosity value, doing so within easy earshot of those who have produced and thrive on this popular culture. They are corrected neither by those who they so uncaringly affront, nor by their parents, who often know little better or, worse still, from whom they derived their transparent wisdom in the first place.

It is perhaps indicative of the rarity of violent displays of anti-foreignism in Hong Kong that one of the most memorable instances remains the E-Sing Bakery poisoning case when, one morning in January 1857, 400 Europeans simultaneously became violently ill. It was discovered that the loaves despatched by the bakery that day had been laced with arsenic. But this was an isolated incident prompted by the sense of indignation felt after the Second Anglo-Chinese War. There were no deaths and there was no clear evidence whether the incident was perpetrated on the initiative of local residents or by Chinese officials outside Hong Kong, but the case raised a lather of hysteria in the European community. There were calls for punitive punishment of the bakery's owner, Cheong ah-lum (a well-to-do moneylender and trader), and his 52 employees. Life for the Chinese became temporarily so uncomfortable that emigration figures doubled.

There have been two major exceptions to the general absence of large-scale racial confrontation: the 1925-6 Hong Kong-Guangzhou Strike and the disturbances associated with China's Cultural Revolution forty years later. Of these, it is perhaps the first that stands out as a crucial test of the colony's ability to withstand the course of events in China.

By the early 1920s Hong Kong was a firm part of a nexus of British trading interests in China. There had been a steady rise in the number and total tonnage of ships clearing its harbour (in 1919 the figures stood at 21,275 and 18,474,996 respectively; fifty years before they had been 4426 and 2,256,049). Increasingly important too was the colony's role as a base for the operations of the established hongs and a local incorporated bank, the Hongkong & Shanghai Banking Corporation, which was first mooted by a group of British merchants in 1862 and came into existence between 1864-6.

A solid foundation of trade and the provision of venture capital responsive to local needs allowed foreign economic penetration to proceed smoothly from the treaty ports into the interior of China. Hong Kong perforce took a secondary role in this process and remained overshadowed by Shanghai throughout the inter-war years. This was natural: Shanghai was closer to the seat of the national government and the heartland of the country's lop-sided course to modernization. Still, to use a Hongkong Bank term, the colony served as something of a 'head office' for many business concerns and became a natural shelter after their eventual retreat from China.

The 1920s were turbulent years for China, a republic only since 1911. War-lords with large personal armies transformed vast tracts of territory into fiefdoms in the north, while in the central region right-wing elements of the Kuomintang, headed by Chiang Kai-Shek, were preparing to deal a deathblow to the left-wing elements in the south. A series of rallies, strikes, protests and marches were simply viewed by the foreign communities of the treaty ports as the effects of Bolshevik-inspired anti-foreignism. In late May 1925, students and workers converged on a police station in Shanghai, demanding the release of those arrested at a protest held shortly before. A nervous British officer ordered his men to open fire. Twelve students were killed. A general strike soon paralysed the city. The Chinese seamen who walked out of British shipping companies in Guangzhou in mid June were followed a few days later by all Chinese workers employed by foreign companies in Guangzhou and Hong Kong. Finally, after the massacre of more than fifty demonstrators by British and French machine guns on the Shakee Road Bridge in Shanghai on 23 June, the confrontation was transformed into a general strike with a full boycott of British goods, focusing principally on Hong Kong.

This action, which lasted fifteen months, led to 100,000 workers leaving Hong Kong for Guangzhou. All commercial and industrial activity was brought to a halt. Foreign residents were left to do their own cooking and housework. The strikers who remained in the colony drew up an extensive set of demands relating to working conditions and civil rights, demanding, for example, an eight-hour day, the prohibition of child labour, the right to vote and freedom of speech. None of the demands was met, nor, at the end of the strike, were any concessions made. The one conciliatory gesture was the appointment of the first Chinese, Sir Shouson Chow, to the Executive Council, a measure designed to restore the loyalty of the Chinese community in Hong Kong. Despite angry expatriates' calls for military action against Guangzhou, the strike had been met with restraint and determination.

There were at least two reasons for the failure of the strike. First, the government of China (which was by the end of the strike in the hands of the right wing of the Nationalist Party) had, in the face of British obstinacy, resorted to a pragmatic line, initiating talks and, finally, unreservedly calling off the strike. More important, however, was the general absence of support from the middle- and upper-class strata of Hong Kong's Chinese population for what was an essentially working-class movement.

This willingness to endure disruption (albeit uneasily, but assisted by the marked avoidance of bloodshed) and to resume 'business as usual' was a characteristic of the 1966–7 disturbances too. Only now are these important groupings really beginning to question the status quo. Unlike the crises of 1925–6 and 1966–7, the present process of transition has forced the Hong Kong Chinese to come to terms with their own identity; to make a choice between being Chinese or being foreigners in their own country. The delicate equilibrium involved in existing as Chinese on Chinese territory but living under a flag of convenience has been broken. Despite assurances from both Britain and the People's Republic of China (PRC) that the status quo will be preserved, there is scarcely a person in Hong Kong who believes that this can be achieved. The status quo, after all, is the quiet assurance that tomorrow will be the same as today; it cannot be promised, it can only be lived. Since the initiation of talks on the colony's future in 1982, daily life has shown that the familiar sense of stability has gone. The year 1997, when Hong Kong returns to China, has become an *idée fixe*. As such, it intrudes constantly, bringing into question not only an ever closer uncertainty, but each tomorrow until then. This suggests that Hong Kong is a paradoxical amalgam of resilience and fragility. For a society that is preoccupied with the present it could not be otherwise.

History is a luxury in Hong Kong. The territory's residents have always lived in an environment where structures are, in Henry James's words, 'expensively provisional'. His description referred to New York, but in his conclusion that the city's buildings were 'crowned not only with no history, but with no credible possibility of time for history' he could as easily have been writing about Hong Kong. Architecture should provide a treasure hunt for those who wish to trace a city's past and orientation for those pegging out their own histories. In Hong Kong this process is more akin to solving a cryptic crossword puzzle, involving the slenderest of clues, a hefty amount of lateral thinking and a strained imagination. Nor is this something new, a result of the rocketing prosperity of recent years.

The colony's first attempts at architecture were blown down by a typhoon in July 1841. It might well have been a sign. Since then any hope of physical continuity has been thwarted by a combination of growth and regeneration.

Murray House, built in 1844 (to house British army officers) and one of Hong Kong's oldest colonial structures, was dismantled stone by stone and stored while the outcome of a debate on where and when it should be reassembled was awaited. On its former resting place will be the new Bank of China, itself a replacement for the old structure that provided delightful counterpoint during the Cultural Revolution by displaying and blaring anti-colonial slogans to the cricketers at the Hong Kong Cricket Club across the street. Nor has that venerable institution been spared. Its familiar corner pavilion has been demolished and its sacred acres are now occupied by a park and by the Central Station of the Mass Transit Railway (MTR). The club itself still exists, but now sits in a discreet corner of Wong Nai Cheung, where the crack of willow against leather and the occasional guttural cry no longer catch the attention of a passing Saturday worker, Sunday stroller or perplexed tourist. Many an idle and probably longing glance must have been cast onto the expanse of green through the windows of the adjacent Supreme Court building. The solemn grey of the court's colonial columns, arches and dome has made it an anachronism in the otherwise haphazard patchwork of colour and form making up Central. The blindfolded figure of Justice still stands atop the entrance, although the process of law that she symbolizes has transferred its business to a dull grey monolith erected on Queensway, the fourth set of premises that the Court has occupied since its introduction in 1844. The Supreme Court building's new tenant is Legco. The question of whether blindfold, scales and sword should symbolize the activities of a constitutional body charting the affairs of state is perhaps best left unanswered.

Across the water, on the tip of the Kowloon Peninsula, stands a solitary clock tower that was part of the Kowloon-Canton Railway Terminus, now dwarfed by a cultural centre that looks more like a ski jump than a home for the arts. The reprieve of the tower was the government's answer to vigorous agitation from a small but vocal conservation society, which called for the transformation of the old terminal into an arts centre or museum. Few now would recognize the tower as an undedicated monument to the many thousands of refugees who caught a first glimpse of their new lives at this very spot. Until the border was closed in 1950 there was a constant flow of Chinese from the interior, to be replaced during the 1950s and early 1960s by carriage-loads of Russians in transit from their former homes in Manchuria, Shanghai and Tianjin to resettlement in the Americas, Australia and Europe. The largely forgotten 40,000 Indonesian Chinese, whose existence was made impossible in their own country after the emergency and genocide of the mid sixties, arrived in shiploads at the nearby pier and took the short walk to the terminus on their way to China; the majority returned to the same station a year or two later because they had not been able to adjust to life there.

Nor does there seem to be any great anxiety to preserve or be reminded of the past. In a place where there has hardly been a year without the initiation of a large capital construction project and where the Government's 1980–1 land transactions yielded almost $7000 million (more, in fact, than was earned through direct taxation), the past seems irrelevant. Museums have been modest in size and scope, usually relegated to the obscure upper floors of public buildings. For some time the Hong Kong Public Records Office (formed only in 1972) was housed on the first floor of a car-park. While the Museum of History now has its own premises in a former military building hidden in the undergrowth of Kowloon Park, the squat, sandy-coloured dome of the Urban Council's Space Museum (where '320 visitors can make imaginary trips into space') occupies pride of place on the shoreline of the peninsula. In a bizarre expression of priorities, the chairman of the council proudly announced, upon its opening in late 1980, that he hoped to see the day when such space museums could be found in every district. And not for the first time have space-age aspirations come into conflict with the earthy sensibilities of the Chinese: residents have dubbed the tomb-like building 'Sales's Tomb' after the chairman. Businessmen with a superstitious bent (and there are few in the colony who are not) are reluctant to occupy office space in a direct line with the museum; it is considered bad *fung shui*.

Many blind spots exist in the society and history of Hong Kong. There is only a sketchy understanding of the complex origins of the territory's population and of its early settlement patterns. Equally, the nature of modern demographic growth is to a great extent disguised. The Government does not like to refer to the Chinese settling in Hong Kong as refugees. The avoidance of such a category ensures that potentially awkward distinctions between economic and political migrants are left unstated and fosters the neutral image of the population as a large amorphous mass. Nor does the Government directly show the refugees in its vital statistics. In its yearly reports, birth- and death-rates do not quite tally with the size of increase in the estimated population, while official immigration figures for most years show that more people left the colony than entered. When there is an imbalance in the other direction, it is usually minimal. In these figures, the refugees occupy a grey area. And yet this element of the population is enormous. In the 1970s a little over 50 per cent of the population was born in Hong Kong, but many people had parents who had come to the colony from elsewhere. And this picture is, of course, based on official figures.

To complicate matters further, villages in the New Territories have enjoyed a special relationship with China. Within the *cordon sanitaire* near the border, where urban dwellers are not allowed without a special pass, farming villages still practise transhumance. In the case of Sha Tau Kok, a town in the north-eastern corner of the colony, the settlement literally straddles the border. Non-residents must have a pass to enter its environs. Farmers crossing the border regularly are expected to have necessary documentation (to confirm their place of residence) for the otherwise unrestricted toing and froing.

There are only fleeting glimpses of another form of transhumance. On a recent visit to sample how the natives of the New Territories viewed the 1997 handover, I met a cheerful young man from one of the old single-clan villages (where inhabitants are from the same extended family, bearing the same surname). I asked if he had any reservations about the future. No, he replied, it promised to be a healthy one. What form of assurance had he that this would be so, I continued. Because the people coming to his village from China had brought only good bodings. Were these villagers who had visited China recently, relations from there or emissaries sent to steady the villagers' nerve? I probed further. They were none of these, came the reply, 'just recent arrivals from China'. My GIS (Government Information Service) guide anxiously sought to correct him: 'There is no longer such a provision for free stay for people from China.'

He obliged, altering his original, revealing reply: 'Yes, I mean people that arrived long ago but have *visited* China recently.'

The most significant historical blind spot concerns Hong Kong's difficult experiences during World War II and the Japanese occupation; a period described quite aptly by one historian as the 'hidden years'. The colony had only begun to industrialize in the years before 1939. Up until then it had concentrated on entrepôt trade, the introduction of industry being largely prompted by the Sino-Japanese conflict, which began with the Japanese occupation of Manchuria in 1931 and the attack on Shanghai in 1932, and the associated chronic shortages of consumer goods in China. Britain had negotiated with Japan, agreeing that Hong Kong should not supply the Chinese Nationalist Government's war effort, a continuation of the by now well-defined policy of remaining detached from Chinese internal politics. The colony did not have the resources to act as a military strong point in the event of its being drawn into a wider conflict, the only regular forces available being the Middlesex and Indian Regiments, the Royal Scots, a small naval force and local volunteers, the latter including separate companies of Portuguese and Eurasians. On the eve of the Japanese invasion, in 1941, these were supplemented by two Canadian regiments made up of raw and unacclimatized recruits.

Japanese forces were already well entrenched to the north of Hong Kong as a result of the Sino-Japanese War that had broken out in 1937. Their initial thrust across the Shenzhen-Hong Kong border came at dawn on 8 December. A brave defence was fought by the vastly outnumbered local forces, most of them operating from the island of Hong Kong itself. The whole of Kowloon and the New Territories were secured by the invading force in precisely four days. On 14 December the Japanese offered peace terms to the besieged island. They were refused. On the same day the British Prime Minister, Winston Churchill, made a typically emotive plea to the colony to resist an irresistible Japanese onslaught even if such resistance should purchase only a few days.

'You guard a link long famous in world civilization between the Far East and Europe,' he said in his radio broadcast. The defence would, he proclaimed, 'add a glorious page to British annals'. The colony obliged. The protraction of the conflict to Christmas Day, when the colony finally surrendered, does indeed stand as a testament to human courage. But in looking at the defence from a broader perspective, it is difficult to avoid seeing the great human cost exacted by Churchill's rhetoric, or that this is a page of history

Britain would much rather forget.

The defence of Hong Kong was hopeless. The main fortifications and heavy guns were all on the southern side of the island. There was no realistic prospect of reinforcement from the sea or support from the air. In spite of this, the Hong Kong Government issued optimistic statements assuring the defenders of relief from British forces and even from a mythical nationalist Chinese army making its way south to the border!

In the course of the hostilities it was brought home that, far from being the front line in the struggle to preserve the British Empire, Hong Kong was one of its loneliest outposts. As one British journalist present during the siege, and subsequently interned, put it: would it not have been wiser to have removed the men and materials for their use in another area of the war effort? Many of those who survived the brutal conflict had three and a half years in internment camps to savour the bitterness associated with such questions.

The years of occupation were exceedingly difficult for the colony. Due to the ferocity of the fighting, there had been much destruction, and the population was rapidly depleted as large numbers of Chinese returned to villages in China. In the course of the next three years the numbers living in the settlement fell from 1,639,000 to 600,000; Hong Kong became a shell. There was little work and a general scarcity of food. Those who remained had to suffer brutally harsh treatment from occupying forces. It was, quite frequently, a tightrope existence. Memories of the occupation run very deep to this day; not only of the hardships, but of the ever-present violence and cruelty. A middle-aged Chinese woman still remembers vividly how, as a child, her mother's hand grew clammy around hers at the sound of a Japanese gendarme's angry bark from across the street and the bewilderment she felt in being pushed away by her mother to a safe distance as he approached. After much shouting from the official, it transpired that, although she had not seen him, she had nonetheless failed to show appropriate deference by bowing. The sharp slap that she received could as easily have been summary execution. The punishment had depended purely on the gendarme's mood.

For foreigners held in internment camps, life was reduced to nightmarish routine. A Portuguese member of the Volunteer Corps described his existence in these years as being a bowl of rice at 4.30 am, with a spoonful of garlic water poured over it for flavour, and then a march to Kai Tak (the airport) to labour for the whole day. In the evenings he would return for another bowl of rice and garlic water. The working 'week' was thirteen days, with a rest day on the fourteenth. When he finally emerged from the camp, his weight had fallen from 182 lb to 96 lb. All that had kept him going was the will to live. Upon release, he was offered a large bag of weevil-ridden rice, which he grabbed eagerly. The bag weighed 7 lb more than him, but he somehow managed to carry it for many yards. A fellow inmate, whose weight had slipped from 150 lb to 44 lb, died in hospital soon after liberation.

The post-war years added a tragic dimension to this already painful period. Those who fought so loyally for the British armed forces have for some years been forced to conduct another campaign: with the Hong Kong Government over pensions. After an initial fund had been set up and divided, the government promised that it would be replenished if it were to run dry. At first a means test was introduced to ensure that those who applied were in need of the money, but this was eventually dropped. After the funds ran out, the government was reluctant to honour its pledge. The matter revolved around a point of principle: did the people in the camps suffer more than those who spent the wartime period in Hong Kong without internment? Only with great reluctance and much public discussion did the government finally give in. But even then a means test was reintroduced for the handful of claimants who had not applied previously.

Worse was to follow. Through the revision of nationality legislation, Portuguese and Eurasian veterans of the battle for Hong Kong were at first excluded from those who had right of residence in the United Kingdom. After much pressure from the veterans themselves with the backing of Legco, this ruling was relaxed by Prime Minister Margaret Thatcher, who regarded the adjustment as both fitting and imaginative. Sixty veterans in all were given full citizenship. Their children too were to be allowed this privilege, so long as they were under the age of eighteen. The youngest of the veterans granted this hard-fought reward was sixty-three and the oldest eighty-five!

The unfortunate controversy over the veterans reveals that while most people in Hong Kong have a vague idea of what the war meant to the colony, no clear picture of wartime Hong Kong has emerged, or is likely to. But the scars are there. To this day there is an undercurrent of hostility against the Japanese, with angry students occasionally raising the issue of the occupation. There are also lingering demands for compensation. Farmers in the New Territories, who were very harshly treated under the Japanese requisitioning policies, still show resentment towards Japanese visitors.

But if the British Government had overestimated Hong Kong's military importance at the beginning of the war with Japan, it patently underestimated the colony's ability to recover after Britain had regained control in 1945. Were it not for the more serious side of this chasm of incomprehension, the events soon after the war have a delightfully comic turn. In his *Chinese Crackers*, published in 1947, journalist Edward Ward described a trip to Hong Kong on board the *Llanstephan Castle*, on which his companions were Victor Sassoon, who had been sent to set up a makeshift newspaper and radio service, a garrison of commandos and a set of 'serious-looking men who still looked a little uncomfortable in their lieutenant-colonels' uniforms'. In Ward's words, the latter were:

'Civil Affairs' experts who were going to put Hong Kong on its feet again. They had been working, almost completely in the dark, for the whole trip. I had watched them at their conferences, stripped to the waist with sweat streaming down their backs, making such plans as they could with the scanty information at their disposal.

Upon arrival, all discovered how misguided their mission had been. Copies of the *South China Morning Post* and the *China Mail* were already to be had; they contained details of the day's radio programmes. With supplies of electricity and water available and policing organized:

There seemed to be nothing for the experts to do. All their plans had been a waste of time. They looked blankly at each other and asked themselves what on earth they had come to Hong Kong for and why somebody hadn't told them about all this before they had started. . . . We had all come with the idea in our minds that the civilian population would virtually have to be spoon-fed. So it came as something of an anti-climax to learn that there had just been a meeting of the golf club in order to elect a new president: that the cinemas advertised full programmes including the latest newsreels: that the Café Lido offered its patrons an excellent cuisine and fine liqueurs and the Siberian Fur Store a wide selection of sables, ermine and silver fox: that a Chinese grocer was celebrating victory by a great sale of provisions, wines and spirits. . . . And lastly, in the gossip column, that 'the problem now will be to avoid looking too fat when they arrive'.

35

To crown the confusion, General Festing, who accompanied the group, was under orders to assume military governorship of the colony. He arrived to find Admiral Harcourt of the British Pacific Fleet installed in Government House. 'Only through a process of tact and diplomacy,' Ward wrote, 'was this awkward situation resolved!'

Hong Kong readily resumed its colonial existence, but from this time on there could no longer be any pretence of defending the colony from external threat. This position later became what may be called the 'indefensible thesis', a key element in the approach adopted by a remarkably large group of British politicians in the negotiations over the future of the colony with Beijing. Another point of concern that had come to the fore by the end of the war was the question of whether the territory could continue as a colony. Although this was in part the expression of anxiety from an America wishing to see post-war China put on its feet, the logic of the argument was nevertheless compelling. Hong Kong, it was argued, was of greatest value to Britain while China was forced to adhere to an old trading system underpinned by extraterritoriality. With the abolition of the old system, British rule in Hong Kong would be an anachronism, if only for very practical reasons: the colony had in the past served as an important transhipment centre for goods destined for Guangzhou. With its new economic freedom, China could develop the port facilities in Guangzhou and starve Hong Kong of that revenue; at the same time, such a development could well result in the eclipse of the colony as the principal port for south China trade.

CHAPTER TWO

Uncertain Decades

In the post-war years, as it became clear that neither China's bankrupt KMT government, nor the socialist government that replaced it, seemed to harbour any intention of taking Hong Kong forcibly, the issue of the territory's defensibility faded. Instead of becoming an anachronism in the context of a revitalized China, the colony became a vital link between a fiscally weak socialist regime and the capitalist world. This role increased when, with Guangzhou showing no signs of economic take-off, the fragile capitalist infrastructure of Shanghai faltered and then fell apart completely in less than a decade of Communist rule. Hong Kong became China's window on the world. The iron guarantee of the colony's security was the economic and, to a lesser extent, political insecurity of China itself.

Of crucial importance to the emergence of Hong Kong's new character was the Korean conflict. When China went to war on the side of the North Koreans in October 1950, its new government was just a year old and had barely begun to introduce a programme of national reconstruction. More significantly, China pitched what weight it had against the United States and its United Nations allies, including Britain. In May 1951 it was to learn the costs associated with such action. The United States introduced an economic blockade of China. Indeed, trade restrictions persisted until the early 1970s when the United States and China were on the road to normalizing relations. As an ally Britain was forced to ensure that prohibited imports to China should not come through Hong Kong. This had two effects. One was that Hong Kong's role as an entrepôt was dras-

tically restricted. Goods were warehoused, bonded and made im-
mobile. Eventually this was to mean that millions of dollars of goods
cost more to store than they were worth, and so they were auctioned
off or simply abandoned. In the short term this was a heavy blow to
Hong Kong's own economy as its single most lucrative market had
disappeared. In the long term it left the colony with little choice but
to gear its activities to more independent forms of trade and new
markets. By doing so, Hong Kong was forcibly set on the path to the
creation of a modern, industrial economy. The embargo also provided the new authorities in Beijing with a swift lesson in the great
value of allowing Hong Kong to remain, at least in a nominal sense,
separate from China. The colony proved to be an all-important middle
ground where the Chinese authorities, through the services of sympathetic Hong Kong entrepreneurs, could secure goods vital to their
country's reconstruction.

How much early capital was made through informal contact with
China can only be guessed. Far more important, however, were the
relations China generated with the local business community in this
way. Businessmen who dipped into the black market were attracted
not only by the profits to be made but also by the opportunity to
become a 'friend of China'.

The realignment of the colony to the new terms of economic and
political coexistence with its socialist neighbour was not without
hiccups. The political changes in China after the war had resulted
in a stream of refugees entering Hong Kong in search of political
sanctuary. As an old Hong Kong hand put it: with the assumption of
power by the Communist Party in China, vanquished KMT officers
and men began to head for the hills; these hills happened to be just
above Hong Kong.

The KMT elements remained fairly quiet for some years, satisfying
themselves with little more than the celebratory display of sentiment
and flag-waving on the nationalist holiday of the Double Ten
(commemorating the start, on 10 October 1911, of the revolution
that toppled the Qing Dynasty). This would come as a response to
patriots of the new socialist persuasion displaying the flags and
slogans of the People's Republic of China on their own national day,
1 October.

In 1956 these shows of political sentiment took on a violent form.
The troubles began in a resettlement estate in northern Kowloon.
As in past years, the predominantly nationalist residents began their

preparations for the celebration of Double Ten. A large flag was raised over the entrance to one of the estate buildings and decorations were pasted on walls. On the morning of the holiday, the flag was torn down by the officer in charge of the estate, guided by a decision of the Urban Council (who were responsible for the resettlement blocks) on 3 October that no flags or decorations should be stuck on the walls 'as they had been found difficult to remove afterwards'. Within half an hour a crowd had gathered in front of the offending official's office, calling for money for the torn flags. A police party arrived and attempted to disperse the crowd, but with no success. Nor did the new flags pasted up by the now frightened resettlement officers appease the crowd, who demanded that firecrackers – an ancient form of apology – should be discharged by the officials.

While an officer went away to buy firecrackers, the crowd grew to over 2000 and the number of policemen present also increased. When the firecrackers finally arrived the crowd decided that there were not enough of them: 100,000 had to hang in braids down the side of the multi-storey building, and images of Sun Yat-sen and Chiang Kai-shek were to be raised over a large nationalist flag. In addition, the offending officer was to apologize in writing in a number of Chinese newspapers. Within hours the resettlement office had been ransacked, a fire started and officials assaulted. Police moving in to bring the situation under control were pelted with stones and soft-drink bottles from the many verandas surrounding the scene. In the course of the afternoon, more police units were brought in to contain the trouble. That evening large-scale rioting broke out on the periphery of the estate. The police, as the subsequent inquiry showed, were able to quell the initial disorder, but their response – reading between the lines – was piecemeal and half-hearted. The authorities too were caught by surprise by the intensity of the troubles. Their hope was that as Double Ten ended, so too would the rioting. Instead, during the night mobs led by flag-bearers 'became very mobile over a widening area of Kowloon, melting away on the arrival of the police, and regrouping in a nearby street to continue attacking vehicles, shops and so on'. Particular fury was vented on business concerns whose owners were known to have left-wing sympathies.

In the early hours of 11 October, violence erupted in Mongkok District and Tai Hang Tung, another resettlement estate. Later that day the rioting spread south, west and east along the Kowloon peninsula. The outbursts were intense and largely spontaneous, a fact that helped to bemuse and severely demoralize the thousand-odd riot police that were active in the streets. Crowds ran like quick-silver through the maze of thoroughfares, seemingly immune to batons and tear gas.

As early as 12.30 pm on 11 October there was a meeting between the Chief of Police, senior government officials and the Commander of British Forces. Because of the fluid tactics of the crowds and the need to 'confine the mobs of rioters within limited areas and pin them down so that the police might be able to bring full force to bear on them', it was decided that troops would be brought in to support the police. While three battalions were preparing to move into Kowloon from their barracks in the New Territories, a new dimension had entered into the riots. A taxi carrying the Swiss Consul and his wife had been stopped by a crowd on one of the main roads. The vehicle was overturned and set on fire. The driver escaped, but his passengers suffered severe burns, from which the Consul's wife later died. In the confusion two rioters had been pinned under the car and burned to death. The Commissioner of Police, having until then refrained from allowing his men to use firearms, now instructed them to secure the thoroughfare, using their guns 'without hesitation and where necessary'. This proved to be a turning point. A few hours later the military arrived and by 7.30 pm had been deployed. Kowloon was divided into three sections. These were systematically cleared of crowds and rioters. By 2.00 pm on 12 October it was clear that the security forces had firm control of the situation.

The most chilling manifestations of politically motivated violence were, however, not in urban Kowloon itself but in the small industrial satellite town of Tsuen Wan to the north-west of Kowloon Point. As in Kowloon, the trouble was ostensibly caused by disputes over national day decorations. Right-wing workers, many dressed in the uniforms normally worn at nationalist rallies, demonstrated in front of a cotton mill on the afternoon of 11 October, demanding that it raise the nationalist flag and dismiss all left-wing employees. By the evening the demonstration had degenerated into a full-scale riot and the mill was sacked; the small contingent of riot police present were forced to retreat to the local police station (manned by only sixteen men). Only the threat of the use of a bren-gun there prevented the station itself from being overrun. In the next two hours, while the police officers waited for military reinforcements to arrive, a mob of over a thousand methodically set upon factories and left-wing premises in the town, beating and humiliating any leftist it could find. After a brief defence by some of its inmates, a leftist trade union clinic was broken into and its occupants assaulted. Six employees were tied together in pairs and dragged away. Four died from injuries sustained. At another group of union buildings a few yards away, twenty-one people were beaten mercilessly by the crowd and the premises set on fire. One of the victims later died from his injuries. The mob then divided into two, one part heading for the centre of Tsuen Wan, while the other made for a village on the outskirts. Assaults on buildings and people continued until the arrival of a detachment of soldiers. After brief resistance, the crowds scattered, leaving their victims lying on the roadside. The rampage had left eight dead and sixty-four injured. The following morning police gathered together over 640 left-wing workers from factories to the west of Tsuen Wan and provided them with shelter in the station compound, where they remained until 14 October.

Although the troubles were extremely short-lived, with the security services having gained control of the situation in the whole of Kowloon as early as the afternoon of 12 October, they had a profound effect on government thinking. The inquiry investigating the rioting placed much weight on the role of the networks of organized crime known as Triads and other criminal elements in co-ordinating and leading the crowds (a conclusion supported by statistics which showed that 75 per cent of Hong Kong crime occurred in the predominantly Chinese and working-class Kowloon, and that of that total 45 per cent was in the northern section, the site of the initial troubles). To an extent this was true. There were many instances of motorists, pedestrians and shopkeepers being forced to buy small nationalist flags in order to protect themselves and their property from the fury of the crowd. But, the inquiry concluded, 'there is indication neither of . . . central control of the riots by a superior Triad or other body nor of any planning of the disturbances before the initial outbreak . . . on the afternoon of October 10th'. Nor was the cause wholly political, as the differences between the events in urban Kowloon and Tsuen Wan showed quite clearly. On balance criminal activities and political debt-settling seemed to be outweighed by the more frightening spectre of social unrest; a conclusion supported by the inquiry's view that '[the rioters'] lack of any definite objective was one of the most important elements in the situation in Kowloon. . . . It made it impossible for the police to anticipate the likely targets . . . or to deploy in advance of any new outbreak of violence.'

After the 1956 riots the police cracked down on the Triad societies, claiming that only small, disorganized groups remained after their action. This was the start of a long-running series of police campaigns against these networks of organized crime, but by the 1960s, despite the crackdown, membership of these associations was estimated at one person in every six of the population. More than fifty large organizations now operate in Hong Kong, under such exotic names as 14K and United Bamboo Gang, controlling a spectrum of illegal enterprises, including vice, drug trafficking, gambling, loan sharking and debt collecting and protection rackets. Much to the frustration of the authorities, their centuries-old rituals and principles have adapted well to the modern business environment.

October 1956 and the preoccupation with the role of the Triads in the disturbances had revealed how frail the colony's social infrastructure was. There was no rioting on the island, and special attention was devoted to ensuring that this should be so. The Assistant Commissioner of Police for the island was warned on the night of 10 October to be vigilant against the spread of trouble to his area. Members of the Special Branch were sent to the scene of the disturbances to provide direct reports about their nature. By sharp contrast Tsuen Wan, with its potentially explosive mix of left- and right-wing workers living in the same factory dormitories, was markedly neglected.

The rioting brought Kowloon to a sudden and virtually complete halt. All forms of public transport stopped, as did the distribution of fresh food, and the operations of almost all the major utilities were seriously affected. The state of medical services was particularly grave. Their capacity to absorb the sudden flood of casualties proved to be inadequate. Had it not been for the fact that military hospital facilities were made available to injured civilians, 'a temporary breakdown' of the main public hospitals might well have resulted. Food supplies returned to normal only on 15 October. Two days earlier large quantities of rice were shifted from the island to the mainland in order to stabilize prices. As rice supplies in Kowloon had not run out, this in itself was an indication of official fears that prices might cause renewed, and possibly broader-based, violence.

In December the Governor Sir Alexander Grantham (1947–57) sent a despatch with the report on the riots to the Secretary of State for the Colonies, which showed that the broader implications for the future of the colony were not lost on him. Grantham eloquently drew London's attention to the immense problems created by the post-war influx into Hong Kong, creating 'conditions of unparalleled overcrowding and the attendant threat to law and order'. He recalled the response of the western world to the recent plight of 100,000 Hungarian refugees and pointed out that Hong Kong had accepted up to six times that number in the space of a year after the Chinese Revolution. The Hong Kong Government, he continued, had done all it could to improve conditions for 'these homeless refugees'. But, he concluded, 'without substantial emigration to reduce numbers or outside help to supplement Hong Kong's capacity to absorb them, the task is slow and uphill. In the meantime the risk of a similar outbreak to that which took place in October will be ever present and require increased vigilance'.

Neither the task nor the risk Grantham warned of were far from government thinking again. Nor were the October events easily forgotten by the police force, for whom the few days of violence were nothing short of a nightmare. Officers were, in any case, not allowed to forget their shortcomings. Shortly after David Wilson, now the Governor, came to Hong Kong in 1977 to take up the post of Political Adviser (a Whitehall appointment to help the Hong Kong Government in foreign policy matters), he was taken on a tour of industrial Kwun Tong in north-east Kowloon. The tour coincided with Double Ten. As he strolled through the area, accompanied by a senior police officer, Wilson noticed the hundreds of nationalist flags flying in the breeze. Why, he asked the officer, did the police not take down the flags? It is difficult to know if Wilson, whose academic specialism was the early Kuomintang, was serious or whether it was an attempt at some very dark humour at the expense of the constabulary. The policeman concerned assured me that it was the former. 'Because,' he replied, 'the last time we tried to do it there was a riot.' October 1956, it seems, was very much alive in his mind.

With the exception of the apparent political undercurrents in the rioting, its characteristics were similar to the 'Star' Ferry Riots a decade later. The troubles had an innocuous beginning and, at least in their earliest stage, an air of good-humoured protest or innocence about them, with many young boys present in the crowds. And, as was to happen in 1966, these scenes rapidly turned into a confrontation with authority. The riots came as a short, sharp shock; not least of all because they seemed to have had the most unlikely origins.

The 'Star' Ferry Company had applied for a fare rise in October 1965, the first since 1946. Despite the modest sums involved, the response on the streets was severe. It began with a lone protest by a hunger striker, So Sau-chung, at the Hong Kong Island ferry concourse with a slogan proclaiming – in English – 'Join hunger strike to block fare increase' painted on his jacket. Within three days the opposition led to sit-ins at both ferry terminals, a march to Government House with a petition to the Governor, a demonstration wending its way through Kowloon and, finally, two nights of open rioting on Kowloon streets. Casualties numbered one dead and twenty-six injured, of whom ten were policemen.

Again a commission of inquiry was set up to investigate the troubles. It concluded that their main cause had been a failure in public relations: protesters had feared that the rise in ferry fares signalled a general rise in the cost of public transport, and so sought assurances that other fares would remain stable; such assurances were slow to materialize. The commission's findings suggested that the rioting had been a spontaneous, ill-informed outburst from a minority of the low earning and idle. To some extent this was right. It had been a small fracture in an otherwise remarkably homogeneous society. Children and adolescents, who made up the majority of the protesters, had had a brief taste of running wild in the streets, their faces reflecting the exhilaration of being able to cast a stone at symbols of authority and wealth. However, there were deeper factors at work. Although the commission rejected economic and social conditions as root causes, there is no doubt that the previous decade had been a period of growth and change. A population increase from 2,440,000 to 3,732,400 had been accompanied by a distinct change in the economy, with manufacturing assuming a far more important role. According to economist E. F. Szczepanik, there had been 2000 factories employing a total of 95,000 workers in 1951. Ten years later the figures had grown to over 5200 and 232,000 respectively. In 1966 they stood at 10,413 and 635,300.

More important than this, however, was the fact that per capita consumption during much of this period had been in decline (at times by as much as 14 per cent per annum). Szczepanik concluded of the period that: 'even on the most optimistic assumption we could only suggest that the "pay-off" period . . . is only just beginning'. There is little doubt that frustration caused by waiting for standards of living to take off was responsible both for the extreme response to an otherwise minor, and isolated, rise in transport fares and the associated revolt against authority.

The police had come a long way in the handling of riots since the chaos of 1956 and had developed hardened techniques of crowd control. New police stations resembled forts, with gun turrets, high walls and strings of barbed wire, a model that is replicated to this day. Given the absence of deadlier weapons than stones and projectiles in the hands of rioters in 1966, it might be asked why the police had so readily resorted to the use of firearms. The majority of those who had been shot at had become involved in the disturbances through curiosity and a search for excitement. Indeed, the riots came as such a shock that a number of theories circulated about their causes. Communists were accused of having paid rioters to generate trouble against the British administration. Police were said to have used their links with Triad organizations to discredit social reformers who had involved themselves with the protest movement against the fare rise. A prominent social activist was rumoured to have orchestrated the riots in order to harm the standing of the police.

The representation of the leadership of the disturbances, in so far as there was one, in the inquiry that followed did little to support either the commission's own findings or the suggestions of conspiracy. Nineteen-year-old Lo Kei and a twenty-year-old Eurasian, Brian Raggensack, were singled out for special attention. Both came from broken families. Lo's father had remained in China till his death in 1961 and his mother committed suicide in Hong Kong two years later. Raggensack was brought up by his mother and had no contact with his father. At the time of the disturbances, Lo was living in 'a rented cubicle with a friend' and Raggensack stayed with his sisters and an aunt. Both had little schooling and an erratic employment record. Raggensack, after brief stints as a nightclub door boy and junior hotel employee, became a 'freelance tourist guide'. Lo had briefly delivered kerosene and undertaken a series of factory jobs.

Both made little money. Their testimony showed that they had been inspired by a chance sighting of the hunger striker and his fellow protesters at the ferry terminals. Associations with other minor personalities had formed spontaneously. Their actions were typical of those who find sudden access to political voice and an opportunity, in their small way, to assume leadership. Their political life, whether bought or genuine, was short-lived: Raggensack slipped back into obscurity, and Lo, like his mother before him, took his own life. Hunger striker So Sau-chung was eventually committed to a mental institution.

The events of April 1966 proved to be little more than a surreal prelude to those of May 1967, into which curiously there was no commission of inquiry. Disturbances were triggered off by an industrial dispute that escalated into a violent clash between striking workers and strikebreakers. The involvement of the police failed to quell the conflict, which quickly spread into a full-blown riot. As in Tsuen Wan in 1956, the political dimensions of the disturbances caused greatest concern. On this occasion, however, it was the colony's left-wing circles that took the initiative. The main target was not rival political groupings, but the Hong Kong Government itself.

There was already a great deal of tension present in the region: four months earlier Macau had been rocked to its very foundations and brought to a standstill by a prolonged and bloody confrontation between Chinese activists and the Portuguese administration. Local Chinese officials who, according to a retired senior Portuguese civil servant working in Macau at the time, 'directly represented Beijing's word' finally concluded that, despite Portugal's offer to immediately ship out its entire presence of about two thousand, the Portuguese should remain, but only after they had been subjected 'to a considerable "loss of face" '.

Although the British administration in Hong Kong was far more restrained in dealing with militancy than its Portuguese counterpart (at the first flashpoint in the Macau disturbances, Portuguese troops had opened fire directly into a crowd of agitators), a confrontation seemed inevitable. In China itself the Cultural Revolution had entered its most traumatic phase. For the disgruntled sections of Hong Kong's workforce and their unions, the disturbances in Macau had proved that a colonial regime was not invulnerable. In the meantime, China was showing a militancy that threatened to spill over into Hong Kong. After the first wave of riots – which this time engulfed Hong Kong Island as well – angry crowds crossed into the colony at Sha Tau Kok and surrounded members of the border police, who later became the targets of deadly pot shots from Chinese border guards.

The four months of disturbances proved to be a supreme test of Hong Kong's ability to survive, more so, perhaps, than that of the Guangzhou-Hong Kong General Strike forty years earlier. In addition to the open confrontations, the police and government faced a concerted campaign from left-wing institutions of every description. Left-wing stores, banks and unions became billboards for anti-British slogans. Left-wing schools served as living public-address systems for the dissemination of Mao Zedong thought to the streets outside and, until an explosion killed a pupil, occasionally as centres for bomb making.

These were very tense months. The short-sleeved white cotton shirts and blouses tucked into blue drill trousers worn by sullen *Maojügend* came to symbolize radicalism as much as the black tin hats and the glossy black wound-rope shields of the police represented authority. Sporadic rioting and curfews were punctuated by left-wing demonstrations and poster and press campaigns. By late June bombs were being planted on the streets. Over four thousand of these were found, often nothing more than a soup tin with a note attached warning away 'compatriots', or a container filled with gunpowder extracted from fireworks – which remain banned to this day – and fitted with crude, unstable detonators. Stones were thrown at foreigners, some of whom taunted the new righteous Maoist order in return. As the stifling months of July and August dragged on, the lines of racial confrontation began to make their appearance in a manner unknown in post-war Hong Kong. The situation was made no easier by the lurid photographs of the mangled body of a British bomb disposal expert, one of his arms blown away by a bomb he suspected to be a fake, on the front page of *The Star*, Hong Kong's first English-language sensationalist tabloid.

1967 has subsequently been depicted as a year of resolute resistance by a government gritting its teeth against anything that the left wing could throw against it. Such a view must be qualified. There are certain members of the administration who did indeed live up to this description. Some accounts suggest that they were a minority. Many more became obsessed by images of impending doom, or were simply paralysed by nerves. Government gazettes for the period show that an unusually long list of senior government officials departed that summer. As one of those who stayed put it: 'Even if they were eligible for leave, it was their duty to remain at their posts if only to set a good example to their juniors and the public at large.'

Amongst those who left during the troubled months were the Governor, Sir David Trench (on regular vacation), and the Commissioner of Police (who was sent away to London 'for consultation' in July and did not return until after the disturbances). These were individuals with at least *prima facie* reasons to be away. Sources close to Legco at the time observed that all but one of the local councillors fled to the United States or Canada to secure a passport.

The struggle between local leftists and government was above all a test of nerve. In some respects it was nothing more than the old-fashioned technique of fighting fire with fire. When the Bank of China set up loudspeakers outside its head office in Central to blare out anti-government slogans and Mao thought, the Government Information Service office, conveniently located across the street from the bank, set up a bigger set of speakers through which they played God Save the Queen and popular music. Within days the Bank's efforts, having been completely overwhelmed, were shut down.

A small anti-propaganda committee was formed to combat the virulent propaganda campaign conducted by the left-wing press. The committee's brief was to generate a public controversy over the disturbances in the local press. Its members were to write letters from bogus Communists, supporting the compatriots' struggle. Then the views of 'shocked' citizens were sent in response. Many of these exchanges were so good that they elicited supportive contributions from genuine leftists. Fully prepared with necessary details, the committee would, remembers one of its number, 'fairly jump in reply'. Amongst the small group making up this committee were two Chinese civil servants, who risked a great deal by working with it. When the emergency finally subsided, they were recommended for honours. These were refused because by then Britain was involved in 'mending fences' with China. One received an honour only eighteen years after he had made his brave contribution, and even then not directly for his work on the committee. The other man is still waiting for some recognition, which he will probably never receive.

In dealing with left-wing strongholds, the action took a more physical form. The Commissioner of Police who left was replaced by a man who was, as one of his contemporaries described him, 'a tough bastard'. When, upon his appointment, he was asked what he intended to do with the new emergency regulations at his disposal, he responded without a trace of indecision that he would move against the leftist organizations. When asked when this would be, his response was simply 'immediately'. When a supplementary question of 'how soon?' was posed, his answer was 'tomorrow . . . morning'. True to his word, the new Commissioner set about methodically encircling organization after organization, beginning with the smallest and working upwards, culminating with the Bank of China on Hong Kong Island and the Trade Union Federation in Kowloon. By the time his campaign ended, Communist activities had petered out.

The China dimension added to the uncertainty. In retrospect it is clear that, as in Macau a few months before, the central Chinese authorities were happy to distance themselves from events in the colony, leaving local left-wing elements to decide the best channels and scope for the struggle, as well as its final objectives. Apart from public anti-British pronouncements and pressure from Beijing to secure the release of those Chinese detained in the colony, the main contribution of the Chinese Government was the discreet supply of funds. Food exports to Hong Kong and entrepôt dealings through the colony were maintained at normal levels. At the time, however, the British administration was very unsure how far the Chinese Government was directly behind the political ground swell in Hong Kong. There were disturbing indicators, such as the uneven course of Sino-British relations in London and Beijing and the course of events in Macau, where a mob had forced the British Consul to stand motionless in intense heat, surrounded by chanting crowds. All this had the effect of making Hong Kong officials very jittery.

The Chinese authorities' most calculated intervention in the political situation in Hong Kong was through the Anthony Grey affair. Grey was a British journalist based in Beijing. Following the seizure of a reporter from the New China News Agency (NCNA) and his trial and imprisonment by a Hong Kong court for unlawful assembly and intimidation, Grey was placed under house arrest in

Beijing. He remained a captive for two years. Some time after he had been arrested, he was used to influence political and legal processes in Hong Kong. At the height of the troubles, a senior civil servant accused the publisher of a left-wing daily of slander and sought a private legal action against him. There was a distinct chance that, when the action finally reached the Supreme Court, punitive damages would be awarded which would knock out one of the most aggressive arms of the propaganda campaign against the government. But then the official was called to a meeting with his superior. The Colonial Secretary was also present at the meeting. The official was informed that information had just been received from the consulate at Beijing. The Chinese authorities had made it plain to a British representative that every action against the leftist publisher would result in a reciprocal action against Grey. This revelation was passed on to the man 'not as a directive, simply as a matter of information'. He was then told to go away and think about it. A few days later he was brought in again and asked what he had decided. When he said that he planned to go ahead with the action, he was told that this might result in 'very serious' repercussions and asked if he had considered these. He was then given fresh news. In a cable from the Ministry of Foreign Affairs to the Foreign Office, China had informed the British Government that: 'For every blow struck against . . . (the publisher) and the . . . (his newspaper), ten blows would be struck against Anthony Grey.' The civil servant went straight home to 'dwell on the inequity of (his) predicament'. After a night of painful deliberation, he agreed to seek a restraint on the order and waive the costs. In return, the publisher retracted his accusations in full.

Although the wounds of 1967 have long since healed, scars remain. The shock of seeing the political system in Hong Kong under such great pressure had been enough to convince thousands of residents that their future could not lie in the colony. Many fled during the early months. Despite the depressed property and stock markets, there was a rash of selling. Those who bought secured bargains: flats and houses were often sold fully furnished, their sellers being in too much of a hurry to haggle or pack their household belongings ready for shipment to their new homes overseas. The flight of people and capital continued through 1968 and 1969, by which date it had become clear to most, including the most faint-hearted, that China was anxious to preserve the *status quo*. At the height of the panic, however, even leftward-leaning business people had begun to purchase insurance. One such person, a property and construction tycoon who finally remained in Hong Kong, visited the Canadian High Commission to apply for an immigrant's visa to North America: 'What financial resources can you produce in support of your application?' asked the consular employee, wearied by an earlier string of applicants and unaware of this applicant's standing in the business community.

'US$5,000,000 . . . in cash . . . immediately. Will that be enough?' His application went through without another word.

CHAPTER THREE

Glittering Refuge

The phrase 'rags to riches; represents the potent, often obsessive dream that provides, ultimately, the only assurance of personal freedom. This dream is very dear to the people of Hong Kong. It explains more than anything else why so many from the territory have been drawn to countries such as America and Australia; societies in which social acceptance is seen to be dependent neither on caste nor class, but on financial success, potential for which seems limitless. Because of its small physical size, the 'rags to riches' dream is all the more potent in the colony. There are probably few places in the world where it is possible to find a man playing tombola with bank clerks and housewives for a line worth $20 and a house of $50 after just having made a million on the stock market, and whose chauffeur waits for him in the club's car-park.

No money, small money, big money and sometimes huge money mingle casually, unconsciously, with one another. Here wealth is inspirational, and the basis of most of the popular folklore. There is virtually no distinction between 'old' and 'new' money: it all amounts to 'live' money; nor is there a social stigma associated with its acquisition. Wealth provides the bench mark, the impetus and the final glittering prize for hard work. Newcomers to the colony may be excused for wondering how, in a place so highly geared to enterprise, coffee shops could do such thriving business during office hours, with patrons seemingly fixed idly to their seats for hours on end. The chances are that they are talking about buying, selling, deals. Nor is there any need to eavesdrop to discover that this is so: the faces are often joyless, as if discussing someone's funeral. Every so often someone walks away to the telephone, or picks up a portaphone, to 'touch base' with the office.

Of course the limitless potential has very definite boundaries. Dreams turn into nightmares very quickly in Hong Kong. There is many a haunted look to be seen, the tell-tale frayed collar and barely perceptible stoop of the shoulders betraying a person on the brink of defeat. More subtle signs are revealed in the popular pastime of counting money to while away the time while travelling by bus or tram: it is the person who is counting and recounting $10 notes (often by turning the fold of notes around to the four corners, earnestly thumbing through each) who deserves a second glance. It is tempting to believe that money comes easily in Hong Kong, derived from the willingness to indulge in opportunism. And there is a certain sector that fuels this image, as there is in any society. But this should not obscure the majority's diligent and dignified pursuit of material well-being, a reflection of the overwhelmingly immigrant character of the society. So many of those living in Hong Kong have arrived with nothing but the clothes on their backs and with only two initial qualities to offer their new home: patience and application. These characteristics are tempered by an age-old Chinese cultural trait of desiring nothing more than a stable environment in which to pursue *sang-i* (business) and being grateful for the absence of natural and political blight. This particular combination gives rise to an atmosphere in which there is a fine balance between an earthy lack of expectations and the promise of limitless potential.

Through the 1960s and 1970s a tiny, slightly-built man made the rounds of office buildings in Central District, providing his own magazine subscription service to office workers. He was neatly dressed and carried a soft-sided plastic case from which he would produce the journals every week and make a note of the delivery on a small square of paper. His charge for the magazine was no less than the cover price, so why anyone should buy from him was not altogether clear. Nor was it clear how he had come to introduce his service to these offices. Perhaps all was explained by his soft, even voice and good spirits. While he conducted this trade, his wife sold newspapers from a street stall in the area. Although he kept an accurate account of deliveries, one day he became involved in a dispute: two office workers queried the amounts they had been charged. He replied that the amounts were right and that he had them written down. As proof, he produced his small square of paper. On it were scribbled rows of circles and crosses.

'This is you and this,' he pointed to the other person, 'is you.'

'But what do these mean?'

'I can't put it any other way. I can't write in Chinese or English.'

At Chinese New Year, he would come for the customary yearly bonus and bring with him a string of children for their *lai si* (a red packet containing a New Year gift of money, ideally freshly-minted notes and coins for luck, given to children and unmarried adults). On one such visit he told the people who had been involved in the dispute: 'I am uneducated myself, but I will make sure that each of them will be educated to as high a level as I can achieve.' Year by year there were fewer children until, finally, he would come alone to collect his bonus. All his children had been educated and some of them had already gone abroad.

This man was Cantonese, one of the millions who found their way into Hong Kong either legally or illegally, many of them unskilled. Of major importance to him and to the thousands like him who are able to transform their marginal and, it must be said, precarious existence into a solid foundation for their families is stability; a guarantee of day-to-day routine. Without it, the minute calculations that go on at all levels of society are impossible. This stability has very little to do with grand political design or macroeconomic models. To most who have come from nothing into nothing, stability is little more than the precise and personal measurement of today against yesterday and the necessary luxury of routine financial return. It was summed up well by a Vietnamese-Chinese friend, himself an illegal immigrant in the early 1970s: 'If I haven't made a dollar today, I won't sleep tonight.'

The need to maintain this certain knowledge of one's place between heaven and earth plays an important part in the lives of unskilled worker and entrepreneur alike. The wave of Shanghainese immigrants arriving in the colony during the early years of Communist rule in China brought with them a considerable degree of skill, particularly in the manufacture and sale of textiles, and were largely responsible for the first plateau of Hong Kong's modern industrial development. The Shanghai businessman brought with him combinations of capital, stock and plant, or in some cases made his way to the colony with little more than a connection with a foreign business that had moved from Shanghai when conditions there had become intolerable.

He represents the more visible form of the entrepreneurial influx, but is not easy to get near. There is the high profile example of Sir Yue-kong (Y.K.) Pao, a man who, like Woody Allen's Zelig, is to be found in photograph after official photograph: at a reception with President Reagan, behind the shoulder of Prime Minister Thatcher, chatting with Premier Deng. The other Shanghai patriarchs, however, comprise an intensely secretive bread-and-butter group involved in textiles, light manufacture and finance.

It is not impossible to get a flavour – albeit at a more modest level – of how the Shanghainese have integrated into society. An example of Chinese Shanghai transposed to Hong Kong is provided by Mr Y, a stocky broad-faced man in his mid sixties, with a manner and slicked-back hairstyle that conjures up images of Shanghai's bustling, waterfront promenade, the Bund, in the 1930s. After the fall of the Qing Dynasty, his family still possessed large tracts of land. Piece by piece these were either sold or given away. Now, to Mr Y, they are nothing more than a memory. Without a trace of emotion or sense of loss, he regarded his family property as 'something like reading a newspaper: you recognize the facts, the history, but it is meaningless to you'. In Shanghai he had served an apprenticeship with a piece-goods merchant, acquiring skills. He learned how to match materials, but not just as an exercise in taste: samples of materials were combined in the swatches in such a way as to make even the less desirable materials attractive, in order, in his words, 'to make the person choosing confused. He would come for blue material, but then begin to think that the less popular brown is "not bad".' Mr Y eventually joined a small Russian-Jewish import/export firm, working with the owner in Shanghai and, after the revolution, with the owner's son in Hong Kong. Before moving to Hong Kong, however, Mr Y had decided, like many other Shanghainese importers, to direct incoming shipments of stock not to Shanghai but to Hong Kong. His decision had been prompted by a simple commercial expedient: Hong Kong provided cheap storage at the time. Once he and the company made the move, he was in possession of sufficient stock to allow his trade to continue virtually uninterrupted. In postwar Shanghai, where commercial conditions were exceedingly difficult, he developed elaborate schemes, juggling Japanese quotas, American servicemen's quotas and PXs (armed forces discount shops), to avoid the pitfalls of dealing with China's trade problems and sagging currency. In the process he was managing to make 100 per cent profit on his goods. But the juggling of these schemes has not changed the yardstick with which he measures the success of his achievements. In earlier times he remembers having earned enough to buy 4 ounces of gold every month. Today, he says, his earnings are the equivalent of 35–40 ounces per year, so to his mind he is not doing so well. Behind this thinking is a spiral of cautionary logic: 'You think,' he observes, ' "I will spend $100 today . . . I will earn another $100 tomorrow." Maybe not!' And he tells you how years ago office workers would buy one cup of coffee per day, but that now coffee is consumed with lunch, at teatime and after dinner. Each extra cup costs money, each cup means added expense. To him this is a hidden form of inflation and threatens to impair his ability to hedge against the unforeseen.

Shanghai has added another indelible stamp to the character of Hong Kong. A tiny fraction of the small foreign community, itself only about one per cent of the population, are Shanghailanders who resettled in Hong Kong after capitalist Shanghai finally ground to a halt in 1953. They make up an exotic racial mix, being predominantly those born to mixed marriages: Russians escaping from the Bolsheviks, Ashkenazi Jews escaping persecution and discrimination in Russia, Sephardic Jews who made the long trek from Baghdad to China via India. They are synonymous with a distinct part of the financial establishment, and are the very soul of the foreign community. Through them the sparkle of Shanghai society, which so dominated foreign life on the China coast, was imparted to the colony, giving rise to much of its own attraction and many of its myths. It is perhaps a mark of the Shanghailanders' impact on Hong Kong that, despite their relatively late arrival, they give the impression that they have always been there.

Aside from the anarchic blend of internationalism that they brought with them, there are charming anachronisms that from time to time appear in their vocabulary. A casual mention of tiffin instead of lunch conjures up a vision of grand Shanghai hotels, waiters in starched white jackets and freshly-typed menu cards in their silver-plated holders. Such phrases also evoke memories of Hong Kong's own past. In a sense this group – now beginning to fade away forever – is a unique, living archive of colonial existence. In them the grandeur of days past mixes in a bittersweet way with a new colonial life in Hong Kong. Most were born, educated and lived much of their lives in China. Those who have met them will know the old-fashioned cheer, the earthy humour and in some cases the odd flash of bawdy behaviour which owes, in all likelihood, a debt to the infamous Shanghai night-life for its inspiration, but is made endearing by a depth of humanity and a pinch of the profound sadness that can only come out of a life lost. Like Mr Y, they are people to whom China has taught its enduring lessons: fatalism, deep attachment to the land, very often the facility of language and Chinese attitudes to class, so different from those of colonial Britons.

Overlapping the exodus from Shanghai was the temporary influx of Russians from northern China. This began in 1952 through the work of the International Refugee Office (IRO) – later replaced by the United Nations High Commission for Refugees (UNHCR) – and the World Council of Churches. The initial brief for these bodies involved a case-load of 2000 people, with a further 3000 applications pending. By the time UNHCR officially closed its door to European refugees in late 1973, 21,000 people had passed through and been resettled in countries as diverse as Australia, Brazil and Switzerland.

These refugees represented a very wide cross-section of Russian society. The majority came from a number of urban centres in Manchuria, the most important of which was Harbin in Heilongjiang Province. If Shanghai was the Paris of the Far East, Harbin was its Moscow. It was a quintessential Russian settlement, founded in the 1890s by the Chinese Eastern Railway on the banks of the River Sungari, in the very heartland of the Manchurian plains. The indigenous population of railway employees was boosted by the arrival of thousands of *émigrés* fleeing the Russian Revolution of 1917.

Russian life continued to thrive in the region in the 1920s, survived the Japanese occupation, World War II, the Chinese Civil War and, for a brief period, even the rise of Communism. However, within a few years of the formation of the People's Republic of China, conditions became untenable. Despite official assurances that nothing would change for the Russians – most of whom were stateless – the Communist victory ensured that everything did. Part of the problem was beyond the control of the new regime: inflation was rampant, leading some Russians to note sardonically that for the first time since they arrived in China they had become millionaires; unfortunately, monthly pay had to be transported in wheelbarrows and millions of yuan were required to buy a loaf of bread! In addition to the natural processes involved in such a change, the Russians were gradually, and in many cases deliberately, squeezed out of all forms of livelihood. By the late 1950s most had unwillingly decided they had to leave. Exit was not straightforward: the provision of a visa often hinged on the willingness of householders to sell their homes to the state. In the case of owners of flats, senior police officers would broadly hint that visas would only be issued if the property were signed over directly to them. Many homes were forcibly requisitioned and levelled, their owners receiving payment based on the weight of wood and metal fittings.

With their final visa and fortnight's transit document to Hong Kong secured, the refugees packed their belongings. Money was not allowed out of the country, nor precious metals or gems; the most that they could bring out with them was five American dollars per person. Life savings were spent on anything. Those who bought Chinese furniture and curios were the luckiest, for they would have something to show for their time in China. Rumours spread of what might prevent exit, resulting in the destruction of reams of personal papers and valuable books, or what was *khodovoe* (saleable) beyond Chinese borders. Many bought as much black caviar as they could lay their hands on because they heard it was in demand in Hong Kong. A thriving trade developed, with refugees buying and selling between themselves once they reached the colony, and finally to restaurants and hotels. Hong Kong's gourmets had never known such a surfeit of this great delicacy.

The majority made the long journey to Hong Kong by rail, while some came by ship from Tianjin or Shanghai. Once in the colony, their short stay visa was extended to allow necessary medical examinations to take place and final approval to be received from the country issuing the migrant visa. Most stayed in Hong Kong for no more than three months. Initial arrivals were housed in hotels with such prestigious names as the Waldorf and Cathay in Causeway Bay or the Shamrock, Metropolitan and Movieland in Kowloon. Later, under the pressure of increasing numbers, others found themselves assigned to an expanding net of guesthouses such as the London Better Home, Manshing Apartment House and Rodo House. Kowloon City Hotel, which stood near the airport, became a village of Old Believers. Behind the exotic names accommodation ranged from shabby hotel to nothing more than a tiny room with little ventilation and a tiled floor for each family. The guesthouses in particular were makeshift affairs, hardly able to bear the strain of the constant turnover in refugees. Spartan communal dining-rooms provided thin soups and even thinner main courses. Bottles of Ajinomoto (Japanese monosodium glutamate) stood on every table.

The Russians' board, food and onward passage were paid for by the UNHCR, which also provided a tiny weekly allowance for small purchases such as toothpaste and occasional sweets for children. At the height of the influx in the early 1960s there were thousands of men, women and children for whom the months of waiting seemed interminable and whose only diversion was to wander the streets peering wistfully into the glittering shop windows. During the humid summer months some of the families would forsake their cramped rooms for the roofs of the guesthouses, where they would while away the long days under improvised canopies and wait for the blissful relief of a gentle evening breeze.

For most, Hong Kong will remain a memory far more vivid than their comparatively brief stay should have allowed. But the experience of poverty in a rich society is hard to erase; especially so when, as if by capricious irony, the doctors to whom the Russians were often sent for their medical examinations and treatment had their offices on the mezzanine floor of the Peninsula Hotel, then as now a show-piece of wealth.

An irony of this episode is that many of the small number of Chinese, Russians and Eurasians who worked long and selflessly to ensure the smooth flow of the Russian exodus had been refugees themselves. One member of the tiny UNHCR office was the daughter of a scholarly Mandarin who, although she had been born in Hong Kong, spent much of her childhood in Malaya and Kweilin Province. To this day she sends monthly cheques to a sister living in Guangdong from whom she was separated before the war. Another Chinese woman, who worked for the World Council of Churches and later the UN, was born to a senior official of the Chinese Eastern Railway. She attended a Russian secondary school and polytechnic in Harbin, departing for Shanghai in 1949 and finally moving on to Hong Kong in 1953. There she immediately found work in the refugee programme; she remembers how she would use her fluent Russian to greet elderly Russian women at the railway terminus, loaded down with bundles and with their heads wrapped in peasant scarves. The women would burst into tears of happiness as they exclaimed: 'How good it is to come all this way and meet a Russian!' Because of the Sino-British Joint Declaration and Britain's nationality legislation, the caseworkers themselves have become refugees again.

The Hong Kong Government, as in most of its dealings with refugees, kept a paternalistic but distant eye on the Russians. Visas were issued with a minimum of fuss and even less aid. The terms of entry to the colony did not allow the holders to work. A greater obstacle to finding casual employment was, however, the general absence of English. A few women were able to find work as cleaners in British households, while groups of Old Believers applied themselves to finding work as labourers. It was with some embarrassment that, following a newspaper story about Russians labouring alongside Chinese in the construction of the colony's first flyover, the government clamped down on the Old Believers' initiative. Had the Russians been given the time and opportunity, as they were in the countries in which they eventually settled, there is little doubt that they would have represented a splendid example of how integration functions at its most basic level in Hong Kong. They are the European minority that has come closest to living through the full rags to riches cycle in China that Chinese refugees themselves have faced in the modern era. Most shared a stoical understanding of the delicate balance that exists between a lost or forsaken past, an empty pocket and the certain knowledge that things can only get better. The Russians also, in a sense, highlighted the stark plight of the many Chinese who found their way into Hong Kong. Despite the obvious hardships that they had overcome, the Russians enjoyed the luxury of refugee status and rudimentary aid. The Chinese were not assured of even this.

By 1968 the flow of Russians from north-eastern China had become a trickle. In that year the exodus of Russians from Xinjiang began, as if China was wringing out every last trace of its former mentor from within its borders. This sparsely populated, windswept region in the north-western corner of the Chinese land mass, with a snaking border shared with Soviet Central Asia, was regarded by Beijing as a potential security problem. Its native inhabitants, in appearance Chinese, had long associations with Russia. There had been much transmigration and intermarriage. Many of the men who lived in the border region spoke fluent Russian, had Russian names and second families on the Russian side of the boundary. The radicalism of the Cultural Revolution, that had so devastatingly spilled over into the internal affairs of Tibet and was forcing the rapid sinification of that country, swept into Xinjiang too. Those who were too close to things Russian were subjected to great hardships by the authorities. As with the Russians of the north-east, the Xinjiang Russians found that there was little alternative but to apply for exit visas. In the late 1970s, with the Beijing leadership fully committed to a policy of 'purifying' the Xinjiang region, the numbers of refugees grew. Hundreds again populated the small guesthouses while they waited patiently for resettlement, the majority finding their way to Australia.

Coinciding with the flow of Shanghainese, Shanghailanders and northern Russians into Hong Kong was that of the Indonesian Chinese. The total number of ethnic Chinese who severed their links with Indonesia and resettled in China, in three waves between 1959 and 1967, has never been precisely calculated. Estimates vary from 100,000 to over 300,000. By the time the movement of Russians had begun to slow down, some 70,000 of these had decided that they had had enough of China and secured exit visas. About 30,000 were able to find new countries to resettle in (Indonesia refused to allow them to return); the others squeezed into Hong Kong. As the Shanghainese before them, the Indonesian Chinese began to form a neighbourhood with its own distinct identity. In the 1950s the Shanghainese had created a Little Shanghai in Causeway Bay. With the coming of the Indonesian Chinese, North Point, the next district along the eastern corridor of the Hong Kong waterfront, became known as Little Indonesia.

The Indonesian Chinese had scarcely settled in when a new group of south-east Asians began to appear in Hong Kong, the Indo-Chinese. Initially, they came in small numbers. After the escalation of the conflict in Vietnam and its spread to Cambodia, the early handful of merchants and professionals who found their way into the colony between 1968 and 1971 became a small, regular flow, conveyed by the steamers that plied the route between Indo-China and Hong Kong. This form of passage, a forerunner of the syndicated operations in the late 1970s, was not cheap. One of the early arrivals, the son of the holder of Saigon's rice monopoly, described how he was approached by a man in 1972. All that was said to him was: 'Do you want to leave next week? I have a boat going to Hong Kong.' The cost of the journey was the equivalent of HK$50,000.

Having agreed, he was directed to a beach outside Saigon, where, with thirty-six others, he was deposited on board the Hong Kong-bound ship. He knew little about his final destination except that a distant relative lived there.

A week later the ship moored in mid-harbour in Hong Kong. That evening, before boarding a walla-walla (a small diesel-powered water taxi), his courier provided a short briefing about his new home: 'On the left is Kowloon, on the right is Hong Kong; where do you want to go?' He guessed Hong Kong, although he had no idea where his relative lived. The courier continued with a warning: 'Look straight ahead when you land, don't look around at the new sights.' Before he left the ship, the courier suggested that it might be wise to leave his only luggage, a satchel, behind to prevent any suspicion being cast his way. The courier added that it would be 'passed on to him'. Guessing that the courier was looking for something more than the protection of the illegal immigrant's welfare, he refused, saying that the bag contained all that he had. He offered the courier US$100 'for his expenses'. It was accepted.

The early Vietnamese and Cambodian arrivals were relatively fortunate. The normal course was to go into hiding, live on money brought out or find work. After a few years, disclosing themselves voluntarily if they were not discovered, refugees would throw themselves on the mercy of the authorities for the right to remain. Following a lengthy, anxious wait, permission 'on the strength of the individual circumstances' was often – if sternly – granted. The numbers involved were small. According to government sources, only 14,425 Indo-Chinese refugees and 'displaced persons' have settled in Hong Kong since 1975. Most of the illegal immigrants were able to assimilate easily, frequently finding that residents they had befriended would produce character statements and petitions on their behalf. The government could be seen to be lenient. However, the influx of the true Boat People, beginning with the fall of Saigon and Phnom Penh in April 1975, has gradually elicited a general hardening of hearts and minds to the plight of the Indo-Chinese refugee.

It has already been mentioned that the Hong Kong Government is reluctant to refer to the Cantonese entering the colony as refugees. In fact they are, and the overwhelming majority are economic refugees; in the same category, ironically, as the long-suffering Vietnamese refugees in the Hong Kong camps today.

Following the introduction of a formal border after World War II, Hong Kong's policy on Cantonese refugees has been consistently curious.

There is no better example of this than the Touch Base policy, which remained in force until 1982. According to this, the II (illegal immigrant) patrols – at first a function of the police, but later gradually taken over by an otherwise redundant military – would work hard to stop a person entering the colony illegally. Anyone caught would, having been questioned to discover their motives, be handed over to the Chinese authorities. Should that person have reached the urban side of the Kowloon hills, however, he or she was deemed to have reached 'home base' and was allowed to stay on in the colony.

In the early 1960s, with the numbers of IIs having increased dramatically as a result of the abortive Great Leap Forward in China (1962 alone saw an influx estimated at over 142,000), the Foreign Office appealed to the Chinese authorities to tighten their own border control, while Whitehall pressed the Hong Kong Government to reduce the flow on its side. One of the priority measures suggested was the construction of a second fence a few yards behind the existing one. The experiences of a civil servant working for the Public Works Department at the time reveal some interesting facets of government policy and the illegal immigration problem. He was summoned to his superior's office one afternoon. There he found that his colleagues had also been summoned. The department head was saying to himself: 'Who knows anything about erecting fences?' and, turning to my respondent, asked, 'You were in the Engineer Corps weren't you. . . ?' Before he could respond, the department head had already begun a flurry of 'You, you and you. . . ' followed by an official confirmation of immediate transfer to this duty. The project, those chosen were informed, was to be initiated simultaneously in three sections at Sha Tau Kok, Lo Wu and Lok Ma Chau. It was to be completed in five weeks. Daily progress reports ('precisely, in feet') were to be relayed to London. This in itself posed problems: how was the length erected to be surveyed when the fence was coming up in three separate sections? Also, nothing had been said in London or Hong Kong about the terrain they would be working on. There were no roads and most of the area was marshy. Nor had any provision been made for the co-operation of the landowners whose property the fence might traverse. Instead, as the fence was erected, a District Officer was to move slightly ahead of the work, negotiating with villagers.

The original fence was of the type that surrounds tennis courts. Large sections had been cut open. In some parts the fence posts were held up by the fence itself. As the engineers and their gangs arrived in the morning they would walk past groups of mainland people huddled together, waiting for nightfall to make the crossing into Hong Kong and an Olympian sprint to 'touch base'. If they were unlucky enough to be rounded up and returned to China, a few days later they would be back at the same point.

The land crossing is a difficult way to enter the colony. Those who have attempted it recall that it is a frightening experience. In order to prevent detection by II patrols, the routes pass through countryside which is densely vegetated and hilly. Even with the assistance of professional guides, the refugees still remember only the darkness and the sensation of moving into the complete unknown. Some of the younger refugees crossed the border by swimming across Mirs Bay or Deep Bay. Confident swimmers set off with little more than a bag containing clothes and a few belongings. The less proficient would use floats, some being nothing more than a large plastic bag filled with an accumulation of ping-pong balls. At the height of the flood of refugees in the 1960s, regular reports were published in local papers of those who did not succeed, whose bodies were found floating in the bays or washed ashore. Families were frequently split up. Less hardy members would make a costly trip by boat, either to Macau – from where special 'travel agencies' arranged the next leg of the journey to Hong Kong – or to one of the outlying islands. Small children would be left behind with relations to wait for the parents to settle down in Hong Kong before formal application was made for their entry. In some cases they were entrusted to women who were entering Hong Kong legally and would bring them into the colony as their own.

With the end of the Touch Base policy, the true image of immigration control in Hong Kong became clearer. Its action had been similar to that of a narrow filter, slowly straining a flood of souls pouring through the apparatus. The true psychological importance of the policy was that it provided both legal and illegal means of finding sanctuary in Hong Kong. Today there is only the legal route, a fact reflected in the 600,000 names on the official list of Chinese waiting to enter the colony to be reunited with their families. In addition, literally tens of thousands of children in China have been barred, probably permanently, from joining their parents in Hong Kong.

The infrastructure that accepts refugees in Hong Kong demands a natural application to work; it stresses the importance of the family while encouraging individualism. In return it offers nothing more than the chance of the daily satisfaction of working for an improved lifestyle. It is the refugee's careful management of these facets of existence that eventually gives rise to thoughts of potential and, coincidentally, explains why 'reborn' Hong Kong entrepreneurs have enjoyed such success. Need encourages flexibility and sacrifice, which in turn lie at the heart of the Hong Kong industrial miracle.

CHAPTER FOUR

A Precarious Society

The 'pay-off' that was promised for the sacrifices made during the lengthy period of reinvestment in the 1950s and 1960s began to find its way into the ordinary lifestyle only in the early 1970s, when the economy began to boom. With one eye on China's simmering power struggle, Hong Kong entered the new decade with some confidence. Following their brief attempt to establish a platform of power during the 1967 disturbances, the unions had been systematically brought to heel. Manufacture began to edge toward the quality market. The advent of denim as a fashion fabric transformed the colony into a clothier to the world. Children the world over were playing with toys made in Hong Kong. In three years of quiet after the trauma of 1967, the government began to release more land, its most valuable asset, into the recovering property market. Major new capital projects were initiated in urban areas. Matching these internal trends, exports grew strongly virtually across the board. The new decade coincided with the arrival of a new Governor, Sir Murray MacLehose, sworn in in November 1971, and a new administrative style.

Unlike his immediate predecessors, Sir Robert Black and Sir David Trench, MacLehose did not emerge from the ranks of career colonial administrators. He had a diplomatic background, having worked in legations both in China and Japan. MacLehose immediately began to dismantle much of the pomp associated with the post. He dispensed with the use of the Governor's limousine for the short journey from Government House to Legco Chambers, preferring to walk there for meetings. A common touch quickly became apparent as the new Governor took regular walks, in short-sleeved, open-necked shirts, through densely populated residential areas. All indications were that here, at last, was a Governor of the people. This in itself came as quite a shock to the colonial system. More so, however, was the sweep of MacLehose's vision for social engineering. An urgent campaign for a rapid expansion in low-cost housing was introduced, followed by reforms to the political structure and a host of government crusades against social ills ranging from drugs to litter. For the civil servants that had to implement policies handed down to them, MacLehose was a Peter the Great playing to their boyars, dragging them into the modern age by their beards.

Apart from the government housing programme, MacLehose's most difficult enterprise was in dealing with the blight of corruption. It was not a new problem, nor was the Governor the first to attempt to tackle it, although his was the most senior and radical initiative. In many respects, corruption within government had less to do with lack of morality than with simple exigency. This had been particularly evident during the Korean War and in its aftermath, when a trade embargo on China led to high levels of smuggling. The situation was not helped by the numerous irrational laws that were aimed at harming China, but in fact rebounded on Hong Kong. For example, under the strategic goods embargo, cobalt oxide was banned because of its applications in nuclear armaments. But this chemical was also used in the blue edging used to decorate enamelware, which was at the time of vast importance to the colony's economy. Hundreds of millions of dollars were involved. Government employees who were on the front line at this time were relatively low paid – in particular the officers from the Department of Commerce and Industry, who dealt with the paperwork for goods passing through the colony, and those employed by the Customs and Excise. An officer holding a senior position earned little more than $500 a month, plus $100 in various allowances. Customs officers earned even less, little more than $400 a month.

One of the early pioneers of anti-corruption work remembered the problems graphically. He began his activities while working for the Department of Commerce and Industry. The chronically overworked department's certification section was a mess. Having completed building up a system for certification that would allow straightforward access and cross-reference, he moved on to Customs. There the situation was a complete disaster. His work, he observed, was: 'like holding a sieve by its solid edge and watching the water run through as I tried to patch up hole after hole'. During his period in office, he created a file for official responses to gifts that were 'beyond reason'. These, in his experience, included jade neck-laces and rings worth tens of thousands of dollars. Such gifts would be returned with a letter, a copy of which was to be filed, explaining why it had been rejected. Of some forty letters that were filed during his time there, over thirty were his own. 'What of the rest of the employees?' he asked. There was, of course, no answer.

Resistance to the reality of the situation was most pronounced at senior levels. One day he was called in by his head of department and a police report slapped on the desk in front of him. He was accused by his superior of 'collaborating' with the police. 'I can recognize your writing, your style in this report.' Although he denied it, the head of department continued: '(It) suggests that the department is riddled with corruption.' Casting a glance at the list of cases quoted in the document, the junior recognized most as those he had investigated himself. He tried to impress upon his superior that the contents of the report were, after all, ultimately the latter's responsibility, but was cut short: 'Oh no! I don't know any-thing about it, it's your responsibility. . . . I have only eighteen months to go before retirement and I'm presented with this as a parting gift.'

The officer was unceremoniously sent from the room, with a parting demand that there be no further spoken contact between the two men before the superior's retirement. However, the officer remained true to his principles, cleaning up section after section with the instigation of criminal proceedings and the dismissal of staff involved. At that time reports were taken up by the Police Anti-Corruption Branch, known to the small circle of activists as the Corruption Branch. Cases referred to it would, the informant knew, simply make known a new source of revenue which the investi-gation officer could tap.

After more than a decade of work against corrupt practices, the civil servant became a focus of attention from the press. In the late 1960s he appeared on a radio programme, in which he suggested that every government department, to a greater or lesser degree, suffered from corruption. Following this radical statement, he received a letter from a senior civil servant – later to become Chief Secretary – strenuously denying that this was the case. A long correspondence ensued between the two men, ending abruptly with the establishment of the Independent Commission Against Corruption (ICAC) in 1974.

ICAC was the result of a commission of inquiry initiated by MacLehose in response to a sharp rise in public disquiet over corrupt practices within the police force, given particular vent in the Godber affair in 1973. Peter Godber had had an exemplary record since his arrival as a police officer cadet in 1952 and had moved upwards through the ranks until, in 1971, he was promoted to Deputy District Commander, Kowloon. He was soft-spoken and of an amiable disposition; a few of the older residents remember him as a young man spending his Friday evenings as a tombola caller at a local social club, earning a meal, free drinks and a few dollars. Godber had been a brave leader of the police tactical unit during the 1967 disturbances, for which he was awarded the Colonial Police Medal. But he was, it was discovered, corrupt. Worse still, having investigated him fully and found a bank account in Canada containing over C$200,000 in early 1973, the authorities had somehow managed to allow him to escape to Britain in June of that year. He had left a further HK$250,000 in his Hong Kong account. The fiasco stirred up a hornet's nest. There was a public campaign to bring Godber back to face justice; posters appeared everywhere depicting him sitting on a pile of banknotes and toasting onlookers with a glass of champagne underneath a final estimate of what he had accrued through his corrupt career ($4,377,248.43). The case caused extreme embarrassment to the governments of both Hong Kong and Britain, not least because of the thorny legal path which led to Godber's extradition from the safety of his comfortable cottage in Rye, to be returned to the colony in handcuffs in January 1975.

The new agency was organized and headed (as the Commissioner Against Corruption) by Jack Cater, one of those who had fought corruption in the early years. Its work showed that, indeed, there was widespread corruption to be dealt with in all sectors of public and private life. Particularly singled out, at least initially, was the police force, where bribery was discovered to be on a scale that made Godber's earnings seem insignificant. So thorough was the work of the ICAC, and so ravenous its appetite, that it became an immense political liability to the government. There were those who considered that, while corruption in and around government was fair game for the ICAC's attention, the private sector with its well-known grey areas was not. Discomfort in the business community grew perceptibly as the commission systematically tackled all manner of bribery, gift giving and tipping. Public criticism of the ICAC became particularly pointed when it was reported that the wave of prosecutions arising from its investigations had extended to doormen and delivery boys who accepted tips. But it was with the police that the ICAC ran into its most spectacular opposition.

For three years the force had watched nervously as the commission dug deeper and deeper into case histories of serving and retired officers. In late October 1977 the tension broke. A large group of angry off-duty police officers mobbed ICAC headquarters, assaulting members of the commission's staff in the process, in an attempt to convince the commission to ease what was regarded within the police force as straightforward persecution. This crude statement of dissatisfaction was supported by a demonstration by over a thousand members of the police rank and file outside police headquarters. The government, fearing a full-scale mutiny, relented within days. Less than a month after MacLehose had made a forceful statement on corruption to Legco, stressing that 'if criminals once believed that the heat was off, we would soon be right back where we started. . . . (P)ressure on all forms of corruption will be maintained inexorably' and making special reference to the 'weeding out of the corrupt' in the police force, the government announced what was effectively a full amnesty for any act of corruption committed by a policeman before 1 January 1977. This episode had a profound effect on ICAC itself: although it still had the same wide-ranging powers, the commission began to shy away from controversy. More cynical observers described the transformation that had occurred as 'from Untouchables to Public Relations'. Jack Cater, who in his first annual report had promised that 'the back of corruption will have been broken in two or three years', became Sir Jack Cater and was appointed Chief Secretary to the colony. A few years later he was moved to the Hong Kong Government Office in London.

Like Cater, with his ambitious timetable for the eradication of corruption, MacLehose has been accused of being too impatient in his desire to see changes occur in Hong Kong's bureaucracy, which he encouraged to respond to, if not slightly ahead of, the dramatic changes in the colony. In retrospect his attitude was correct, although his reportedly imperious methods caused considerable resentment in the ranks of civil servants who had to implement his 'diktats'.

In the critical early years after 1949, Hong Kong's achievements were nothing short of miraculous. Over 1,500,000 refugees squatting on the hillsides in difficult conditions nevertheless focused their energies into broadly productive pursuits, a fact that still leaves more thoughtful civil servants of the period with a sense of wonder. With a sharp, and sustained, growth in population and a new role as workshop to the world, Hong Kong was exposed to attendant pressures. The colony had to show itself to be constantly competitive (which included maintaining lean wages) and increasingly profitable (to attract vital foreign investment, which between 1950 and 1960 accounted for a large proportion of the five-fold increase in local capital formation). Vital to the evolution of a supercharged economy was the fact that the growth of a sophisticated money-making operation was based on rather primitive financial legislation. This was not accidental. In a conversation with a visiting banker, a Financial Secretary who presided over Hong Kong's economy during one of its most spectacular spurts of growth outlined the rudiments of how he thought the government's part in the system worked. When the banker registered his surprise at the colony's financial system appearing so crude, the Financial Secretary responded in a matter-of-fact voice: 'Yes, and we've purposely left it so.'

Spending by the government has been particularly channelled into education and housing, two areas that are vital for the colony's future. On the one hand, low-cost housing subsidises the poorer sections of the working class; on the other, education is the key to progress in an economy which has lost its competitiveness as a source of cheap labour and must therefore move into increasingly more sophisticated forms of production. Virtually no buffers have been built into the government's financial system to protect the population should there be a major recession in the economy. Social welfare hovered at around five per cent of total expenditure during the late 1970s and early 1980s. It is highly unlikely to expand in the coming years to allow the evolution of a large-scale safety net that could come into play should it prove necessary. There is not even appropriate institutional machinery which could be activated in the event of a major economic slide. Government policies are, in short, a calculated gamble on the strong.

The scale of the potential problem is not easy to assess. There is little way of judging accurately how many lead a marginal existence in a society where the gross domestic product is about HK$70,000 per person, placing Hong Kong second only to Japan in the economies of the Far East. But there are signs that many only just make ends meet, and these people are not necessarily the obvious examples so often quoted by western journalists, the derelicts sleeping on the street, the 'cage dwellers' in their cramped dormitories, or even the five-member families occupying minute low-cost flats. Some time ago I stood with friends waiting for a lift in the building they lived in. The building itself is one of the many monoliths that appeared in the 1960s: occupying a huge block of land, its dozen storeys are decorated by little more than yards of dirty windows. Within is a society in miniature: shops on the ground floor, multi-floor restaurants immediately above, and then storey after storey of lower middle-class flats, many of them converted into guesthouses, offices, travel agencies and keep-fit gyms.

While we waited for the lift to arrive, one of my companions, a Singaporean Chinese, was approached by a wizened old man and they began a polite conversation. I did not pay much attention. When we entered the lift, the old man followed. He also followed us out when we reached our floor. While we busied ourselves with the door, our new companion asked my friend for a few dollars, which she gave him. He wished us all good night and made for the lift. As much of the conversation in the lift had been about the building, I asked if he was the caretaker. No, she replied, he was the *former* night-watchman. The old man had been retired recently. He had no family to look after him, little money and few prospects of finding new work. There was no pension to fall back upon, so he resorted to the only avenue available to him: he had created a small workload for himself by becoming something of an unofficial watchman, relying on the generosity of his former tenants to grant him face and a little money for his reduced livelihood. My companion had parted with her money with little hesitation. Inside the flat, her mood was tinged with melancholy. This, she reflected, was an unfortunate characteristic of Hong Kong life. Even such an old person could not look forward to the financial security and rest that his years deserved; he had either to continue searching for work or face the deeply unpalatable prospect of seeking out charity. And lest I thought that this was an isolated case, she added: 'Do you see how many old people are still working? They can't afford to stop. They need to work to stay alive. Food is not so important, but it's where they will sleep that matters. How will they afford a roof over their heads?'

Coming from Singapore, her outlook was attuned to such problems. There her future was not so insecure. The government runs a strictly administered central provident fund which, because she had already worked there for over twenty years before coming to Hong Kong, guarantees her a pension if she returns to Singapore one day. And the family home had been purchased with the aid of an incentive scheme operated by the government. In Hong Kong there are no such assurances. There is only the hope that the working life will provide a little fat and that, if need be, the family will provide shelter. It is a stark image to wake up to each morning as old age approaches.

In a way, this is an encapsulation of the harsher dimension of life in Hong Kong. The younger working population are no more secure. The worker has few rights in the areas of job security, severance pay, compensation (notably in the event of industrial accidents) and benefits, and the absence of a private or public pensions mechanism means that each person entering the job market is living very close to the edge. Here again is evidence of the government's gamble on the strong.

While Hong Kong's economy is functioning normally, there is little reason to consider the implications of this system. Even when a rare recession has gripped the economy, its effects have been limited. The most important indicators of what might happen in the event of a crisis are the disturbances which took place after the slumps of 1965 (the 1966/67 riots) and 1981 (the 1982 Christmas 'disturbances'). Although neither has been accepted by the administration as stemming, even indirectly, from economic factors, the connection cannot be totally disregarded. The rapid increase in the population and the spread of densely populated low-cost housing areas all add fuel to a conflagration that can be sparked by virtually anything, given a sufficiently sharp fall in the economy.

The unstated nervousness that exists in official circles is, however, linked to a still grimmer picture. A rapid and sustained slide in the economy, it is suggested, will result in nothing short of social disintegration of catastrophic proportions. Whereas even forty years ago farms in the New Territories were able to supply a considerable proportion of Hong Kong's food, today the colony is entirely dependent on a constant flow of imports. In the event of economic collapse, the argument goes, millions of Hong Kong people would rapidly be faced with starvation because of disruptions in supply and an inability to pay for what little is available; the alternative would be a chaotic exodus of people into the neighbouring Chinese provinces. Because the colony is extremely crowded, it is a latent time bomb. Neither the police force nor the British garrison could, under the circumstances, control the explosion. A harsh response from the security forces would have the effect of escalating the strife.

Sir Murray MacLehose is perhaps the most notable exponent of this school of thought. Indeed, much of the personal weight he threw behind social legislation – and especially the plans for the breakneck expansion of low-cost housing – suggested that this apocalyptic vision occupied a central position in his thinking, and particularly so in the latter part of his governorship. It certainly helps to explain why an otherwise forceful, wilful leader should have compromised so drastically on the issue of the 1977 police revolt against the ICAC. A senior local politician who worked with MacLehose throughout his time in office contends that this had two effects. It left some strongminded local leaders with the feeling that the Governor was 'timid, fainthearted', a great failing in the eyes of a population used to, and in many cases expecting, unassailable strength in the supreme leader. As important, however, was the loss of the ICAC initiative and the lasting position of strength held by the police ever since. 'He should have held out . . . , perhaps by giving in slowly, granting limited concessions initially. . . . Instead (he granted) the full amnesty.'

It seems he acted in this way not from an error in judgement but because of a fear of upsetting the long-term stability of the police force. As we shall see later, MacLehose's fears also seem to have had a considerable influence on his part in the shaping of the British approach to post 1997 Hong Kong.

But in society at large such preoccupations were distant, if they were present at all. The Communist-induced troubles of 1966/67 had receded. China seemed happy to allow the situation in Hong Kong to continue on the same footing that had existed since the territory first came under British sovereignty. This appeared to have been officially confirmed when, after five years of troubled relations, a communiqué was signed by China and Britain in Beijing on 13 March 1972. Diplomatic representation was raised from chargé-d'affaires to ambassadorial status and the document asserted 'the principles of mutual respect for sovereignty and territorial integrity, non-interference in each other's internal affairs and equality and mutual benefit'. Coming on the heels of the historic Nixon visit to China the year before, this communiqué has been associated largely with Britain's extrication from the 'two Chinas' conundrum. Through this agreement Britain finally abandoned all pretence of maintaining full relations with both Beijing and Taipei, thereby formally abandoning Taiwan as an independent entity. But the March accord also had important implications for Hong Kong. Five days before the Sino-British communiqué was signed, Huang Hua (the PRC representative to the United Nations) made a statement to the UN, by which China asserted that:

. . . the questions of Hongkong and Macau belong in the category of questions resulting from the series of unequal treaties left over by history, treaties which the imperialists imposed on China. Hongkong and Macau are part of Chinese territory occupied by the British and Portuguese authorities. *The settlement of the questions of Hongkong and Macau is entirely within China's sovereign right and does not at all fall under the ordinary category of 'colonial Territories'.* Consequently, they should not be included in the list of colonial Territories covered by the Declaration on the Granting of Independence to Colonial Countries and Peoples.

Britain made no protest at the wording of the statement, which was passed by the countries present. Hong Kong had, in effect, been transferred into the same category as Taiwan for the purposes of the March communiqué. The statement also insisted that 'The United Nations has no right to discuss these questions'.

Huang Hua's statement was greeted warily in Hong Kong, but most attention was focused on a vague conclusion that 'with regard to the questions of Hong Kong and Macau, the Chinese Government has consistently held that they should be settled in an appropriate way *when conditions are ripe'.* Thus, while Hong Kong had been formally removed from the category of colonial Territories and, from about that time, the Hong Kong Government began to refer to the place as a territory rather than a colony, the population was allowed to think that its future remained wholly open. If China had not seen fit to assume control of the territory, and had actually refused Portugal's open invitation to take back Macau, why should it be concluded that conditions would become ripe sooner rather than later? Little heed was paid to the curious confluence of the UN statement and the March communiqué.

*Author's italics.

CHAPTER FIVE

A Halcyon Interlude

For over nine months after Premier Zhou Enlai died in January 1976, the political situation in China see-sawed between the pragmatism of Deng Xiaoping, Zhou's recently rehabilitated heir apparent, and the extremism of Mao Zedong's wife Jiang Qing and her loosely-knit group of radicals, the 'Gang of Four'. While Mao remained alive the power struggle persisted in the very bowels of the Party structure. After the Great Helmsman's death that September, his widow made a concerted drive for power. Her ascendancy, however, was short-lived, and in October she and the 'Gang of Four' were arrested. When the news reached Hong Kong, there was a collective half-sigh of relief. A struggle that had begun with the Cultural Revolution and resurfaced in the demonstrations in Beijing after Zhou's death had, at least temporarily, been halted.

Political undercurrents in China are studied very carefully in its refugee outpost. A large and avariciously inquisitive press ensures that the population is, by Chinese standards, remarkably well informed. In addition, there are also the personal barometers of political change in China: hundreds of thousands of people return to China each year for Chinese New Year, the most important of Chinese festivals. With the gradual opening up of China since Deng Xiaoping's accession to the Chinese Communist Party throne, many thousands more have come to take other holidays there too. In addition to the more subtle forms of measuring relaxation of political and social restraints, many of the visitors use such standards as the availability of taxis on the streets of Guangzhou to estimate how conditions have changed. For example, a young woman said to me: 'A few years ago there wasn't a taxi to be seen. Now there are almost as many as in Hong Kong. Guangzhou has changed a great deal.' She was university-educated, but she used the same yardstick that scores of others less well-educated than herself would employ in talking about change in China.

Why, I reflected silently, is it always a television, queues or taxis that are used to measure how a society develops in the socialist context, whether it be China, the Soviet Union or Albania? Particularly so when, virtually in the same breath, the woman had spoken angrily of how the reception she received from China Travel Service while booking her ticket for Guangzhou had been marred, as so often happens in a state-owned concern, by an indifference bordering on rudeness.

In Hong Kong, the property, stock and gold markets had begun to boom in sharp succession. It was truly a golden period for the economy, buoyed up by a major increase in industrial production. Following the recession of 1974–5, domestic exports for 1976 showed a 43 per cent growth over the previous year. Growth throughout the manufacturing sector was uniformly high, but textiles, plastics and electronics led the field. Production continued to rise steadily until 1983, when domestic exports rose above HK$10 billion for the first time. Moreover, this figure represented a 48 per cent increase over that for 1982. The financial sector also began to take off. Between 1977 and 1978 there had been 74 licensed banks in the colony. In 1979 this number rose to 105 and in 1982 to 128.

The property market reached its peak in 1981 and slumped slightly – due to a glut of all but low-cost housing – the following year. Before the slump, a rent spiral had pushed Hong Kong prices to those of Tokyo, New York and London. As with most other markets in Hong Kong, it was one in which fortunes were made and lost virtually overnight through buying on the margin. A speculator would secure a row of unbuilt houses or flats by putting down a tiny deposit, hoping to sell them at maximum profit before full settlement or huge interest payments were due, or the market went into decline. Hong Kong Land, which had started life as a modest expatriate-run concern in Central District, briefly became the largest international property company. Other companies with less honourable pedigrees also built up immeasurable prestige through property dealings. The most significant of these was the Carrian empire, run by a Malaysian national George Tan. Until the property bubble burst in 1982–3, companies such as these appeared to wheel and deal in a way that suggested there was no ceiling to property prices and rents. The slump revealed both the honourable and the less than honourable to be massively over-exposed, committed to expensive projects which will not realise their pre-crash value and, in the case of Carrian, guilty of suspect bookkeeping (see p. 96).

The stock market too showed a resurgence of interest after a severe slump in the early 1970s, when thousands of small investors had their fingers burned and some bigger players who practised highly geared buying – subsequently severely curtailed by the introduction of tighter legislation governing trading on the seven stock exchanges – had gloomily sat calculating how many years' salaries would be devoted to repaying brokers. From 1980, with gold prices beginning to move on the international market, a formal venue was provided for those who wanted greater returns from trading in gold through the opening of the Hong Kong Commodities Exchange gold futures market.

This boom was remarkably visible on the streets. Goldsmiths' shops and jewellers showed display cases full of every conceivable form of gold. Imperial Russian gold roubles jostled with Krugerrands, Chinese wise men, deer, tigers, horses, fish and exotic birds; all competing in twenty-four carats for the attention of passers-by. Black plastic boards announcing the day's price for 99.999 per cent pure gold occupied prominent places in the displays. Excited groups gathered round the boards at lunchtime to discuss what they could have earned in the past twenty-four hours and what the prospects were for a further jump. After lunch, the conversations about personal holdings would continue in the office. Smug 'market makers' would lecture office boys and anyone else who would listen about the foolproof systems they had devised for their daily purchases of a tael or two. At the height of the fever, strategically placed television screens displaying the latest share prices also bid for the hapless office worker's attention at lunchtime. A Swiss watch agency occupying a prime corner location in Central entered fully into the spirit of the age by setting up a board to give pedestrians an idea of lunchtime and closing share prices in addition to their latest line in timepieces. Architects added to the general euphoria by planning walls of golden glass to encase their latest projects.

In 1979 Hong Kong's entry to the ranks of the First World was marked by a large international charity, which ceased gathering aid for the colony and began to collect funds from it instead. The Hongkong & Shanghai Banking Corporation, Hong Kong's quasi-central bank and ever the leader in anticipating new epochs in the colony's economic history, took the controversial step of demolishing its 1930s head office at 1 Chater Road. The building, whose distinctive terraced shape was synonymous with generations of children's piggybanks and the background to millions of snapshots, was razed in 1981 and work began on a structure that is to take the bank into the twenty-first century. Built to a radical glass and metal design by Norman Foster (a partner of Richard Rogers, the architect of the Pompidou and Lloyds buildings in the 1960s), the new bank was to become a disturbing omen of the future. The difficulties encountered in raising the building, deferred schedules and rocketing costs coincided, unfortunately, with the most tempestuous stages in the resolution of Hong Kong's fate. To many residents the building and its construction has come to epitomize their own insecurities.

The years 1976–82 saw the flowering of a large middle class and a new breed of local entrepreneur. Young, western-educated and well-travelled, the new class led the way in undermining the old colonial values and sensibilities. This development was linked to a fruitful symbiosis of Western banking and Chinese industry. The sharp rise in productivity in 1976 had shown that, of nearly 800,000 registered factory workers, only eight per cent were working for foreign-backed concerns. The rest were employed by indigenous industrialists. The Hongkong Bank had played a particularly important part in the rise in prosperity. Through dogged determination, and perhaps a little good fortune, the bank had become broadly involved with fledgling industry in the late 1950s and early 1960s. One of its coups was to have opened a branch in Mongkok, a district sitting neatly between the two principal areas of industry, Kwun Tong and Tsuen Wan. To this branch would gravitate Cantonese manufacturers looking for venture capital for whom the more straight-laced Central District was less convenient.

The growth of these relations, and the subsequent expansion into the commercial sector, was in later years to lead to a change in the position of the 'princely' hongs in local society. The swift evolution of a sizable Chinese commercial aristocracy led to an assault on the commanding – and for over a century unassailable – place held by expatriate companies in Hong Kong's life and economy. It is fitting that the first blood, involving the hong of Hutchison Whampoa, was drawn by Li Ka-shing, the most illustrious of the early manufacturers. Under British leadership, the hong had expanded rapidly, buying up company after company in the 1960s and 1970s. Somewhat nervously, the Hongkong Bank had backed the purchases and maintained the funding of wholly-owned Hutchison companies that seemed to be unlikely to realize a return. By 1981, technically controlling over half the Hutchison stock, the Bank called a halt. Bill Wylie, an Australian known for his skills as a 'company doctor', was brought in with a brief to turn the operation around. This he did. However, even with Hutchison shares rising to new highs, the Bank began to sell off its holdings. The principal purchaser was Li. According to a source close to expatriate business circles, Li's successful takeover of the company 'ruffled many feathers in the Establishment and hongs'.

Similarly, Y. K. Pao's purchase of the controlling interest in two companies, Kowloon Wharf & Godown and Wheelock Marden, raised fears of further encroachment on this expatriate preserve. As the circle tightened, Jardine Matheson and Hong Kong Land purchased into one another so as to prevent any attempt to scale these bastions of hong power. Ironically, the cross purchases were much to the disadvantage of Jardines, as the collapse of the property market was to show. The turbulence of the early 1980s brought down both Trevor Bedford and David Newbigging as the taipans* of Hong Kong Land and Jardines respectively. Both companies underwent a flurry of pruning and reorganization, largely under the tutelage of Simon Keswick, a member of the controlling branch of the Jardine family. The takeovers and skirmishes helped in a most spectacular way to reinforce the image that, at last, Hong Kong was entering a post-colonial epoch.

Parallel to these developments was the emergence of a strong, readily identifiable Hong Kong popular culture. In some respects this can be traced to one major watershed. In late 1967 wireless television was introduced to the colony by a Chinese company, Television Broadcasts Limited (TVB). This was an important change in itself. Up until then, television came via the expensive, and geographically limiting, medium of cable. The cost of renting a television together

---

* From the Cantonese *taai-paan*, or boss, a term adopted by the West to identify the heads of the handful of British-owned companies.

with the cable service was, in the mid 1960s, $55 a month; at the time, an unskilled worker earned an average of $42 for a six-day week and a skilled worker $102. Viewership in the tens of thousands before 1967 had increased to two million three years later. In 1976 90 per cent of households owned a television set. Today that percentage is approaching 100 per cent. This remarkable growth provided a ready medium for the emergence of a broad veneer of national identity that links ramshackle squatter huts and isolated fishing villages.

TVB's earliest broadcasts brought with them fitting signs of what was to come. While the highlight on Pearl, the English-language channel, was the Beatles singing *All you need is love*, the Chinese channel (Jade) launched *Enjoy Yourself Tonight*, a series that was to become one of the main arteries of the new popular culture. Its modern forms of variety drew huge audiences each evening and launched many a career.

There was one other important development that can, essentially, be traced to the arrival of TVB. The mass audiences it generated also created mass markets for a new wave of singers and film makers. In fact, the first generation of these was not altogether new. Samuel Hui, Hong Kong's first superstar, who was to span both music and cinema during the 1970s and 1980s, had originally found limited fame amongst the middle classes in the 1960s singing in English with the Lotus. This was one of many groups spawned in the 1960s on the back of Beatlemania in the colony, all of which ended up, relatively quickly, as resident bands at tea dances and nightclubs.

Hong Kong's appetite for western popular culture has long depended on its consumption, digestion and dispersion by the colony's middle classes, but this process was never particularly efficient while there was a free flow of people across the border with Guangdong Province. In both spiritual and practical respects the cultural and educational roots of most of the population were in China, with those who could afford it gravitating to Chinese universities for higher education and cultural sustenance. Following the tightening of border controls after World War II, the situation changed radically. The middle classes could no longer look to China for either education or a living culture. They became dependent on things foreign and were forced to find their own centre of gravity.

The first hesitant steps in this process were greatly eased by the emergence – particularly noticeable during the Korean War – of a string of educational benefactors, most notably the Ho Tungs, and by the early film-makers (many, such as the prolific Shaw brothers, bringing their expertise from Shanghai), whose output of 310 films in 1963 was exactly double that of the United States!

From these beginnings grew the intellectual and technocratic stratum which came to man TVB and other popular media, the means by which Hong Kong-centred culture and entertainment were gradually disseminated to steadily growing audiences. It was also this group that in the 1970s instigated a return to the Cantonese language as a vehicle for the creative process.

Samuel Hui and his generation of entertainers, many of whom had spent time in America or Britain as well as having received a formal western education, successfully transformed their music, complete with marked western influences, into a refined form of Cantonese entertainment. The same blending of old and new occurred in film. The formula films of the Shaw Brothers, many of them in the Mandarin dialect, owed much to the chivalric myths and fables of Imperial China.

The arrival of new attitudes in Hong Kong film-making can be traced to the return of one of its young sons, Bruce Li, at the end of the 1960s. Although he was born in San Francisco, Li spent much of his childhood working in Cantonese films in Hong Kong. In the early sixties he returned to the United States, where he drifted from college to the teaching of a martial art that he himself had developed (Jeet Kun Do, combining Chinese Kung Fu with Korean Karate). Among his students were Hollywood celebrities, through whom he found his way into two television serials and a feature film.

The resumption of his film career in Hong Kong was a revelation. To his hybrid combat art, Li had brought an equally hybrid acting technique. The result was an entertainment form that was as acceptable to western as it was to Chinese tastes. His first film, *Big Boss*, broke all attendance records in Hong Kong. In *Fist of Fury*, Li showed precisely why the colony's youth came to regard him as an icon in the 1970s. In this follow-up to *Big Boss* Li's fictional hero fighting for the honour of the underling in a foreign land was seen to represent the Chinese struggle against foreign imperialists in the 1930s. Defiantly, Li hurls himself in a flying kick into a hail of bullets fired by an execution squad of sinister foreigners. The film provided the opportunity for a fresh popular assessment of the heroism of generations of Chinese struggling for national integrity. Li could be seen as a synonym for the Boxers who, in their rebellion at the turn of the century, charged fearlessly into rows of foreign guns.

While his later films betrayed an impatience to expand the scale of the productions by using Hollywood actors and more exotic foreign locations, Li's screen persona appeared to dig deeper into its Hong Kong roots. His characters remained nothing more than the simple Hong Kong man transported abroad, whose inability to speak English (Li spoke nothing but Cantonese in his films) was made up for by self-confidence, quick-wittedness, purity and courage, set off by touches of mock self-deprecation.

The emergence of a nucleus of young talent helped to confirm Hong Kong's unique position amongst overseas Chinese communities, spawning and dominating modern Chinese popular culture outside China itself. The new self-confidence showed itself in less attractive ways too. The colony's blossoming economy provided many thousands of the expanding middle classes with the opportunity to holiday abroad. *Nouveau riche* travellers took with them the trappings of wealth that stood out dramatically in the poorer Asian countries which became the initial targets for the colony's multiplying tour operators. The Philippines, Thailand and Malaysia became the playground of bands of young Hong Kong visitors sporting loud casual clothing and jewellery and oozing confidence. For a time, they ran the risk of becoming as unpopular as the American tourist of the 1960s.

By the early 1980s, this popular culture had reached maturity and the colonial image had been all but discarded. Hong Kong had its own thriving music, film and publishing industries, with indigenous film stars who could draw massive audiences. As a result cinema owners became less inclined to order expensive foreign films, concentrating on B-grade movies to augment local productions. English-language television channels were similarly affected, losing both viewers and funding to their Chinese counterparts. The English-language services provided by the government radio/television station (RTHK) face an uncertain future.

This was not a wholesale rejection of western culture and practice. Far from it. Foreign ideas were imported in ever increasing quantities and efficiently adapted to the needs and whims of the population as a whole. Fast food flourished, putting paid to early foreign scepticism about local response to this new 'cuisine'. And in a society which, it has long been held, is morally conservative,

Chinese editions of *Playboy* and *Penthouse*, featuring photos of nude Chinese celebrities, can now be bought on every street corner. This is a far cry from the days when Chinese student teachers were encouraged to hold mock tea parties at which their British teachers would oversee decorum and the proper pouring of tea!

By 1982 Hong Kong had already shown itself to be a mature, modern consumer society. The growth in national wealth enabled a far broader band of the population than ever before to indulge in sophisticated western forms of consumption. It required little prompting. Even before the boom conditions of the late 1970s, Hong Kong had been known for its brandy drinking, having for some years held the world record for per capita consumption. Subsequently, VSOP and Napoleon became the standard fare, with Cognac, that costs the equivalent of an office worker's monthly salary, being reserved for special occasions. Such expensive tastes are not confined only to those who can afford them. Chinese parties are egalitarian affairs, where chief buyers will happily rub shoulders with office boys. Both fill their water glasses with hefty measures of the liquid gold, add a lump or two of ice and drink like the genuine cognoscenti they are! Western 'convenience' foods have been readily accepted, but remain just that: convenient.

Food in Hong Kong, as it has always been in China as a whole, serves as a remarkably accurate gauge against which the individual can assess personal and general progress. In 1984, I sat in a restaurant with a group of self-proclaimed elder statesmen of the business world. To the accompaniment of measure after measure of fine Scotch (a suitable lunchtime aperitif), they spoke of Hong Kong and food. There were happy boasts about the quality of eating in Hong Kong ('the finest in the world'), the quality of southern soya sauce ('the finest in China . . . essential for good cooking'). Then, as if speaking of the rarest and most fragile commodity, they turned their attention to the preparation of fish. One knew a restaurant where the preparation of seafood was the best in Hong Kong (and, by extension, the world). But he could not quite trust the quality of the fish, or its freshness. To ensure that his palate was not compromised, he would regularly make his way to a special fish market to purchase live baby garoupa at a final cost/weight ratio that might come close to the price of silver. With the fish still alive, my gastronome would rush to the restaurant, where it would be killed, cooked and served in no longer than four minutes. By the time he had eaten it, the cost of the fish was that of gold. While telling me the story, his meal arrived: a lunchtime special of spaghetti bolognaise.

Advertising agencies recognized the need to change their focus. More often than not, it was a Chinese that appeared merrily quaffing XO cognac in magnificent European mansions. Cigarette advertisements set on yachts in exotic places balanced occidental faces with Chinese faces. The message, for those that read anything into advertising, was clear: Hong Kong people had made it, they had found a well-deserved niche in international society.

CHAPTER SIX

Booms, Bubbles and High Fliers

Hong Kong's arrival in the First World coincided with the coming of age of monetarism. In the late 1970s, Professor Milton Friedman visited the colony to film a television documentary. With a twinkle in his eye, he stood in front of a television camera on the 'Star' Ferry concourse, marvelling in reverent tones at the results of 'total freedom' and a 'pure *laissez-faire* economy'. In his commentary he extolled Hong Kong's virtues and pronounced that it had become what all capitalist societies should aspire to: a synthesis of economic and political freedoms, unfettered by a demanding government. It was a veritable monument to the glories of individualism unbound. There was a supreme irony in Professor Friedman's choice of location for his ill-judged conclusions on the political and fiscal freedoms in evidence in Hong Kong, as it was this very spot which had seen the start of the 1966 riots, sparked off by dissatisfaction with economic and social conditions.

But even away from such sensitive areas, on the substantive point of personal freedoms it would be misleading to regard Hong Kong as the best example of a society whose government remains aloof from the political and economic pursuits of the individual. As one experienced civil servant observed, the government has 'a finger in each and every area of activity'.

On the surface, at least, the government does hold to the spirit of a market economy, as, for example, by showing little sympathy to businesses that fail. Indeed, it is the general willingness to adhere to the principle of the survival of the fittest that has generated much of the acclaim about Hong Kong enterprise. As with simplistic images of political freedom, however, the picture of a government that does nothing more than passively hold the ring for rampant economic individualism is not an accurate one.

In reality, the Hong Kong Government operates at both the general and the individual level in the economy. It allows inequities to be generated, thereby providing the environment in which the rudiments of *laissez-faire* capitalism can thrive, and it maintains the infrastructure that allows society to function. On the other hand, it also intervenes to offset the harsh results of exploitation, providing the barely perceptible safety nets for those who fall out of the system. The process engenders a constant weighing of bureaucratic procedure against the humane aspects of policy; a process of selective non-intervention. Because there is no welfare state that will automatically act as a buffer against the bureaucracy's mistakes, the judgement exercised must be very keen.

Today there are over 20,000 illegal industrial enterprises in operation in Hong Kong, employing over 100,000 people. Existing legislation provides for their closure and yet they are allowed to continue, despite a strong case for shutting them down. The workforce involved is small enough to be absorbed by the legal labour market. And if these industries were shut down, their less desirable aspects, such as the fire and health risks associated with running an enterprise in a flat on an upper floor of a residential tower block, could be avoided. But their destruction could also mean, in a sense, the elimination of the very basis of Hong Kong production.

A granny rushes out to the street corner to pick up a bag of plastic parts, returns to her home and begins to assemble plastic flowers, recruiting members of her family along the way. So far, all is legal. Then the same granny begins to subcontract, hiring other grannies to assemble bags of flowers. That is illegal. This process, *sans* grannies, extends to manufacture too. A factory may subcontract the manufacture of components in homes. Apart from the advantages of cheap production, the result is fumes, danger and unsavoury individuals loitering in the area. All this has to be taken into account by the bureaucrat and weighed against the economic and social gains derived.

The advantages are in fact considerable. Piece-work and subcontracting are often the vehicle through which arrivals can earn a meagre income or families can top up their joint earnings. Access to such work, which requires little more than unskilled but willing hands, is often by word of mouth. Someone has a brother, sister or cousin who is available to do the work and is put in touch with their friend the foreman. The factories themselves can concentrate on producing parts, while the 'take-away' assembly line is scattered across hundreds of homes or, less often now, seen at rickety tables or seated on tiny oblong wooden stools on the pavement outside. Overheads are reduced, production is efficient and dispute-free, prices are kept sharply competitive and a vital first rung of the ladder is provided for new unskilled labour.

Seasoned government officials recognize that, although Hong Kong is made up of a remarkably resilient, sturdy people, the colony's infrastructure is very fragile. There seems to be no pattern to it, no rhyme or reason. But at heart it is highly patterned. And as with a fine weave, the pulling of one thread will lead to consequences elsewhere. Segments will fall apart or fray around the edges. So while the government appears to have no involvement in the process, it is ever-present, continually tinkering to ensure that all manner of excess is avoided.

The symbiotic relationship between business and government is greatly facilitated by the absence of an elected government. There are considerable advantages in the monopoly of power enjoyed by the appointed bureaucracy. There is a very strong strand of continuity, with officials departing from office only through natural attrition or, very rarely, by demonstrating total incompetence. Relations created between the private and official sectors can therefore evolve through the years without the possibility of a rude interruption at the ballot box or, with the occasional change of government, a sharp turn in political direction being imposed upon the bureaucracy. Because there is no elected government to take into consideration in addition to the civil service, the avenues of power are clearer and efforts to influence the exercise of that power can, as a result, be more focused.

How this works in practice is clearly demonstrated in what one retired civil servant described as the 'parallel escalator' phenomenon. Chinese business people choose a person of similar rank in government with whom they will carefully develop a close friendship. This twinning occurs early: by their mid to late thirties possible 'horses' within junior government ranks are carefully eyed and approached. If all goes well, the two individuals' careers will develop in parallel, eventually giving the businessman access to a high-ranking official and vice versa. If a successful symbiosis does not take place at an early stage, there is little chance of barriers being crossed later.

But even such carefully cultivated relationships often fail to bridge cultural barriers or to be more than skin-deep. According to one former official, the Chinese often see themselves as skilfully pandering to the vanity of the foreigner, whom they may secretly regard as obnoxious – 'pig-faced', in the popular derisive term. A friend who worked in the civil service described how he met the Chinese vice-chancellor of a university, a man he greatly admired, at a cocktail party. The conversation drifted to the situation in China. The expatriate expressed views that differed greatly from those of the Chinese academic. As the latter remained silent, the propositions were laid on thick and fast, my friend thinking that he was winning the argument. They parted. Nothing was said until my friend got home. There, his Chinese wife – who had stood silently beside her husband during the discussion – pointed out how loutish his behaviour had been. She confirmed that the academic had not been convinced. Courtesy towards my friend had compelled him to be silent. As if to underline her husband's barbaric behaviour, she spoke of her own embarrassment and disagreement with some of his views.

The oiling of the relationship between a Chinese businessman and an expatriate civil servant can go on with little understanding by the expatriate of what is happening. Only after he has left the civil service do the true feelings of the Chinese become evident. Suddenly, the expatriate finds himself without the circle of friends he thought he had gradually built up over the course of his career. To many this comes as a traumatic experience, and particularly so for the colonial mandarin.

This might suggest that the foreigners are the manipulated rather than the manipulators, and to an extent this is true. Expatriates who come to work in the Hong Kong Government are very much refugees within a refugee society. Many have been attracted by the financial glitter and the promise of career mobility denied them at home. Most come as strangers to the society and culture, relying on their wits to pick up what is usually an imperfect understanding of colonial life from their peers. Hong Kong is seen as a glorified transit camp: a place to earn and save and perhaps even to enjoy life, but never to regard as home. Some might claim that they would like to retire in the colony and a handful of senior government officials do so. But in reality retirement usually means joining the private sector, where expertise gained in the civil service is applied to lucrative consultancies. Some time ago senior government officials were not allowed to return to the colony for a few years after the end of their contract, during which time their information and contacts would become stale and an overlap of interests be avoided. More recently there have been complaints that senior civil servants are returning early and blurring the line between the private and public sectors.

For the Chinese population money is everything. Only after big money has been made does a successful Chinese begin to look around for other 'trimmings', such as honours or political position. The methods they employ to acquire status are remarkably straightforward, indeed even predictable. Apart from the 'parallel escalators' approach, there is the simple expedient of gaining recognition by spending money. Donations to worthwhile causes in Hong Kong never involve the casual dispersal of millions of dollars to favourite causes. Most benefactors require a significant return for their money and are as careful in giving away the allocated sums as they are in making them in the first place.

Giving money away in Hong Kong is the easiest method of attracting attention and prestige. It is based on old principles of Chinese philanthropy, but in the limited confines of Hong Kong donations are governed by a precise cost/benefit table. Sums of about $100,000 will be rewarded with considerable exposure in the press. The donor of $1,000,000 will be regarded very creditably in senior government circles as well as earning considerable public acclaim. Those who give $10,000,000 and over are rewarded with massive exposure and have their names enshrined on buildings or associated with institutions, very often accompanied by their father's name as well. The agencies receiving the donations are, needless to say, only too happy to provide the appropriate publicity. For they are well aware that this is how the whole community service runs: every donation, gift or pledge must be reciprocated by some form of favour, whether it be a plaque, corner-stone or dedication. As a person close to the process observed: 'Often the representative will be passed on to the (potential benefactor's) public relations man, whose ears are like radar dishes anticipating any indication of a return for the donation.'

Somewhat more pointedly, a civil servant who was placed in charge of a major hospital appeal in the 1960s described how many of the pledges were made on the understanding that the favour might be reciprocated at some stage. On the other hand, he too had handed out a pile of favours in the past 'which might be zeroed in on – within institutional precincts of course! – one day. I remember them all!' Reflecting on this process, he concluded that this is 'how (the Hong Kong) Government by and large works; it may not be the most efficient system in the world, but it does work'.

Such precision even extends to the ritual of giving at the level of the ordinary household. At first sight there is a bland uniformity about the exchange of gifts in Hong Kong. Shops are filled with boxes of Danish cookies and Dutch sweets, and standard bottles of expensive drink. At festival time there are massive sales of these items, suggesting a distinct lack of imagination on a very broad scale with very little attempt to search out unique, or tailor-made, gifts. However, there are two points to appreciate about this habit. First, all the goods that achieve such blanket popularity are, to a very discerning Cantonese taste, superior and therefore both safe and prestigious (and practical: the same box of chocolates, bottle of brandy in ornamental packing or tin of biscuits may come full circle a year or two later!). Second, it is easy for the recipient to judge what value the donor has placed on the friendship or business association and the state of his finances. In Hong Kong life there is little room for ambiguity in such important matters.

This all ties in with what can be described as Hong Kong's cult of 'the best'. Status can be accurately judged by people low and high on the wealth ladder by a calculation based on outward appearances – the value of the Rolex on the wrist, the make of the suit and tie or dress, the model (and year) of Ben-zee climbed into. If they are not sure what constitutes 'the best', they can now buy one of a number of suitably titled monthly magazines that will give them the information. Brash signs in the colony's underground railway draw the attention of commuters to Ceaser's (sic) World International, 'The world's most luxurious resort hotels where Only the Best will do!'. From office boy to company executive, very few will be unaware of what is 'the best'. Ironically, many foreigners, and especially government employees, choose to disregard the importance of icons of status. While middle-class Chinese aspire to buy Gucci, their European counterparts roam the street markets in search of fakes and factory rejects in the righteous belief that the genuine item is just not worth the expense.

But if the trappings of status are easy to read, so is the negative side. There are those in the colony who are immensely rich and yet have had few formal honours bestowed upon them and have not been invited to join social and political bodies. In most cases it seems the reason must be their lack of contribution to Hong Kong life. When discreet enquiries are made to various government officials on this point, the answer – as in one particularly prominent case – is often a blunt: 'What has he done for Hong Kong?'

Those who do give freely and whose names adorn the entrances of numerous hospitals and institutions may not always be seeking personal advancement, but their donations usually involve a strong element of self-interest. One millionaire was motivated by a lucky escape at the time of the Japanese invasion. Together with many other Chinese residents condemned to death, he was marched down to the edge of a nullah (an open conduit) to wait his turn to be bayonetted or shot. While the guards were busy with one of the other victims, he did a backward somersault into the nullah. Although he hurt his ankle, he was able to complete his spectacular escape in a hail of Japanese bullets. As a result of this reprieve, the man committed himself to donating large sums of money to the community every year. But, as it was pointed out to me, 'this was not done because of a great sympathy for the downtrodden, but as a tribute to his early salvation'.

In this environment the Honours List is more akin to a bazaar than the honourable institution it is supposed to be. Nominations are initiated at a fairly high level and any one person may be proposed up to four times for a particular honour. On the fourth attempt, if the application is still unsuccessful, the person proposed may be recommended for a lower honour. A government official whose job it was to nominate business people for honours described a telephone conversation with a businessman who had been informed that he had been nominated for a lesser honour. After circling the issue for a time, the man asked if he was talking to the person who was responsible for nominations. When the latter answered that, indeed, it was he, the caller continued by asking if he had been nominated for a lesser honour:

'Yes.'

'But this other award is senior, isn't it?'

'Yes.'

'So I would refuse?'

'Yes, but refusal may mean it will be years before another is offered to you.'

'I see. But if I accept it, I may not become . . . [the senior title he hoped for].'

'That is correct.'

The individual concerned refused the honour, only to receive the one he wanted soon after. The official responsible for the original nomination was at a loss to understand how this had happened: 'he may have had contacts elsewhere in government, or used other means to secure this extraordinary decision.'

All that could be done was for his department to lodge an official protest.

Such precise judgements are made at the other end of the scale too. There, middle-aged office messengers who have to support a family on $2500 a month have other decisions to make; how to get to work cheaply, for example. Often this means that they have to leave their homes in low-cost housing estates – mostly miles away from the business districts – at 7 am in order to start work at 9 am. They could cut their journey time considerably by using the underground, but for them the cost of travel is the crucial factor. Compared with $2.50 for a two-hour journey by bus and ferry, the underground at $3.50 is a luxury.

All this suggests a far more ordered, perhaps even rigid, society than that which Milton Friedman would have us believe exists in Hong Kong. The fluid character of the economy, in so far as it exists, lies in another area.

The key to the prodigious growth of Hong Kong's industry, and indeed its service sector too, is its ability to shift quickly in anticipation of international trends in demand. As the emphasis moved from tin and metal goods to plastics, human hair products and simple electronics, the labour force mastered new techniques with a minimum of fuss and with little attention from factory owners to formal technical qualifications or relevant experience. The highly adaptable nature of Hong Kong manufacture is not so much the result of preference as of necessity. Little research and development is done in the colony, but there seems to be the ability to pick up new imported technology, adapt it swiftly to marketable products and capitalize on international demand. The crucial element is timing.

A sense of timing permeates all economic activities, from the manufacture and sale of radios and watches to dealing in gold, currency or property. In the late 1960s a friend who sold office machinery visited the tiny premises occupied by a plastic-flower dealer, Li Ka-shing. He found Li hunched over a set of brass scales, juggling with the minute individual plastic blooms which made up a twig of artificial flowers in an attempt to find a maximum return on minimum production and freighting costs. While he worked to find the perfect balance, he shook his head and absent-mindedly offered an observation: plastic flowers, he said, were no longer a good area to be in; it was time to move into property. 'A decade later,' my friend reflected, 'I'm still selling office machines at a penny profit and he has become a multi-millionaire.'

Hong Kong is small enough for the cult of the personality to be of considerable importance in business. Sitting at his desk in one of the high-rise buildings of Central, the modern Chinese tycoon uses his skills to draw the public along: entertaining and impressing, demonstrating prescience, wisdom and guile. In contrast to their role in other major business capitals, anonymous corporations take a back seat in Hong Kong. All attention is focused on the strength of the individual financier. This business culture fuels meteoric rises in company fortunes and also leads to breathtaking collapses.

There has been no better example of this phenomenon in recent times than George Tan and his Carrian Group. Tan is a moon-faced, amply-toothed Malaysian Chinese. His arrival in Hong Kong was tinged with an element of mystery, as was the source of the funds which he wielded so proficiently in his spectacular rise. In 1979 he took over a property company called Mai Hon Enterprises. At the time of purchase the company had reported a modest profit of HK$3,800,000. Its most attractive feature, as it turned out, was its listing on the Hong Kong stock exchange. Under Tan the company's name was changed to Carrian Investments Limited. The new title came from Chinese terms for 'the best' and 'peaceful'. Initially, only 'the best' seemed appropriate as Tan's operation set off on a feverish programme of deals and takeovers. Two years later Carrian had diversified into everything from shipping to Japanese soft-core pornography. Net profits had risen to HK$626,000,000.

In June 1982 shareholders' funds had reached an astounding HK$3.5 billion. Public interest in the fortunes of Carrian had grown greatly when, in early 1980, with the property bull market gaining pace, Carrian bought a single building in Central District for HK$998,000,000. Nine months later the same building was sold for

HK$1.68 billion. This was widely hailed as a coup. After the collapse of the Tan 'empire' it proved to have been something of a sleight-of-hand, a successful manoeuvre which gave Tan both publicity and, more importantly, leverage with the banking community. Greater borrowing facilities were used to maximum effect in 1981 when Carrian made a series of quick raids into a property market whose prices were, at least in part, fuelled by Tan's own self-advertisement. Between January and December 1981 the value of the company's shares tripled. There were distant warnings about Carrian's lack of a sound operating base and of the absence of recurrent earnings, but for bankers and share-purchasers in Hong Kong Tan could do no wrong.

Under the umbrella of Carrian Investments Limited, controlled by the mysterious Carrian Holdings, which in turn was held by the shadowy Carrian Nominee, Tan's group bought up taxis, coaches, shops and cafés. All were decked in a sickly high-street green and emblazoned with the company logo. Before his fall, it was difficult to go anywhere in Hong Kong without being reminded of George Tan and his business wizardry. Niggling worries about where the company would find the expertise to run such a diversity of operations occasionally crept into public thinking, but such doubts were quickly answered: management skills could be bought! People were not preoccupied with the soundness of Tan's operating base, or with the fact that most of his profits were of a windfall nature, but with the source of what appeared to be a bottomless pit of funding. A popular rumour at the time was that Tan's business received cash transplants from the coffers of the Marcos family in the Philippines. Tan allowed the guessing to go on. In the meantime, he ensured that his company's image was further enhanced by increasing its charitable donations from HK$250,000 in 1980 to HK$1,900,000 in 1981. Appropriate publicity followed.

The bubble finally burst in the autumn of 1982, when the property and share markets nosedived. For some months Carrian's image was represented as that of an essentially sound company that had been caught by the markets. Conditions, it was said, had been exacerbated by Prime Minister Thatcher's discussions with the Chinese Government about Hong Kong's future. Carrian's bankers attempted to rescue the company, but it became increasingly clear that there was very little substance to it. The company's main asset was its new headquarters in Wanchai, and even that had been used to secure a US$83,000,000 syndicated loan from a subsidiary of the Hongkong & Shanghai Bank. In addition, some of the other loans had been secured against Carrian shares. Irregularities in the company's finances began to become apparent and more questions were asked about Tan's ultimate backers. These remained as elusive as they had been from the start.

Trading in Carrian shares was suspended in January 1983. Four months later, an official inquiry was ordered into the Carrian Group's affairs. While the creditor banks nervously rescheduled their loans, the affair took on a more sinister form. A representative of a subsidiary of the Bumiputra Bank of Malaysia, itself one of the main creditors, was murdered in his luxury hotel in Kowloon and a senior lawyer who had advised Carrian was found dead in his swimming pool with a manhole cover tied to his neck. A year after Carrian had first found itself in financial trouble, the Hong Kong authorities took firm action: in September the company's headquarters were raided and documents seized; a few weeks later, George Tan and his chief executive Bentley Ho were arrested under the Thefts Ordinance. The final tally for Carrian's losses amounted to well over HK$3 billion. When trading finally resumed in the company's shares, they were virtually worthless.

The legal tangle that arose from the Carrian affair was a drama in itself and continues to this day. The most expensive criminal action in the colony's history, with costs estimated at well over HK$100 million, was brought against Tan, one of his lieutenants, two accountants and two business associates. They were accused of conspiracy to defraud investors and creditors. In September 1987, after eighteen months of proceedings, the presiding judge deemed that the defendants had an insufficient case to answer and acquitted all six. In March 1988, following months of widespread vituperation, he submitted his letter of resignation to the Chief Justice.

What was so remarkable about the Carrian affair was not so much the bubble that had been created as the fact that the good and the great in Hong Kong's financial circles had been so readily seduced by Tan. Even at the pinnacle of his powers, Tan had presented a less than solid image. His empire's logo had come from the first Carrian company, a pest control firm, and its English title sounded as if it was still intimately tied to that business.

The character of Tan himself should have raised a question or two. The avaricious nature of his deals and the mystery about his sources of finance were coupled with a whirligig manner that suggested anything but substance. Shortly before the collapse of Carrian, Tan was interviewed by Robert Cottrell for the *Financial Times*. He was described as 'an energetic man . . . (who) paces the room while he talks, rattles off a calculation with one hand while slapping the table with the other'. The business aspirations voiced by the chairman of Carrian were reminiscent of a child given a minute to collect as many items in a toy shop as possible. Once this round of frenetic shopping was over – which Tan suggested would be in less than five years – control of the organization would be handed over to the company's management.

Some years after the bubble burst, one of Tan's senior employees revealed further facets of his boss's character. He depicted a man 'backed with money from somewhere', whose financial ingenuity 'left the casual observer breathless . . . or so people thought'. Within his inner sanctum, Tan revelled in the ostentation that befits the *nouveau riche*: a richly appointed office, tables loaded with expensive offerings from his senior staff on his birthday, Davidoff cigars by the caseful. Yet Tan was a rough man, whose provincial background readily showed through. His aide writes of how he invited a senior representative from a German bank to lunch in the Carrian dining-room. A fish-head curry had been served. Tan announced to his guest that it was best eaten with the fingers. 'By the time I returned (to the dining-room),' wrote the employee, 'George (Tan) had immersed himself . . . using all ten digits as his eating utensils. In courting new banking relations, it wasn't my idea of a good impression.'

There is a certain rough diamond quality about most of those who wield immense economic power in Hong Kong. Financial fiefdoms emerge; pretenders palpably mark time in the wastelands, waiting for an opportunity to build up their own closely guarded islands of influence. In some respects, these people resemble the war-lords who dominated the early history of the Chinese Republic. Power is acquired by men with little or no formal education, whose ultimate goal is to obey no authority other than their own. Most are comparative newcomers to Hong Kong, arriving from China soon after World War II. Most have become prominent relatively recently, in some cases as late as the 1970s.

The richest and most influential of the new men, Li Ka-shing and Y.K. Pao, have already been mentioned. In 1987 *Fortune* magazine estimated their personal wealth at US$2.5 billion and $1 billion respectively, ranking them among the hundred richest men in the world. Li, who came to Hong Kong from his native south China, is of an extremely modest bearing. His physical appearance is that of a benign schoolmaster, with a distant but not unfriendly gaze from behind thick dark-framed glasses. Apart from his passion for making deals worth hundreds of millions, now mostly in cash, his lifestyle is ascetic. He lives in an old two-storey house, purchased at the time he abandoned making plastic flowers for property development. In his interview with *Fortune*, he confesses that: 'My living standard in 1962 was maybe even higher than today. A simple life is more enjoyable.'

His rise in the business world seems to bear this statement out. At a time when Hong Kong Land was involved in intricate redevelopment projects, many with long-term obligations that were to become severe liabilities when the property market slipped in the early 1980s, Li took a different and essentially simple tack. Rather than retain his properties and become another glorified landlord in competition with Hong Kong Land, Li opted to search out strategic sites, build them up quickly, and then sell off the entire premises. While Hong Kong Land continued to add to its prestigious portfolio of up-market office space and luxury shops, Li built for smaller offices and lower middle-class shoppers. Indeed, one of Li's early coups was to focus on the MTR (Mass Transit Railway), buying up land over the proposed stations. When the bottom finally fell out of the property market, Hong Kong Land was left with a large number of new buildings and a severe liquidity problem, while Li's company Cheung Kong had overflowing coffers with which it could entertain new, and ever more spectacular, investment schemes. He has not looked back since.

Li's nature is succinctly displayed in an anecdote that was circulating in Hong Kong not long ago. One lunchtime Li took some businessmen to eat at the Renaissance, a prestigious restaurant hidden in the bowels of Wanchai that boasted the finest food and most exquisite cellar in Hong Kong, and millions spent on decor, cutlery and crockery. As with most places in Hong Kong, however, it began to serve specially priced business lunches quite soon after it opened. Li was approached by the wine waiter and asked what he and his companions would like to accompany their food. Li responded that the waiter should choose a suitable wine for them. This was duly brought to the table, shown to Li and poured into the glasses. It was very good. Li asked the waiter to bring more of the same. At the end of the lunch the bill arrived: over £2000 for a small business lunch. Li was reportedly mortified. Upon checking the bill, he found that most of the cost had been the bottles of wine; some early Château Lafite that had pride of place on the quite remarkable wine list. Li quietly paid, but walked out in a black mood.

At sixty-eight, over a decade older than Li, Y. K. Pao – or Sir Y. K. as he is known (he was knighted in 1978) – is of a more outgoing nature. Indeed, by comparison with Li he is almost flamboyant. Very much the elder statesman of the Hong Kong business community, he plays the role with aplomb. The son of a Shanghai businessman, Pao arrived in Hong Kong shortly before the Communists came to power in China. Instead of pursuing the banking career his father had mapped out for him, Pao, then in his thirties, was drawn to shipping. In 1955 he bought his first vessel, which was chartered to the Japanese. This presaged a clever system of leaseback that Pao used to build up World-Wide Shipping. The Japanese, in effect, financed the growth of his business, with the ships he owned and operated being constructed in Japanese yards, and chartered by Japanese concerns.

Sir Y. K. is never short of sage advice, folk wisdom and business tips: 'When money is losing value, that's the time to borrow. When inflation is halted, don't borrow.'

Such glibness has done much to irritate some of his fellow shipowners in Hong Kong. In a decade that has been an unprecedented disaster for international shipping as a whole, with many Hong Kong owners going to the wall, Pao managed successfully to turn his losses in shipping into considerable gains in property, hotels and public transport (the 'Star' Ferry and Hong Kong Tramways are controlled by him). For a time he was owner of Hong Kong's 'Harrods', the Lane Crawford Company. At least part of the secret behind this remarkable turnaround was the fact that, from as early as 1980, the Pao organization began to sell off its fleet while other shipowners, such as his main rivals the C.Y. Tung group, held on to theirs in the hope of a recovery in the market. While the Pao organization was moving from strength to strength, the head of the Tung group, at one of the difficult sessions devoted to rescheduling his company's US$2.5 billion debt, could only gloomily state that he was presiding over a slow death.

Pao's business is run on traditional Chinese lines, being very much controlled by the family, and above all by Pao himself. Because he has three daughters but no sons, Pao has encouraged his sons-in-law to take a prominent part in the running of the group.

Pao is a complicated character. He traces his family roots to Judge Bao Qing, a 'wise and learned' man who was a member of the scholar-gentry class and who, according to Pao, enjoyed a status equivalent to that of a prime minister; a man, moreover, who had little interest in money or power, and above all simply wanted to do his job. Pao's own bearing would suggest that he identifies with these ideals. The ready smile and grandfatherly appearance, however, conceal another less reconcilable feature of his character. As this is written, Pao is losing a most unusual court case. He is responsible for withholding many millions from a construction company and architect who have completed a long row of interconnecting complexes known as Harbour Centre and Harbour City on the western side of Kowloon Point. Pao justifies his action on the basis that his company has been deprived of income because the aesthetically pleasing string of semi-circular buildings with their sweeping panoramas of the harbour underutilized valuable ground space. The dispute has been bitter and has led to a sharp decline in the health of the architect concerned and given him prolonged financial worries. The architect also had a large share in a small but profitable supermarket that was ingeniously sited in the space beneath the main staircase to the Ocean Terminal, Hong Kong's first shopping promenade (also owned by Pao through the Hong Kong and Kowloon Wharf & Godown Co.). Needless to say, he found that the lease was not to be renewed. Wharf insisted that the supermarket could not be put up for sale as a going concern; the premises had to be stripped to a bare shell.

A more enigmatic billionaire, whose stature is likely to increase greatly as Hong Kong approaches 1997 and its handover to China, is Henry Fok Ying-tung. Fok, who is three years younger than Pao, also arrived in Hong Kong after the war. Unlike Pao, Fok had none of the natural advantages provided by a father with a business background. He came from a poor southern boat family and had almost no resources during his early years as a trader in Hong Kong. Fok is a retiring man who steers well clear of publicity. Details of the business he pursued in his formative years are murky. What is known is that he developed his capital base during the Korean War, when he also built up his business links with China. In some thirty years Fok has expanded his activities from oil and construction (in which he controlled much of the import of building sand from China) to transport and gambling.

With the voluble Stanley Ho, whose Sino-Portuguese background and connections with Macau provided a suitable springboard, he holds the gambling franchise in Macau and, conveniently, controls the lion's share of transport to the Portuguese colony. The hundreds of thousands of Hong Kong residents who flock to Macau each week for their regular fix of gambling (a few, in fact, have been so absorbed by gaming that they have taken it up as an ordinary job: the 8.00 am hydrofoil to Macau, at their desk by 9.30, a short break for lunch – often taken as a sandwich at the gambling table – and home on the 5.30 service!) virtually need never leave Fok's and Ho's warm embrace. They are transported to Macau by their Shun Tak vessels. There is then a short ride by cab or pedicab, a service not within Fok's and Ho's organization, to the Lisboa Hotel, which houses casino, restaurants, accommodation and, if required, diversions of a less expensive sort. There is little reason to leave this controlled climate, except to clear the head and refill the pockets. A minute's stroll from the Lisboa are pawnshops filled with jewellery, watches, pens and cameras left by other hapless gamblers. Until recently it was impossible to cash Hong Kong cheques or gain access to Hong Kong accounts while in Macau; so for the desperate it was either borrow or pawn.

The Lisboa is a curious building. For many years it served as a gaudy beacon on a Macanese coastline that had otherwise barely entered the twentieth century. Circles and rectangles mix uncomfortably, dressed in garish yellow and highlighted by a confusion of small white arches. A golden ball radiating shafts of metal on the front of the building is said to represent a tennis ball, tennis being one of Fok's burning passions. There is a story that the billionaire keeps a smaller but more valuable 'tennis ball' in a glass cabinet in his marble and crystal front hall. This 24 carat sphere was intended to be a trophy for the first of his professional tennis partners who could help him win the 'Grand Slam' of major Hong Kong tennis tournaments in the same year.

But these are the minor indulgences of a man of a uniformly modest manner and an otherwise simple disposition. From time to time Fok's lack of pretension has had comical results. His interest in tennis led him to play in inter-club tennis leagues. At five o'clock on a weekday afternoon, his stretch limousine, known by his players as the 'minibus', would transport the team to the match venue. On one such occasion, having earlier warmed up on its own dusty clay courts, the team arrived at the front door of a club still adhering to its strictly non-Chinese membership policy. At the door was the club manager, observing the arriving players with a distant glance. Fok led the group into the clubhouse. As he passed in front of the manager, the latter motioned him to stop and pointed at a small trail of clay left by his tennis shoes. Fok was outraged, but asked for a dustpan and brush. After he himself had swept up the clay under the uncomfortable gaze of his team-mates, he walked through with one of his employees at his side: 'Find out how much this place is worth,' Fok muttered, 'I'm thinking of buying it.'

Under the circumstances, it is understandable that Fok is not an Anglophile, although he owns a large mansion in Britain. He has maintained a tactful distance from the colonial administration and vice versa. His links with China, on the other hand, have grown significantly since his early trade contacts. As well as substantial business deals, which now include contracts for the construction of hotels and leisure facilities, particularly in the south of the country, Fok is also noted for his generosity towards China, which has greatly increased Chinese interest in him. According to those close to him, this largesse is based on a straightforward premise: as a great deal of money is being made from China, so must a share be returned. According to the same sources, about 5–10 per cent (or roughly $1 billion to date) of his earnings find their way back to China.

Because of his interest in sport – his other passion is soccer – Fok has concentrated particularly on providing the country with sports facilities and stadia. And it is sport and finance that tend to dominate Fok's formal links with China, rather than overtly political issues. Even though he was nominated to the Basic Law Drafting Committee (BLDC), the body responsible for drawing up Hong Kong's post-1997 constitution, by the Chinese authorities, his main contributions have come during sub-group meetings on the subjects he knows best. His politics, in so far as they can be identified at all, are centred on an old-fashioned notion of patriotism. In one of the few interviews that he has allowed, published in the *South China Morning Post Review*, he summed up his position: 'I don't believe in fate. Neither do I understand politics. But I do live in Hongkong and I'm Chinese. I have always wanted to do something for the mother-land and the compatriots.'

Not surprisingly, his political gestures tend to be oblique. In 1985, the same year that he was co-opted to the BLDC, he helped to fund the Hong Kong Institute for the Promotion of Chinese Culture, which is intended to reveal to the world the splendour of Chinese culture and to encourage cultural exchanges between Hong Kong, China and Taiwan. The latter function, in particular, slotted neatly into the slogan of 'one country, two systems', a statement of China's intention to reunify with Hong Kong, Macau and, most important of all, Taiwan.

Fok's approach is likely to pay considerable dividends in the long run. By avoiding an excessively politicized stance on events in either China or Hong Kong, he has avoided the stigma attached to those who, like Pao, have attempted to keep a foot in the British, Chinese and Hong Kong camps and have in the process come to be regarded as inscrutable, and perhaps even opportunistic, by all. Fok prefers to skirt such contentious issues as the future form of the Hong Kong polity altogether: 'If the policies and measures of the Hongkong Government and requests and actions of the people were in line with the aim of maintaining the territory's stability and prosperity, there would be no difficulty in Hongkong becoming a Special Administrative Region.'

Such statements, when matched with his simple patriotism – he has totally avoided any British orders of merit – make Fok a safe choice for increased public authority in Hong Kong; a conclusion seemingly supported by his election to the Chinese People's Political Consultative Conference Standing Committee in 1980 and the BLDC in 1985. Most recently, he was chosen as one of sixteen Hong Kong delegates to the National People's Congress, China's law-making body.

But it is not only within the formal areas of Chinese politics that Fok has made his mark. Much publicity has been made of Sir Y. K. Pao's audiences with China's paramount leader, Deng Xiaoping. Fok, in a somewhat less obvious way, has also left an impression on the present Chinese leadership. When Deng visited the Shenzhen area in 1984 to assess progress in this Special Economic Zone at first hand, he stayed at one of Fok's hotels. His official functions in-cluded attending a football match, at which he and Fok sat side by side.

Fok takes this side of his activities very seriously. Perhaps the clearest indication of just how seriously was to be seen when Mao died in 1976. Those in his circle report that Fok's look was sullen. His balding pate, which is normally quite healthy and shiny, was dull for months on end. His face was drawn and his mood chronically bad. Gradually, and this is said to have taken some time, Fok established contacts with the new leadership. As he did so, his colour improved.

Of the other financial barons, there are two individuals worthy of note. In a sense, they occupy the middle ground between the hongs and the Chinese tycoons, belonging strictly to neither category. One is Lawrence Kadoorie. Although Sir Elly Kadoorie & Sons is still ostensibly a family business, with Lawrence (aged eighty-seven) and his brother Horace (eighty-five) maintaining a joint bank account and equal shares in the business, day-to-day control of its interests is very much in the hands of the former. Both still live in their father's shadow. Sir Elly, a Sephardic Jew, was born in Baghdad and made his way to Hong Kong in 1883, while still in his teens. He built up a business as a broker in Hong Kong's early boom period and went on to become a very successful financier. His operations spread to Shanghai, where the bulk of his activity became focused. The main office was there, and that was where most of the deals were made, particularly in property. There was also an early association with utilities through the ownership of the Shanghai Gas Company, an involvement that continues today with the family's control of the China Light & Power Company. This important monopoly supplies electricity to Kowloon and the New Territories, and therefore to an overwhelming proportion of Hong Kong's population and industry. The family lived in Shanghai in a palatial mansion, the centrepiece of which was a magnificent marble hall.

Sir Elly died when he was only fifty-seven. In his thirty-five years in the Far East he had not only built up a financial empire but had also acquired a reputation as a great philanthropist and pre-eminence in the high society of the China coast, particularly in the elegant circles of the racing fraternity. His philanthropic activities, which centred on education and medicine, led to numerous honours, including a knighthood in 1917. His obituary states that he had been 'a familiar and widely esteemed figure, the loss of whom will be keenly felt'. Ten years later, the Hong Kong Government honoured him by creating a Kadoorie Avenue in Kowloon.

After World War II Lawrence and Horace Kadoorie began to concentrate their activities in Hong Kong, but the shift was not fast enough to prevent tremendous losses in Shanghai as a result of the Communist takeover. These losses included extensive property holdings and the investment in the Gas Company. What was left of the family fortune in Hong Kong was gradually expanded to its current level, not so much with the entrepreneurial flair that characterized their father's work, but with dogged determination. Moreover, despite their attempts to take over their father's philanthropic reputation, the brothers' public image does not sparkle in the same way as Sir Elly's did. Horace, regarded as 'the true farmer of the family', has long devoted himself to a pet project, the Kadoorie Farm and Botanical Gardens in the New Territories. And, indeed, it is in the area of farming, and mainly through a system of agricultural loans, that the brothers' own philanthropic work has been of greatest importance. Honours have come late to the brothers. Lawrence, who has done best in this respect, received his knighthood when he was in his seventies, becoming Lord Kadoorie nearly a decade later.

Kadoorie occupies a remarkably distant place in Hong Kong affairs and, judging from some of the responses I have had from people that have had dealings with him, there is little warmth expressed about him. From time to time he has publicly proffered advice to the people of Hong Kong, and especially so in his recent strongly expressed stand on the need to avoid all political change in the run-up to 1997. His advice has increasingly tended to fall on deaf ears. His own record is in part to blame. Freshly ennobled, he was to make his maiden speech in the House of Lords on the important occasion of the 1984 debate on the Sino-British settlement on Hong Kong. He was unable to deliver the speech because he had, one assumes inadvertently, failed to swear his allegiance in advance of the session. Newspapers in the colony have also been critical about the little time that he and others spent in formal session with the Basic Law Consultative Committee, which was set up by China as a forum for the discussion of Hong Kong's future constitution.

At the time of this criticism Kadoorie had already weathered a broader public protest. His electricity company had signed a huge contract with the Chinese authorities to build a nuclear power station at Daya Bay, a few miles along the coast from Hong Kong. In the wake of the Chernobyl disaster, serious doubts were voiced in

Hong Kong about the suitability of locating the plant so close to such a densely-populated area. Protests reached a climax with mass rallies and a petition signed by over a million people against the project. Although Kadoorie himself was not singled out for criticism, his name was unavoidably associated with the scheme.

Even within Hong Kong's small Jewish community, Kadoorie has managed to generate a surprising amount of ill-will. As the head trustee of the Sassoon Trust, which controls a HK$500,000,000 site in the Mid-levels of Hong Kong Island occupied by the colony's Synagogue and Jewish Recreation Club (the latter, ironically, funded by Sir Elly), Kadoorie has co-ordinated talks with a number of property companies since 1985 for the redevelopment of this pocket of Jewish culture, much in the way that Hong Kong Land dealt with the Hong Kong Club. In doing so, passions have spilled over into the press and drawn in the two Chief Rabbis of Israel and the Chief Rabbi of Great Britain. The move to preserve the Ohel Leah Synagogue, a much-loved structure and one of only two remaining Sephardic buildings in the Far East, was defended by the Israeli Rabbis, who forbade its destruction. The head trustee chose to ignore this judgement, announcing that he would only consider the views of the British Chief Rabbi. In July 1986, Sir Immanuel Jakobovits (now Lord Jakobovits) wrote to the members of the SOS (Save Our Synagogue):

Your letters . . . reached me while I was in correspondence with Lord Kadoorie regarding the redevelopment of the synagogue site. He had asked me for guidance to ensure that he would act in compliance with Jewish Law. I asked for certain clarifications, especially since I knew from previous representations to me on behalf of several members that there was some considerable disquiet over the proposed transaction. But before he could reply to my questions, Lord Kadoorie informed me that his enquiry had been overtaken by events and that an agreement with the developer had just been signed.

Because of his wealth and status, Kadoorie has quite naturally been the target of a stream of people looking for funds. His way of dealing with these is in itself revealing. Those who channel representatives of bona fide charitable concerns in his direction find that the dictum 'time is money' operates in reverse in his case. A visiting Israeli rabbi made such an indirect approach to Kadoorie and was pleasantly surprised when he was informed that he had been granted an audience. Excitedly he told his sponsors that half the battle had been won.

They, on the other hand, took a less optimistic view, but the rabbi refused to listen. 'Why would such an important man grant me his valuable time if he wasn't at least interested in my cause?'

At the appointed time, he made his way up to the smart bronze-faced St George's building that houses the nerve centre of the Kadoorie operation. The rabbi returned a different man. During the half-hour audience he had barely managed to get a word in and had been treated to a stream of sage advice on fund raising and the world at large. The meeting ended with a polite 'thank you for coming'. Not a cent had changed hands.

The jestful Hari N. Harilela is a complete contrast to the dour Lord Kadoorie. 'Doyen of Hong Kong's Indian Community', 'Hong Kong's Indian Chief', 'Sindhi Onassis', 'Indian Merchant Prince' and 'Golden Boy of Hong Kong' are just some of the exotic titles lavished on the redoubtable Mr Harilela. Born in 1922 to a Sindhi gem merchant who brought his family first to Guangzhou and then, after his trade failed in the wake of the Great Depression, to Hong Kong, Harilela started in a very humble way selling everything from newspapers to eggs. With a small amount of capital accumulated, he and his five brothers – Mohan, Gary, George, Peter and Bob – moved into the silk trade and custom tailoring (conducted under the euphonic company title of Harilela's Custom Tailors). The fact that this business was a great success owed much to the large numbers of British and American soldiers and their wives who flowed through Hong Kong during the Korean War. By 1960, when Hari first entered the property and hotel trade, the Harilela brothers had the largest tailoring business in the colony.

His sense of timing in moving from the retail trade was near-perfect. Today the family owns hotels in Hong Kong, Singapore, Malaysia, Thailand and Canada, the majority run in association with the American Holiday Inn Group. While Hari concentrates on the property portfolio, interests in other areas, such as restaurants, travel and estate agencies and dealings on the stock market, are farmed out between his brothers. By the early 1980s the Harilela operation was worth over HK$2 billion, while Hari's personal wealth was estimated at over HK$500,000,000.

In his rise to financial success, Hari could not be accused of being discreet. All six brothers and most of their families live in a three-storeyed, forty-bedroomed and forty-bathroomed mansion that can best be described as a cross between a Moghul palace and a Texas ranch. Gold-leaf tables, a bedroom (Hari's) adorned with thousands of strings of pearls, crystal chandeliers and French antique furniture setting off a Chinese artist's rendition of a scene from *The Rubaiyat of Omar Khayyam* are just a few of the many notable features. The music room, befitting the scale of the accommodation, is a miniature concert hall, complete with stage. The car-park in the basement has space for twenty vehicles.

Harilela's attitude to wealth and the influence that it potentially allows suggests that it is all still a great novelty to him. Honours too are taken very seriously. As well as his OBE and appointment as a JP, Harilela's 'profile' lists a knighthood of the Cordon Bleu du Saint Esprit, the Silver Dragon Medal (from the Scout Association, of which he is honorary president), a Medal of Merit (from the Hong Kong Girl Guides Association, of which he is honorary vice-president) and an International Humanitarianism Award from the Anti-Defamation League of B'nai B'rith. Other recipients of the last award, the profile notes, include American Presidents Eisenhower, Kennedy, Johnson and Ford.

Behind the pomp and show is an essentially simple man. When Harilela was asked what had been a particular inspiration in his life, his response was the reading and re-reading of *The Count of Monte Cristo*, which 'gave me a lot of courage in my convictions'. His company headquarters, while lined in gleaming marble and chrome, is located in an earthy Kowloon cul-de-sac, not far from the sites of his early tailor's shops. The neighbourhood mix includes girlie bars, discotheques, fast food shops, fruit stalls and Ned Kelly's, an Australian pub. When I interviewed him the sound system of the discotheque below his office was being tested for that evening's entertainment. When I walked into his room I noticed that my choice of seats was limited: a plastic strip marked 'Hari N. Harilela' reserved the settee farthest from me. When he came to join me, Hari picked up the strip and sat down on the reserved seat. Perhaps it was the place most immune to the throb of the disco's booming bass.

The hongs come at the other end of the spectrum of Hong Kong's big business. Although, particularly in recent years, the activities of Chinese tycoons and the British concerns have tended to merge at the edges (Pao, for example, was recently replaced on the board of the Hongkong & Shanghai Bank by his chief son-in-law, Helmut Sohmen), the hongs are still something of a world unto themselves.

In many ways, these companies form the backbone of foreign life in the colony. The scale of their operations has grown from an early role as China coast trading firms to encompass virtually every area of manufacture, service and construction. In addition to their economic influence, these concerns – of which Jardine Matheson and John Swire and Sons are the most prominent – represent a strong political caucus too. The companies' taipans wield great influence, both formally and informally. Historically the senior management of the trading houses were rarely slow in making their displeasure known, in a most militant and public way, to governors bent on introducing liberal measures. The hongs are also immersed in myth and fable, and have achieved a place in colonial mythology comparable to that of the Gibraltar apes. Without them there would be no colony. The word hong might even suggest that the colony owes half its name to these houses. In fact, the hong in Hong Kong should read *heung*, or fragrant, deriving either from the lyrical fragrance of the harbour – *kong* – or the more practical allusion to the territory as an ancient centre for the making of joss sticks – also called *heung*.

The hongs' image of permanence has been tarnished somewhat by the decision of Jardines, the oldest hong, to move its base to Bermuda in March 1984 (and by the decision of Jardines' sister company, Hong Kong Land, to follow suit five years later). But the mentality which would insist that Hong Kong means little without the hongs' presence refuses to change with the times. I was emphatically reminded of this while interviewing a semi-retired hong man who, coincidentally, was also a senior civic official. The urbane public image apparent in speeches laced with Shakespearean references was instantly replaced by the language and style of a living caricature of a hong man. He was a cross between toastmaster and streetfighter with a brusque and aggressive pattern of speech punctuated by expressions such as 'frigging' and, in referring to recent political developments, 'pissing in the wind'. When I pursued the question of the rapid evolution of local politics after the signing of the Joint Declaration, the corporate ego of a century-old pedigree shone through: 'the politicking may cause the whole place to collapse. But it is companies like Jardines, the Bank and Swire that will make it a success.'

I could not help wondering why, if the picture really was one of such certainty, Jardines had felt so threatened by the encroachment of local Chinese business interests in the early 1980s, or why it should have moved its corporate base. No doubt the two Chinese secretaries who happened to be in the room when their boss made his confident observation had similar thoughts.

Between them, the 'independents' and the hongs occupy the heartland of Hong Kong life. But there is little heart to be felt amongst them and little room for sentiment or loyalty to a community. In discussing the problem of nationality with various tycoons, I was struck by their curious combination of simplistic political analysis with ever so sharp calculation. Hari Harilela has been engaged in a long campaign to convince the British Government that the 15,000-strong Indian community has a legitimate case for special treatment in 1997 when they become, to all intents and purposes, refugees. He spoke of the lack of response from Prime Minister Margaret Thatcher. Despite his attempts to see her, his only contacts have been with the Foreign Office. Thoroughly frustrated, he had concluded that the Indian community's woes are all due to Mrs Thatcher's refusal to reconsider a decision: 'If I could sit with her like this,' he suggested, motioning to an empty chair opposite (I imagined a little plastic strip with her name on it), 'I'm sure I could bring her around.'

It was in his use of himself as an example of why the Indians would not consider moving to Britain en masse that Harilela's mind showed itself to be at its sharpest. He pointed out that for £150,000 he could get right of residence, but that he would have to live in Britain for nine months of the year for five years. This would be undesirable. He owns a company in the United Kingdom which, he says, earns only £100,000 a year. Of this sum, 50 per cent is lost in corporation tax, and another 50 per cent (now 40 per cent) is held back in personal tax. This leaves him with an income of £23,000, of which a further £2000 is taken up by audit costs. And as a non-resident he cannot claim tax allowances on his car or home. Overall, his total income in Britain was little more than £150 per day: 'But for the length of time I stay there, that amounts to only £4500 a year; which isn't enough to run a house even.'

It is hard to reconcile the cause Harilela champions, and his own precise calculations concerning a potential refuge, with his public pronouncements of confidence in Hong Kong's future. A year after we discussed these matters, Harilela told a local newspaper that: 'I will still be around. I know there's a lot of fear, but I think the

Chinese are sincere. China needs Hongkong very badly as a political doorway.' The only common denominator in these views seems to be thoughts of doorways!

On another occasion, just as the discussion of the issue of Hong Kong's future first came into prominence, I spoke to Lord Kadoorie about the gradual erosion of British nationality in the colony. Since 1962, in line with immigration policy in the United Kingdom, British passports issued in Hong Kong had inexorably moved from full parity with those of the United Kingdom to a situation where people who were British citizens on paper had no automatic right to enter Britain. A succession of Immigration Acts, guided by Labour and Conservative Governments alike, had introduced entry vouchers (1962), defined Commonwealth immigrants as a 'problem' (1965), removed the right to enter except by virtue of immediate descent (1968), and confirmed patriality and 'right of abode' as applying only to those who were born – or whose parents were born – in the United Kingdom (1971). In 1972 illegal immigration was made a crime and the police were given the right to hold a person suspected of it indefinitely.

At the time I saw Lord Kadoorie, Margaret Thatcher's government, as it had pledged to do in its first election manifesto, was enacting legislation which would ensure unwanted Britons could be kept out of Britain. In the course of our discussion I expressed my misgivings about Hong Kong-British nationality, the inequities of which were about to be enshrined. Lord Kadoorie corrected me: 'No, it isn't *Hong Kong*-British, it's *British*-Hong Kong . . . British-Hong Kong.'

I didn't argue with this fine distinction. Nor did many other Hong Kong residents as their freedoms were gradually withdrawn over the years. They were aided in their belief that all would be well by public and private reassurances from the likes of Lord Kadoorie: that the changes were only on paper and that the value of British nationality had not altered. The thrust of the legislation, however, was clear. People in Hong Kong who had been born on British territory, or who had subsequently sworn allegiance to Queen and country, were, finally, to become bona fide second-class citizens. I remembered Lord Kadoorie's words with an inward half-smile when, less than three years later, the nearly 3.5 million BDTCs (British Dependent Territories Citizens) as they became known, were informed that they were to be designated Bn(O), or British-national (Overseas), after their handover to China in 1997. In the eyes of the overwhelming majority of those affected by the law, this was a further demotion. They were, through this legislation, truly left in limbo: after Hong Kong becomes officially Chinese they will have the right to hold a British passport, but not to reside in Britain. It did not take long for the more cynical to expand the acronym into an alternative title: British – no.

Yet those who offer reassurances are often the appointed, and at times self-professed, leaders of the colony. They are looked to for wisdom, guidance and inspiration. Those who are less than charmed by such leadership look on in a haze of fatalism and dis-belief. When discussing one such member of the billionaire's club with a friend who had lived through the changes in Shanghai after the Communist takeover and who was now contemplating the pros-pect of perhaps being alive for what he regarded as the replay in Hong Kong, our conversation drifted briefly to the new Governor. Sir Edward Youde had just died and there was considerable debate in the Hong Kong press about who should become the new chief executive. My friend suggested that Mr X should be made the new Governor. I asked why, not having heard this person touted as a potential candidate. Was it because he had some special acumen, or the general approval of the population? 'No', was the matter-of-fact response. 'He would immediately hand Hong Kong over to China.'

This was a strong reminder of the absence of trust in Hong Kong politics. It is understandable: secrecy is an important element in any financial centre's *modus vivendi*. In Hong Kong, where tycoons and hong men all do business in the few square miles of Central, often within earshot of each other, there is hardly room for faith in either institutions or individuals. There are simply too many rumours, too many telling anecdotes circulating to allow public figures to remain with their reputations intact. Secrecy, then, offers protection, a veneer of respectability and, more often than not, an edge on the competition. It is guarded jealously and, because the players in busi-ness are generally those in politics as well, there is a natural, if unhealthy, tendency for secrecy to spill over into the political system too. Under these circumstances, politics is a game of doublespeak.

Nowhere is this more plain than with respect to the colony's future after 1997. By March 1972 China had done nothing to re-assure the colony that it would be free to continue its existence, except to say that the Hong Kong and Macau questions would be dealt with 'when conditions were ripe'. Indeed, Huang Hua's statement at the United Nations less than ten years before should have alerted the population to the inherent difficulties in perpetuating the status quo after the New Territories' lease ran out. Instead, the popular view focused on the fact that, despite the existence of ideal conditions for resuming sovereignty – for example, at the time of the Cultural Revolution – China had chosen to allow the status quo to persist. In the face of this ineluctable evidence, statements at the UN were to be regarded as nothing but ideological acrobatics to facilitate the tacit partnership between a socialist China and a capitalist Britain.

Clients and visitors engaged in small talk at a dinner table would ask their hosts about the future of the colony: what bearing had the lease on its fate? The answer was invariably simple and persuasive. Hong Kong was too useful to China; it was inconceivable that it would kill the goose that laid the golden eggs. Therefore, the lease was immaterial. In any event, 1997 was a long way away and much might change in China itself: just look at the differences already evident there since the Cultural Revolution. Further evidence came from the experiences of the colony's Portuguese neighbour, Macau, 50 miles away: Portugal had, after all, offered to return the territory after the disturbances there, but China had refused. People in Hong Kong are generally very proud of their city, and of their ability to command an encyclopaedic knowledge of their tiny environment. The dense traffic in inquisitive visitors provided the sharpening stone on which the argument could be finely honed. It could be easily summarized: Hong Kong would be because it was.

The major personalities in the business sector played along with this point of view and continue to do so with alarming unanimity. Tycoons who were displaced from Shanghai by the Communist tide, incurring substantial losses in the process, and who had to rebuild their fortunes, are now professing confidence in China, and in Hong Kong's absorption by that country. How close is their public optimism to their inner thoughts? Frequently, the marriage is not altogether a happy one. The voluble Hari Harilela has often gone on record that he is confident in the future of Hong Kong. Privately, he regrets the British Government's decision to make a top-level approach to China about 1997. Had the approach been low-key, he suggested: '(China) wouldn't have talked of an extension of Hong

Kong's existence for fifty years, but about a continued British presence for another fifty, seventy years.' There was more than just a trace of sorrow in his expression. As for his own plans, his reply was non-committal: he was in no hurry to make up his mind. That may well be true. With hotels, businesses, funds and homes all over the world he can well afford to wait. In his own words, he and his wife could become 'citizens of the world'. So might all Hong Kong's super rich.

It is even less easy to fathom the true views of the most tight-lipped, men such as Pao, Li, Fok and Kadoorie and the taipans of the hongs. Pao's family fled from Shanghai. Fok, as we have seen, turns green when the management in Beijing changes; and that is while he is within the relatively stable confines of a British Hong Kong. What will his colour be if a similar change of leadership occurs when Hong Kong is formally part of the People's Republic? The Kadoorie family is well aware of the fickle nature of transitional politics. In February 1988 it was announced that Lord Lawrence had put in a claim for much of the 'substantial' trading company that his family lost to the Communists after 1949. He was, however, reportedly 'reluctant' to say how much was being claimed. The memory of the lost millions is still, it seems, vivid and painful. The hongs also lost money in the collapse of Shanghai. Simon Keswick, the last taipan of Jardines, the hong that suffered most, was both philosophical and positive in his attitude to the great losses that his company, and family, has sustained in China. When asked if he had lodged a claim, his response was: 'They are old ghosts. These things are in the past. We are going to let bygones be bygones.'

It is an attitude that has been characteristic of his public approach to the colony's handover, suggesting a constructive frame of mind and an eagerness to develop a healthy working relationship with China. Against this, however, there is the fact that Jardines has transferred its capital base offshore. There is also other evidence to suggest that the public pronouncements may not be in total harmony with private opinions and fears. A social activist and a champion of the underdog described how, shortly before Margaret Thatcher's fateful trip to Beijing and Hong Kong in 1982, she and a colleague received invitations to lunch with Simon Keswick at his penthouse suite in the Connaught Centre, his company's Hong Kong headquarters: 'I was staggered,' she said. 'In all the time I have spent in Hong Kong – over thirty years – I had never been invited to such an event.' Being astute, she realized that the purpose

of the invitation was not altogether social. The answer to her mis-
givings was not long in coming. In the course of the afternoon, the
Jardines taipan took her aside and warned: 'We must *all* work to stop
Communists from taking this place. . . . At all costs.'

This story is illuminating, and not only because it clearly differ-
entiates between the public and private faces of business leaders
such as the taipan of Jardines. It also reveals the mentality which
has worked – in both the private sector and the government – to
keep China and Hong Kong separate in the crucial years when, with
the handover a *fait accompli*, the two might well have been encouraged
to genuinely get to know one another. Nor would such a process
have been assisted by a note handed down to his staff by one major
company's taipan after the initialling of the Sino-British agreement.
From that day no one was to issue a pessimistic view of the future:
optimism by edict!

CHAPTER SEVEN

Uneasy Dialogue

E ven before 1979, and the initial diplomatic forays into China, the bland reassurances about the colony's future were hardly convincing. Apart from the question of China's future intentions, they all rested on the important assumption that *Britain* saw itself as having a long-term role in the colony. Such an assumption could not easily be made. At about the same time as the Communists took power in China, Britain had embarked on the 'fashionable' course of decolonization. One of the early targets for decolonization was Hong Kong. Soon after diplomatic relations with the new Chinese Government were established, Britain floated the idea of creating an independent Hong Kong. A note was received by the British Government to the effect that this was an impossibility. Ever since then Chinese thinking on Hong Kong has been strongly influenced by the fear that British negotiations were aimed at creating an independent territory.

After the traumatic riots of 1966 and 1967, which had shaken the colony's very foundations, a more subtle initiative came from a most unlikely quarter: the hongs. A well-researched, top-secret document written by the heads of one of the major hongs was circulated to a handful of leading British politicians. The four-page paper appeared curiously simple and, at least at first sight, did not seem to deserve the secrecy attached to it. Basically, it was a detailed calculation of British financial interests in the colony, showing that these were not all that great even taking into account such major capital assets as the airport. Leaving aside such invisibles as the civil service, the most valuable asset was concluded to be the colony's air rights. Three years later Sir Murray MacLehose arrived in Hong Kong. As

116

seasoned observers have pointed out, there was no pressing reason why the British Government should have looked to the diplomatic corps for the new chief executive: there were sufficient candidates in the colonial service for a suitable appointment to be made from its ranks. The British Government obviously had a purpose other than the governing of Hong Kong for its new appointment.

Here the picture becomes murky. While Hong Kong enjoyed rapid economic growth and stability, 1997 was discussed in whispers and uncomfortable circumlocutions in the inner recesses of government. Rarely has a topic of such potential general interest been shrouded in such secrecy. Little substantial detail can be gathered from the official documents of the period. In December 1975, for example, a Defence and External Affairs Sub-Committee met at Westminster. William Rodgers, then the Labour Government's Secretary of State for Defence, together with a number of government officials, was cross-examined by MPs about the future of the British military presence in Hong Kong. The cross-examination touched upon the status of the colony after 1997. Rodgers was asked for the government's philosophy behind the retention of British forces in Hong Kong. His reply, as printed in the minutes of that meeting, is telling:

My philosophy I think would be that at the moment there are three parties to an unarticulated understanding. One is London, another is Peking and the third is Hong Kong, and the unarticulated understanding is that the status quo should remain ∗∗∗ because it is of convenience. In a situation of this kind, if some part of the status quo is unreasonable it will upset the other parties and they may feel it necessary to look at the situation in a new light ∗∗∗ .

The asterisks in the reply represent 'a passage, word or figure' left out at the request of the Foreign and Commonwealth Office. In this way the general features of the tripartite relationship were allowed to emerge, without giving away any substantive information about Britain's own position on the 1997 question. Later at the same meeting another government representative, a Mr Hawley, was asked if, assuming that the tripartite interest existed, 1997 no longer had any relevance. He replied:

The year 1997 has official relevance, and one cannot just write it off. Everything would turn on the political relations between the three members of the tripartite interest.

The statement and restatement of the tripartite interest is of importance. What is clear is that Britain recognized the delicate balance that existed between the three interested parties and how easily it could be upset. What is not clear, however, is the level of commitment that Britain felt to its colony. That remained elusive. When the Head of the Hong Kong Department, Mr O'Keefe, was finally pressed on the question of whether policy decisions were being reached 'on the assumption that there will be a continuing British presence in Hong Kong, irrespective of any date . . . refer(red) to', his answer was laced with ambiguity and, thanks to Foreign and Commonwealth Office censorship, omission:

I think these decisions are taken because there is faith in the future of Hong Kong, and the only policy we can now adopt is one of regarding the future of Hong Kong as a viable entity. More than that one cannot say ***. The decisions are taken in the interests of the people of Hong Kong ***. There is no other viable policy.

In sum, these officials were saying that the maintenance of the status quo in Hong Kong depended on the inaction of the three interested parties. Intriguingly, they were also saying that 1997 was not a meaningless date and that the preservation of the status quo through inactivity would, eventually, have to be complemented by some activity. But surely whatever action was taken would disrupt the balance of the status quo? And if action were not taken then that too would upset the status quo as land in the New Territories could not be safely leased beyond 1997.

Discussions such as these confirmed what had been felt by a number of Hong Kong politicians for some years: that the only way of producing a satisfactory result would be through a finesse. In essence, the dilemma was how best to neutralize 1997 or avoid its import altogether.

In January 1978 the Governor was visited by a member of the Legislative Council. The audience lasted some 45 minutes. The subject of the meeting was precisely the issue of how a suitably structured finesse might be worked. The councillor was a lawyer himself, but had enlisted the help of a team of lawyers to draft proposals, which he then took to London for vetting by well-known QCs who have subsequently become high court judges. The conclusion reached by these eminent persons was that the proposals were indeed workable under British law.

The document was based on a simple premise: that a resolution of the 1997 issue had to be made to allow growth and reinvestment to proceed uninterrupted and that such a solution had to be arrived at by 1981, 1982 or 1983 at the very latest. How was this to be done? The document assumed that China did not want to scuttle the existing arrangement in Hong Kong, nor did it want further open dealings with Britain over the colony. Such views, together with a belief in the importance of the status quo, were widely held in Hong Kong.

The intention was, therefore, to test China's willingness to entertain an extension of the leasehold without drawing publicity to it and, more importantly, without forcing China to make a direct and open proclamation about the sanctity of the New Territories' lease.

The plan was ingenious in its simplicity. Leaseholds in the New Territories that were submitted for extension were to be drawn up to or a year beyond June 1997. This was to be done discreetly with a few test leases. If there was no adverse response from China, more such leases would be created. If there was *still* no response, a similar lease for a New Territories' holding would be presented directly to the Chinese Government.

The beauty of this scheme was that it was fully in accordance with the general parameters of leasehold in British law. A lessee, at the time, was allowed to extend a lease beyond his or her own tenure and the sub-tenant could enjoy that extension. Indeed, even a squatter could sub-let, and the sub-lessee would enjoy legal protection. This would then allow Britain to freely issue leases beyond 1997 and at the same time obviate the need to enter into formal negotiations with China, which would *certainly* have to include the question of sovereign rights. Given China's UN statement, no public proposals that impinged upon Chinese sovereignty would be acceptable.

MacLehose's response to the councillor's plan was most promising. He disclosed that he had had thoughts on the entire question before taking office. Turning his attention to the document itself, the Governor suggested that 'at two or three points' it came very close to his own views on the subject. Encouraged, the councillor pressed on by asking if he could in due course enquire about progress on his proposals. MacLehose's response was that he would be 'empowered by the governor' to approach him direct.

The viability of the plan appeared to be supported by events in China. In the early 1970s the country began the process of opening up to the outside world, notably with the normalization of relations between itself and the United States. At the same time there was a steady dulling of the ideological glint of Maoism, and especially so after the replacement of the 'Gang of Four' by a more pragmatic leadership. A year after it was installed, this leadership, under the chairmanship of Hua Guofeng, spelled out its intentions for Hong Kong. In his Report on the World Situation to the Communist Party, Hua pointed to a directive he had issued which instructed that the status quo should be maintained and that the problem of recovering Hong Kong and Macau should not be mentioned 'in the next ten or twenty years or even a considerably longer time so that Hong Kong and Macau may enjoy a period of relative stability for development'. In the same report he argued that great progress had been made in Sino-British relations 'where the question of Hong Kong is concerned' and that the colony would play an important role in China's expanding trade with the outside world and import of western science, technology and equipment. Significantly, Hua placed Hong Kong in the timetable for another, and more important, task: 'Some advocate,' he said to the assembled Party members, 'that we proceed with the recovery of Hong Kong after liberation of Taiwan. Although we have not expressed it publicly, the possibility cannot be entirely ruled out.'

Here was as clear an indication as was ever likely to come from the People's Republic that it was willing, indeed eager, to leave the question of Hong Kong on the back burner of history. Such an exposition of China's views on the colony's distant future all but begged a quiet British approach.

By the mid seventies, however, there had been hints that Britain's intentions for Hong Kong were not altogether compatible with the idea of prolonging a British administrative presence in the colony. The most important development was the establishment of the Diversification Committee within the Executive Council. Contrary to the notion of preserving the status quo, the committee's brief was to broaden the colony's political arena through the creation of District Boards, which were to serve as elected representative bodies at a local level. In addition, the committee was charged with devising a framework for bringing a hitherto excluded majority into the political system. There was said to be a need to bring the system of government into the twentieth century and to provide suitable political safety valves for pockets of discontent. However, these steps could also be regarded as moving towards at least a *de facto* form of independence for Hong Kong. At the very least, such developments were likely to help upset the status quo and might, in turn, disrupt the delicate tripartite balance so important to Hong Kong's future.

The committee's brief had been enough to warn the councillor that all was not quite right. As a result, he had begun to dump his considerable personal local holdings and used the proceeds to establish himself overseas. He notes with bitterness that the Governor, while remaining silent on the subject of perpetuating the leasehold, advised him informally that he should reinvest in Hong Kong 'because things will be all right'. Similar advice, he later discovered, was proffered to other members of the business community.

By the time the first of the crucial years had arrived, the Governor had already made his historic trip to Beijing in 1979 for an audience with China's paramount leader, Deng Xiaoping. The result was encouraging. The Chinese leader had, MacLehose said, asked him to convey a message to investors in the colony: they were to continue investing in Hong Kong's prosperity and not to worry about the future. 'Put their hearts at ease,' were the words that were to be passed on to the worried business community. But MacLehose failed to pass on another important piece of information: he had asked the Chinese leadership about the possibility of prolonging a British administrative presence in Hong Kong beyond June 1997. The response was that China intended to recover sovereignty.

The assurances did instil hope in the faint-hearted, who were satisfied that a British official had broached the thorny topic of 1997 and, however vague the Chinese response, had at least not been rebuffed outright. This was sufficient to re-establish confidence, mirrored in rocketing property prices in 1980. Shortly after, Hong Kong Land went ahead with record bids for a piece of reclaimed land in Central on which they were going to erect Exchange Square, their curvaceous, glistening centrepiece of a financial centre. Others were less satisfied with the results of the MacLehose mission and were puzzled by Hong Kong Land's willingness to invest so heavily in an uncertain future. The government had a right to grant leases on Hong Kong Island beyond 1997, as it was held by Britain in perpetuity. But it was very well understood that there would be little point in Britain holding on to this land, once the leased territories had reverted to China. The colony would have lost most of its industrial land and infrastructure. Indeed, it would have lost its very *raison d'être*.

And what of the ingenious plan that MacLehose had responded to so favourably? In 1981 the councillor asked the Governor what progress had been made on his proposals. MacLehose's response was short. Whitehall, he said, had dubbed them unworkable under British law. So ended the chance of a soft diplomatic option.

Politically, all was quiet from the time that MacLehose visited Beijing until 1982. Property prices rose to unheard of levels. Not even the nationality legislation pushed through Parliament in 1981 to, as cynics observed, finally set Hong Kong British nationals on their own feet, seemed to have much effect on the buoyant mood. In January 1982, the first of the diplomatic set pieces took place. A senior delegation travelled to Beijing to initiate new talks on the question of Hong Kong. Again, the British were encouraged to convey to the population of Hong Kong that its fate was secure. Again, however, the issue of 1997 was a sticking point. By this time, both Britain and China recognized that it should be fully explored. Hong Kong markets were buoyed by the favourable news. That summer Sir Murray MacLehose finally left his post, having served a record term in office.

The arrival of the diplomat and sinologist who replaced him, Sir Edward Youde, was upstaged by two other developments that summer. A group of left-wing glitterati who paid homage to Deng in Beijing were told that China would be reclaiming sovereignty, but intended to keep Hong Kong's socio-economic system as it was. In July a prime plot of land in Central was sold to the Bank of China for its new headquarters for much less than the market rate and with a lease running only to 1995. These two events together were sufficient to suggest that all was not well.

In August Britain revealed that Prime Minister Margaret Thatcher would raise the Hong Kong question when she met senior Chinese leaders the following month. Experienced Hong Kong officials winced at the idea of talks being initiated at such a high level. The preferred system for the Chinese, they observed, was to seek out a go-between through whom the general theme could be discussed. The announcement triggered a sharp fall in the value of stocks, property and the Hong Kong dollar. The trial of nerves in Hong Kong had well and truly begun.

Precisely what Mrs Thatcher's role was in the ensuing diplomatic scrap remains an area of contention. The superstitious in Hong Kong flinched as they watched her stumble and fall on the steps of the Great Hall of the People. It was a bad omen. On the eve of crucial discussions the British leader had shown weakness. Her inauspicious entrance, however, presaged a calamitous exit. Following some constructive discussions, resulting in the agreement that talks should be initiated to deal with the Hong Kong question, Mrs Thatcher apparently behaved with extraordinary naivety: during her audience with Deng Xiaoping she referred to the importance of the nineteenth-century treaties governing Hong Kong, treaties which had been weighted heavily in Britain's favour. When her words were translated for Deng his response was said to be so violent and filled with expletives that the interpreter could not translate it for her. As if to make it clear that she meant what she said, Thatcher repeated her statement in Hong Kong a few days later and, for good measure, stressed the moral responsibility that Britain felt for the colony and its people, promising that there would be full consultations on Hong Kong's future. Rather than taking heart from such reiteration of commitment, popular opinion in Hong Kong sent the stock market crashing and the Hong Kong currency sinking to an exchange rate against the American dollar that had not been seen since the 1956 riots.

Some have depicted the 'Iron Lady' as having taken the only course open to the British side. With Beijing adamant about resuming sovereignty over the colony, the only possible stance was to adopt as strong a bargaining position as possible and proceed downward from there. Others have suggested that, fired by the Falklands spirit, Mrs Thatcher disregarded prudent advice from her close advisers and decided to launch a headlong attack on what she saw as China's Argentina-like folly. Others still, who are more suspicious of British motives, conclude that her conduct in Beijing was premeditated. According to their hypothesis, she knew full well that reference to the sanctity of treaties which the Chinese believed had been secured at gunpoint would provoke a furious response and a refusal to entertain any thought of a continued British presence in Hong Kong after 1997. Such an approach, moreover, would have another advantage: by raising the matter of the treaties, Thatcher would initially narrow the focus of the talks from the vague Chinese position of taking Hong Kong 'when the time was ripe' to a specific timetable which would end on 30 June 1997.

Certainly, the Falklands War had a great deal to do with Mrs Thatcher's personal approach to the Hong Kong question. But its effect was not as crude as has frequently been suggested. Mrs Thatcher, despite her flag-waving traits, is a canny politician. A

military solution to the Falklands crisis was both feasible and by
and large had popular backing. Hong Kong, on the other hand, was
neither defensible nor, should it come to it, recoverable through
force of arms. Without a military card in her hand, the game was
automatically limited to diplomatic double bluff. Moreover, in judging the effect of the Falklands crisis it is probably more appropriate
to see the war as a near defeat, rather than a glorious victory. The
Foreign Office had co-opted a number of legal experts and sinolo-
gists to its advisory team in the months preceding Thatcher's trip to
China. This group prepared a long and detailed document on the
approach the Prime Minister should adopt with the Chinese leaders,
who were to be allowed maximum 'face' and dignity. Much to the
frustration of the enlisted specialists, Thatcher was still furious at
the way in which their kind had landed her in the Falklands predicament two years earlier. According to one of the recruited
specialists, instead of allowing herself to be briefed she rushed into
the Foreign Office, blamed them for her embarrassment over the
Falklands and announced that she would tackle the visit to Beijing
in 'her own way'. The rest, the specialist concluded bitterly, was
history.

As it happens, Mrs Thatcher's 'own way' was very much in character. Experts of her own choosing were invited to Downing Street to
provide the necessary briefing and guidance. One in particular, an
experienced China-watcher and former correspondent with a London
newspaper, had been summoned on a number of occasions. This
adviser complained that Mrs Thatcher had done little listening and
most of the talking at their sessions.

Whatever her underlying motives were in raising the question of
the treaties, Mrs Thatcher's approach soon made its mark. Reporting
in *The Guardian*, Robert Whymant noted that during the banquet
on the first day of her visit she referred to the 'happy record of contacts between China and Britain in the nineteenth and early twentieth
centuries'. On a visit to Shanghai, she noted the role of Britain's
empire builders in 'bringing Britain and China closer together' and
paid tribute to the taipans of old (most of whom had built up their
businesses on opium sales). Such public relations exercises alone
were sufficient to ensure that her negotiators should expect little
assistance from their Chinese counterparts in crossing the political
minefield of nineteenth-century treaties and leases.

While they avoid reference to the more blatant of Thatcher's historical, and historic, indiscretions, those charged with completing the difficult task that she set in train do regret her statements in Beijing and Hong Kong. One senior official to whom I spoke during the closing stages of the nightmarish process two years later tactfully referred to her pronouncements as having gone 'farther . . . than her political advisers would have liked her to have gone'. The gaff, he said, was not due to some Falklands-induced bravura. She had intended to say that the treaties were something 'to be taken into consideration'. However, under pressure from headline-hungry journalists after her meetings, she had gone 'a little too far'. Her words had immediately been picked up by the Chinese propaganda machine, who interpreted them as meaning that Britain would negotiate *only* from the treaties. This, he assured me, was not in fact true.

If the population of Hong Kong was shocked at Thatcher's poor grasp of historical realities, it was to be dismayed by the lack of interest and impatience that she was to display during her visits to the colony and in her subsequent dealings with its politicians. During her two visits to the colony – the first by an incumbent Prime Minister – she performed the requisite round of official and social duties: eating spring rolls at receptions and greeting curious youngsters. However, her mood in Hong Kong appeared far more detached and aloof than might have been expected from a Prime Minister who advocates *laissez-faire* economics visiting the most successful exponent of her cherished principles.

The explanation will come as a surprise to people in the colony: according to those close to her, she hates Hong Kong. The hatred stems, it is said, from the contempt she holds for the colony's successful businessmen and financiers, whom she regards as being opportunists unfamiliar with her much-vaunted ethic of hard work. She frequently refers to these individuals as 'second class'; people who have been able to make use of advantages created for them by circumstances and British protection, and who would be unlikely to survive or prosper in the 'real world'. According to the same source, the 'second-class' label is not limited to the private sector alone. In private Mrs Thatcher refers to the colony's administration as 'Hong Kong County Council'.

Having set the tone for the subsequent negotiations, the Prime Minister withdrew from active participation. The controversy she generated, however, refused to die down. China launched a sustained press campaign against the Prime Minister herself and the ideas she had raised, focusing mainly on the treaties and British responsibility for Hong Kong. Both positions, the Chinese press argued, were blatant encroachments on Chinese sovereignty over Hong Kong. As the Chinese line hardened, being expressed in language which was reminiscent of that heard during the Cultural Revolution, so hopes of a compromise on the status quo receded. China announced that the return of the colony had become its main objective, although it aimed to preserve Hong Kong's stability and prosperity. While Britain remained tight-lipped, Hong Kong showed its view of such a proposition in the most effective way it could: the stock market fell to the 1980 level, while the colony's currency slid to its lowest rate ever against the American dollar.

The next nine months, culminating in the reinvigorated talks – the so-called 'second phase' – in July 1983, were marked by a three-way test of nerve. While Britain and China seemed to have reached deadlock in their discussions, they nonetheless tested their views of the situation through the media. China suggested the nebulous concept, attributed to Deng Xiaoping himself, of 'one country, two systems', by which Taiwan, Hong Kong and Macau would all exist as virtually unchanged capitalist enclaves within the broad embrace of the motherland. A high-ranking Chinese official assured the colony that this concept would be accompanied by another: 'Hong Kong people ruling Hong Kong'. Shortly after, Britain was warned that, should it continue to prevaricate, China would be forced to act unilaterally in recovering Hong Kong before 1997. By way of response, the British side floated the long-held 'three-legged stool' notion of the status quo – much as it was outlined by William Rodgers in 1975 (with Britain, China and Hong Kong each representing a leg) – as a possible basis for the discussions. This initiative, however, was interpreted by Chinese officials as a suggestion of power sharing beyond 1997 and was roundly rejected. It was abundantly clear in late December 1983 that any form of official British administrative presence after 1997 was completely unacceptable. Hong Kong's business community reacted to the news in the way they have always done, through the stock and currency markets.

From July 1983 to September 1984 there were twenty-two rounds of bilateral talks, mostly referred to by the catch-all phrase 'useful and constructive'. According to sources close to the negotiating process, the formal sessions held during the day contained very little of substance. Much of the time was taken up by courtesies and formal translations. Broad points and outlines would be exchanged on these occasions, while the main discussion took place during the lengthy dinners afterwards. The results of this 'talking turkey', as a Hong Kong civil servant aptly described it, were then taken up by the negotiating team and relayed to their nerve centre in the Hong Kong Government Offices and to London.

Between August and September 1983, Britain appeared to be shifting very slowly from its original hardline position on sovereignty to advocating a residual official presence after 1997. Rumours about the conflicts of interest, and China's irritation, regularly swept through Hong Kong at this time, often as a result of indiscretions by the Chinese authorities themselves. As they did so, the markets continued their slide. By late September one American dollar was worth nearly ten Hong Kong dollars. The Chinese press accused Britain of using the 'public opinion card' and the 'economic card' to exact concessions from China. What it failed to observe was that the game of show-hand poker (in which most of the players' cards are displayed for all to see) was being played not so much with the British Government as with a semi-orchestrated group of Hong Kong's own politicians and financiers, who were dumping their holdings in Hong Kong dollars and shares in order to force China's hand. Britain was simply marking time. The trick seemed to work to some extent. In October the Chinese Foreign Minister Wu Xueqian announced that China wished to talk to Britain about 'the prosperity and stability of Hongkong up till and after 1997'. Between November and December, the mood in Hong Kong lifted considerably. Talks at the end of the year ended with a joint communiqué that included the word 'progress' among its achievements.

Why Britain took so long to concede on sovereignty remains something of a mystery. The common explanation is that Britain was clutching at any straw in an attempt to perpetuate its institutional links with the colony. And yet there are those who point to signs that this was not so. Before his visit to China as Leader of the Opposition in May 1974, Edward Heath informed two senior members of the Legislative Council that China would definitely take Hong Kong back in 1997. After his trip to see Deng Xiaoping in September 1983, Heath passed through the colony and recommended that the people of Hong Kong should view their future realistically. At a meeting with the Senior Unofficial Members of Legco and the Unofficial Exco Members in London in May 1984, the former Prime Minister amplified these thoughts by confirming that he had known since 1971 that the British Government was ready to cede sovereignty to China in 1997.

One of the two Legco members who had been made privy to Heath's earlier candour saw Britain's actions, after a few years of reflection, as a sell-out. He saw the references to nineteenth-century treaties as a deliberate move to incite China so that Britain could then appear the reasonable party in a dispute of its own making. Any chance of a quiet deal, and continued British presence, had both been eliminated. Moreover, by resisting China in the early fruitless talks, it had become possible to dispense with Hong Kong in an acceptable fashion through a show of defending democracy and moral principles. There was the added bonus that China was pleased with the final 'breakthrough' when it eventually occurred. In the process, Britain had been seen to have absolved itself of the burden of empire with its international image untarnished.

Such an analysis cannot be discounted completely simply because of the degree of subtle control that Britain exerted upon the talks, while simultaneously professing to be in a weak, virtually untenable situation. One of the principal architects of the British side of the 1984 agreement concluded during the closing stages of the talks that it had been an achievement of great significance when viewed in the light of 'the campaign of seduction' waged by the Chinese Government for the hearts of Hong Kong people and its having 'hammer[ed] the shit out of the negotiating group' in the preceding two years. Under these exceedingly difficult conditions, he said, Britain's Foreign Secretary Sir Geoffrey Howe had managed to secure a detailed undertaking from the vague ideas that China had first proposed.

By remaining obstinate in the face of steadily rising Chinese ire, the position of the British team had become stronger. China's frustration had led to a public warning of a unilateral declaration of its plan for Hong Kong. This intention, my informant told me, had been tempered by Britain's own 'card', a threat to reveal information about the nature of draft proposals that had been handed to Britain, most of them 'ludicrous in nature', which would surely result in Hong Kong taking fright at China's world-view. Equally, if China had made a premature declaration of its intentions, the effects would have been very similar. When China added another condition – that the agreement should be completed by the end of September 1984, in time to be ratified by the National People's Congress – the pressure to take British views into account was increased. If Chinese negotiators proved too difficult, China would have faced a twin disaster: revelation and non-completion.

During the closing stages of the talks, in August 1984, I spoke to an Unofficial Member of the Executive and Legislative Councils. He expressed his frustration at the 'short lead' that council members found themselves on in the course of the negotiations. The collapse of the Hong Kong dollar in late 1983, he said, had been fuelled by an influential group of Unofficials. The intention had been to use it as a bargaining weapon against China but the Bank of England had intervened to prevent the situation from becoming a full-blown crisis. In early 1984, while a group of Unofficials were in London making their views known to the government, a hint was made that the same tactic might be used again to force China into a more sympathetic position. On the way home, the Unofficials found that they were sharing a flight with a representative from the Bank of England: '(At that moment) we knew the game was lost', the Unofficial concluded.

But if Britain's intention had, from the start, been to ensure that it had no residual role in the colony after 1997, what was its true goal in the talks? The agreement aimed for was to ensure that the formula governing Hong Kong's existence until then should continue: that China would always have the ability to take Hong Kong, but would refrain from doing so. This, an official involved in the negotiations pointed out, was the underlying premise during the 1967 disturbances, and should continue to be so. The terms of the agreement would fulfil the function of preserving this mood of 'certain uncertainty'. Beyond that, Howe and his group of negotiators would not go.

The path to an acceptable document was strewn with obstacles. Some concerned Britain directly, such as the question of how existing leases were to run beyond Britain's tenure in Hong Kong. The issue of air rights was equally complicated. Over the years, Britain had been using the lucrative Hong Kong air routes as a bargaining counter for its own purposes and the problem of whether third-party rights would be accepted by China remained unresolved to the eleventh hour. Thorniest of all was the nationality issue. Britain had been steadily devaluing the Hong Kong British passport. This in itself was not a great problem, as China seemed relatively happy to allow ethnic Chinese who held foreign passports to reside in Hong Kong, and was willing to write a detailed guarantee of their right to leave into the agreement. The quandary was largely a British one: once 1997 arrived, the value of these British passports would be uncertain in the eyes of foreign immigration authorities as the nationality (British) would be unrelated to the normal place of abode (Hong Kong). If these passports were not sufficiently well-backed, there would be a strong chance that those who held them would be turned away by immigration officials abroad. Britain had therefore to decide what sort of declaration was to be formulated to ensure that the passport remained useful. China, in turn, would be wary of granting holders full right of abode in Hong Kong unless Britain would adequately back its own passport. These hurdles were to remain even after the Sino-British Joint Declaration was signed.

On two occasions, Sir Geoffrey Howe made the trip to Beijing to sort out obstacles that threatened to prolong the stalemate. His second visit, on the eve of the twentieth round of talks, was a masterstroke. Since the impasse over sovereignty, China had been calling for the creation of a Joint Liaison Group, which would oversee the transition of the colony to Chinese rule, have wide-reaching powers and be based in Hong Kong. The British side held out against this proposal, fearing, quite rightly, that such a body might be regarded by the population as a quasi-government. During his July visit Howe finally agreed to a watered-down form of the group, which would commute between Beijing and London, and then be established in a permanent office in Hong Kong for the final decade. Restrictions on the group's powers were to be written into the final agreement. In return for this concession, Howe demanded a detailed, unambiguous twelve-point statement that he might deliver to Hong Kong en route to London. He got a ten-point statement, which was to become the basis for the Sino-British agreement.

With the exception of the complicated questions of land leases, civil aviation and nationality, the remaining contentious issues were resolved in a novel way. Howe sat in a room adjoining that where the negotiations were held. While the negotiators argued out the remaining points, fresh compromises reached at these unusually busy sessions were taken to him directly for instant approval. At the end of his stay Howe saw Deng Xiaoping, who concluded that their meeting, and by implication the talks themselves, had been 'conducted in a spirit of mutual understanding and accommodation'. The end was in sight.

However clever the negotiators, or sincere their intentions, the nature of the talks was pernicious in the extreme as far as the people of Hong Kong were concerned, for they had been left to guess at what lay behind each hiccup, each controversy and each compromise that arose in the two turbulent years. Those who in 1982 had looked forward to a resolution of the 1997 problem were, by September 1984, left wondering what the motives of the British and Chinese really were. The superhuman work of the colony's Governor Sir Edward Youde, who combined the shuttle diplomacy necessary to graft Hong Kong opinion on the negotiations with frequent briefings to Whitehall and Mrs Thatcher without neglecting his full Governor's portfolio, went some way to reassure nervous Hong Kong citizens that their interests were, somehow, being represented. During the fraught days of the Sino-British impasse at the talks, it was Youde who had to confront the press corps ravenous for news and report that the session had been 'useful and constructive' while British and Chinese delegates marked time inside, doing nothing more than drinking cups of tea.

Youde, as leader of the 'Hong Kong County Council', had succeeded in gaining the admiration and confidence of the Prime Minister through his unerring judgement and advice. But that in itself was not enough. True to form, the Prime Minister had not changed her attitude to either business people or politicians in the colony. Often, the individuals themselves were at fault here. A Conservative MP long familiar with Hong Kong commented ruefully how ineffectually most of the visiting Legco members conducted themselves in dealings with the MPs they came to lobby. Most of them had, he said, simply 'whinged and whined'. During one visit, a senior Legco member had caught the attention of the Prime Minister. Taking advantage of the opportunity, he pursued the matter of the minority nationalities in Hong Kong and their hopes of being treated as a special case under the nationality legislation. He caught her ear three times during the audience. At first, the Prime Minister assured him that up to 50,000 people would be given special rights. He persisted. On the last occasion she chewed his head off, angrily telling him to stop harping on the same theme.

For the most part, Hong Kong's legislators were content with conducting skirmishes against what they regarded, in many cases quite rightly, as the overbearing and patronizing attitudes of British politicians. Edward Heath was the target of such an attack when he passed through Hong Kong after a felicitous audience with Deng Xiaoping in 1984. Heath, who was staying at Government House, was invited to a dinner hosted by the members of Umelco (the joint Legislative and Executive Council body). The former Prime Minister, it is reported, was full of optimism about Hong Kong's future as he sat down to dinner. Two of the senior councillors launched into him, expressing their scepticism and insisting that the Hong Kong legislative chambers should be allowed to check the agreement that he seemed so happy with. Heath flew into a temper and went off, according to one of the two sceptics, 'to join the boys from Oxford and Cambridge at the bar'.

The same councillor recounted his first visit to Whitehall to see the 'FO clique', a term he applied to the Foreign Office's Hong Kong team. He described their tiny office where 'a secretary was working frantically . . . and others not so frantically'. A calendar from 1968 was hanging on the wall. Beyond the office portals, he observed, were long corridors, decorated with 'paintings of viceroys, but with floors dirty and walls cracking'. He relished every minute observation he had made of the flawed surroundings.

By far the most ingenious dig at the British Government was perpetrated by a Legislative and Executive Councillor who, angered by the seeming indifference of the British Government towards over three million of its charges, was instrumental in forming the Hong Kong Citizens Society in May 1984. The principal object of the society was, according to its constitution:

To protect the interests and promote the status and welfare of Hongkong British Nationals . . . and their families . . . as a body of persons both while Hongkong remains under British administration and thereafter.

A well-known British advertising company, with strong connections with the Conservative government, was then approached to investigate the possibility of its handling the presentation of the association's case in Britain. A guarded reply was received, but was soon followed by another letter in which one of the company's directors concluded that he was still undecided, although in favour in principle. The councillor then wrote a 'by way of information' letter to Sir Geoffrey Howe, explaining that he was in the process of hiring the advertising company to represent his association. Soon after, a telegram was received from the advertising company, informing the councillor that it was inappropriate for it, at that time (being only a few months before the signing of the Sino-British agreement), to accept the brief. The councillor confided that he had had no intention of spending a vast amount of money on such a campaign; he simply wanted to use it as a barb against the Thatcher government.

Such was the relationship between what were, at least on paper, partners with common aims and shared principles. Hong Kong politicians looked for holes in the hall carpet at Whitehall, while their British counterparts observed the antics of the colonials with irritation. Impressions of the Hong Kong leaders were not improved by the style in which they conducted official visits to Britain. A Hong Kong journalist friend described how in 1984 he had waited outside a reception that was to be attended by a group of councillors and a selection of British dignitaries. As he stood there, he observed ministers of state arriving in minis, some of the guests even on bicycles. By contrast, every member of the Hong Kong party had made the short trip from their five-star hotels in sleek, chauffeur-driven limousines.

The differences and antagonism between rulers and ruled have subsequently been papered over, but are still there. Relations between China and Britain, however, achieved new heights as a result of the agreement. The fiery recriminations and icy anger that characterized relations only a few months before were forgotten as the two sides stood in harmony, on 26 September 1984, watching the chief negotiators initialling the Joint Declaration. So warm was the mood that, as the chief negotiators Zhou Nan and Sir Richard Evans exchanged copies and shook hands, the Chinese representative moved to give his counterpart a comradely hug. Sir Richard saw this as a sign that they were to exchange kisses too, and duly pursed his lips. Zhou hurriedly withdrew.

The document contained few surprises, being largely a more detailed rendition of the ten-point charter that Sir Geoffrey Howe had presented some months before. As those who had worked on it had intended, it reflected the Hong Kong of 1984, assuring its citizens of the rights and freedoms they enjoyed at that time and projecting these to a promised fifty years beyond 1997. It was all manner of assurance to all manner of people, mixing generalities that were likely to stand the test of time with copious detailed assurances that were not. This in itself was the result of the interests of the three parties involved. Hong Kong leaders had, almost from the start, pressed for detailed, wide-ranging talks, culminating ideally in a fully resolved blueprint for Hong Kong's future. Britain, on the other hand, was more interested in producing a document containing the broad strokes of general principles. China was in favour of drawing up the vaguest agreement possible.

Frantic crowds of residents who were both anxious and curious to see the document converged on distribution points to collect their own copies. The attendance at a race meeting that evening slumped by an unprecedented 8000. Solemn full-page notices were placed in the press on the following morning drawing public attention to the British promise that the people of Hong Kong would have a say in their own future. Interested parties were invited to send written comments on the agreement. But before they put pen to paper, they were to know that there could be no detailed change to the document. To ensure fair play, an Assessment Office had been set up to mull over the opinions expressed and to present a report on the people's final verdict. Inexplicably, the Assessment Office announced that only signed submissions would be taken seriously. And, as if to give the whole exercise the kiss of death, it was initially stated that these signed submissions would not be destroyed after the assessment was completed.

A fairer, more realistic device to gauge the attitude of the population of Hong Kong to the agreement would have been a referendum. Why was one not conducted? The accepted wisdom, as with most difficult decisions such as this, was to say that 'China would not agree to one'. In fact, one of the senior Hong Kong officials that I spoke to at the time confirmed that China had vetoed the idea of a referendum. But, he added, even if there had been agreement, electoral rolls were only just being drawn up at that time. If a referendum were thought necessary, the government would have needed at least six months of preparation for such an exercise. 'Even then,' he concluded dryly, 'depending on the response, the results would be open to question and interpretation.'

Three months after the agreement was initialled, Margaret Thatcher returned to China for the first time since her disastrous performance in 1982. On this occasion, however, there were no appreciable gaffs, nor any Chinese vitriol. She was greeted as a worthy statesman and a friend. Hong Kong watched as the Prime Minister and the Chinese Premier Zhao Ziyang exchanged signed copies of the agreement. In the midst of the backcloth of officials stood the diminutive shape of a glowing Deng Xiaoping, whose ambition, it turned out, had long been to see the return of Hong Kong to China's bosom.

Mrs Thatcher's personal farewell to Hong Kong was as hardened and detached a spectacle as might have been expected, given her sentiments for the colony. Beijing and the signing of the agreement had been ring two of a three-ring foreign affairs circus. The week before, Mrs Thatcher had entertained Moscow's rising star, Mikhail Gorbachev, in London. After Beijing, she intended to fly on to America for talks with President Reagan before returning home for Christmas. In this grand scheme of things, a short overnight stay in Hong Kong was nothing but a stopover with barely enough time allowed for a press conference. There was to be no general address to the people of Hong Kong, and no direct account of the transition.

On the morning of 21 December I queued outside the old Legislative Council Chambers, where her meeting with the press was to take place. Around me was an overseas journalists' road show, garb frayed through the rough-and-tumble of postings in the inner reaches of Asia. Conversations were predictably far removed from Hong Kong's preoccupations: expense accounts, hotel prices, the odd bit of gossip about mutual acquaintances – indeed, anything but the fate of those around them. In her preamble Mrs Thatcher assured the audience of the value of the agreement in perpetuating Hong Kong's free-wheeling lifestyle. She assured the people of Hong Kong that 'Britain will administer Hongkong wisely and well between now and 1997'. Somewhere near me came a mutter: 'that will make a change!' She then went on to assure the colony of Britain's intention to ensure 'the widest possible acceptance of the agreement in the rest of the world'. Another tiny, irreverent voice advised that the process might best start in Hong Kong itself.

Answers to possible questions had not been very well rehearsed. One of the questioners wanted to know who would be involved in the proposed Joint Liaison Group. Mrs Thatcher responded evasively but pronounced one certainty: the Governor would definitely be a British representative. The Governor, sitting a few feet away from her, looked surprised at this sudden co-option:

'That hasn't been decided yet', he pointed out to her.

'We haven't decided. . . I see. I should be absolutely astonished if the Governor is not on it.' She fudged and bullied on.

The cost of this poor preparation was made clear time and time again as enthusiastic, earnest local journalists asked one awkward question after another. She was asked about MacLehose's mission to Beijing in 1979. Why were the people not told, the questioner asked, that China intended to regain sovereignty in 1997 and had the silence anything to do with the formulation of the Nationality Act that had been introduced soon after? The Prime Minister's response was remarkable. She did not know 'the content of any talks which Lord MacLehose may have had'. This suggested that MacLehose had failed to write up his talks with the Chinese leaders, or failed to pass on his thoughts to Whitehall, or omitted certain points (as he had done in his public statements in Hong Kong), or Mrs Thatcher had simply failed to notice the existence and implications of his report when she was preparing for her trip to Beijing three years later. Not wishing to go into such nuances, she proceeded at a tangent: 'We must now turn our eyes to this agreement. Our task is to implement this agreement which has been overwhelmingly accepted by Hongkong as a whole.'

At least one line had been well rehearsed. She then returned to the question of the Nationality Act which, she concluded, 'was passed by the British parliament in the light of circumstances at the time'. The astute did not fail to notice that this answer did not exclude Hong Kong as a major factor in the drafting of the legislation.

A few questions later, a journalist from a highly reputable Asian weekly, whose family had escaped from China after the takeover and had suffered from Chinese persecution, asked Mrs Thatcher whether it was morally defensible to deliver over five million people into the hands of a Communist dictatorship. The Prime Minister, whose own views of Communism's ability to change its spots are well known, chose to respond in bluster: 'Can I say this to you? What do you think would have happened if we had not attempted to get an agreement? 1997 – 92 per cent of the territory would automatically have returned to China without reassurances. . . . I think you would have had great cause to complain had the Government of Great Britain done nothing until 1997 and I believe that most of the people, indeed, the overwhelming number of people in Hongkong think the same. You may be a solitary exception.'

At the end of the session I slowly made my way from the chamber. While the reporters rushed off to file their stories, I stood not far away from the front entrance of the Legco building, waiting for the

Prime Minister to emerge. There, in front of the concrete canopy where the official car would collect the Prime Minister's party, I had earlier noticed the signs of a protest building up. A small group of simply dressed people and some children were preparing banners and conducting agitated conversations under the watchful gaze of the many blue-uniformed police officers that peppered the area. They needed to do little else, as the party exhibited no aggression, only helplessness. By the time I had returned to the scene, the group had grown slightly and had already begun to chant. The sound was mesmeric. The group were led by a man with a thin, brittle voice, declaiming betrayal, loss, abandonment. His cry was so anguished, so funereal that, even if she could not understand what was being said, surely Mrs Thatcher would gather what it was all about: this tiny cluster of people had come to mourn the passing of Hong Kong. The Prime Minister's manner betrayed nothing as she moved swiftly to her car. The words she had uttered in the chamber only minutes ago to the slighted journalist echoed about the tree-lined concourse: you may be a solitary exception. . . .

CHAPTER EIGHT

End of a Charmed Existence

A few weeks after Mrs Thatcher had announced to Hong Kong and the world that the Sino-British Joint Declaration meant stability and prosperity, I stood outside a Hong Kong hotel preparing to board a taxi for the airport. At the head of the rank was a typical Hong Kong cab, held together by putty, electrical cable and a prayer. The hotel doorman asked where I was going and leaned through the passenger window to tell the driver. As I was settling into my seat I caught the Cantonese for 'keep' or 'hold'. I guessed that, thinking I was a tourist, the doorman might have signalled to the driver that he should inflate the fare and that they would share the spoils later. As we set off, the driver asked if I was leaving and how long I had been in Hong Kong. I replied in Cantonese that I had lived in Hong Kong for many years and had, in that time, learned the language. His reply, in English, was curious: 'It's good to be able to speak. . . . It's convenient.'

I replied that it was not so much convenient as important, but my response seemed to make little impact. He asked where I lived now. I said England and, for good measure, added that I taught at a university.

'What subject?'

'Politics.'

This interested him. Perhaps I could give him my views on the future of Hong Kong. I told him that I thought that the talks and the agreement might have gone in a different direction, leaving Hong Kong under notional British rule beyond 1997, which would have made many people in the colony much happier. This provoked a furious reply. The British, he said, were 'fucking bastards' and did not deserve to be in Hong Kong any longer. Although I had detected a deep-seated loathing of the British in conversations with Hong Kong Chinese before, I had never heard such a plain statement of anti-British sentiments. The taxi-driver went on to explain that the British had done little for the Chinese in Hong Kong and, in return, had gained much from the colony. By way of example, he spoke of the billions of dollars that Britain earned stationing its garrison in Hong Kong.* At least when the Chinese took over this burden would be removed and the money might be put to better use. As an afterthought, he said that the Hong Kong situation would not stretch to 1997, but would be resolved well before then. I asked him if he would prefer control of the colony to be in the hands of the colony's legislators, the members of Legco and Exco, who had been so heavily criticized by the British. No, he replied, he did not trust them. I wondered if he had been born in Hong Kong (thinking that, if he had, there might be some naivety in his views of Chinese rule). No, he was born in Guangdong and had slipped into Hong Kong as a teenager. Our trip to the airport turned out to be too short. On board the plane, with some time to sit back and reflect, I thought about this chance encounter, wondering if I had just met an example of the new post-colonial Hong Kong Man; a bitter realist with no illusions about the future and only a little hope that somehow he might be able to preserve his hardly-won identity.

I thought of another such chance meeting in 1982, in the depths of the expatriate thieves' bazaar known as Stanley Market: rows of concrete-shelled shops snaking around narrow cement paths, their designer-labelled wares clamouring for the attention of the passer-by. Mrs Thatcher had only recently set the tone of the Sino-British talks and I was interested to see what response there might be on the streets. In one of the emptier, more secluded stalls I struck up a conversation with a shop owner. He was in his late twenties and, from what he said, had spent most of his life in Hong Kong. He had built up his trade from virtually nothing to this light, airy shop with rows of clothes on hangers and purpose-built changing rooms in the back. Progress, he said, had not been easy. He and his partner did not own

---

* At the time, Hong Kong shouldered 75 per cent (or HK$1.7 billion per annum) of the cost of maintaining a British garrison of 9000 men, most of them Gurkhas, in the colony. This division of costs has long been deeply resented, many being convinced that Britain profited from this arrangement.

the property and the rent was high. His ambitions were modest. He planned to build up some capital and go it alone in a few years time. What, I asked him, were his thoughts about 1997 and his own future. Was he not worried about the possible return of the colony to China? No, he replied, the prospect of such a development did not worry him at all. In fact he was looking forward to it. That would at least give him an opportunity to move freely around his own country, and perhaps even set up a little business there.

In case I had not guessed it already, he added that he held a CI.* He had no need to elaborate: travel abroad was possible, but it was not as simple as buying a ticket and going through the formality of getting a tourist visa. A CI was no guarantee of receiving a visa, or of trouble-free entry to the country concerned once it had been granted. His freedom, he suggested, was not altogether boundless.

Nor did he seem to be worried that it was likely Hong Kong would become part of a communist political system. His answer to my question was both considered and disarming: 'I am a small man. I have no strong political beliefs. Why should I worry about such things?' I tried to find him again two or three years later, but without success. Perhaps he had made his fortune sooner than he had thought possible and moved on. Perhaps he had reassessed his views of the political situation and had taken advantage of a cousin living in Canada or America. After my encounter with the taxi-driver, I wondered if the shopkeeper had become a shade more cynical with the passing of time.

It is not only people that move on in Hong Kong. The city itself changes very rapidly, favourite corners disappearing between one visit and the next. I remember a noodle shop on Cameron Road, in the tourist district of Kowloon, that I had walked past thousands of times in my youth, often pausing to use the public telephone that sat conveniently half in and half out of its premises. The eating area was tiny, with space for no more than four or five small tables. A chef stood in his cubbyhole of a kitchen, tossing noodles from a steaming vat and leaving the shop's larger window permanently dripping with condensation. On the other side of the narrow entrance was an even smaller cubbyhole occupied by the ubiquitous cashier. This humble establishment was a constant reminder of a

---

* Certificate of Identity: a travel document issued to those in Hong Kong who wish to travel but are not eligible for a British passport. In effect, these people were second-class citizens who have now, with the most recent amendment to Hong Kong-British citizenship, become a third-class category.

street that had long since disappeared, the ghosts of the demolished buildings all crammed into this timeless noodle shop. I discovered I was not alone in my affection for it: many other soup noodle gourmets had singled it out as the spot for a quick and appetizing snack. For some reason, I felt sure it would always be there, but only a few days after I had taken my last meal there it had gone, its shell taken over by a factory outlet, one of a dozen or so selling garment seconds in the area.

Only the expatriate clubs and bars show a bizarre sense of continuity. People can return to their old haunts after an absence of years and be greeted as if they were only there a week or two ago. For a large proportion of the colonial section of society events in Beijing had little meaning. While Hong Kong buzzed with controversies over 1997, the hub of colonial life continued very much in the way it always had: self-contained and self-obsessed. Predictably, this group showed the most agitation over the security of their pensions.

This is not to say that the events of 1982–4 did not take their toll on the colonials too. They have always liked to be regarded as the salt of Hong Kong's earth, the local European colour. But the years of uncertainty destroyed their aura, showing them to be an anachronism. There could be no clearer indication of this than the fissures that became particularly evident in 1984 between the British expatriates and those who aspired to be British. The latter – who might be Chinese, Indian, Pakistani, Singhalese, Portuguese or Eurasians – have played a vital role in cocooning and nurturing the expatriates in an otherwise alien environment, oiling the channels of communication between the foreign 'masters' and the local populace, introducing the new expatriate to the social round and providing the essential requirements of life in the colony. In return, the members of this sub-class have sought to emulate the expatriates and seek acceptance from them.

The relationship is normally a smooth one, ruffled only by the occasional inadvertent slip of the tongue, a racial slur or an unkind dig. When the slips occur they are quickly glossed over as being the result of drink or poorly chosen words. The remarks are neither forgiven nor forgotten, simply set aside. The injured parties could look to their British education, their mastery of a provincial British *bonhomie* and, most importantly, their British nationality for reassurance of their equality. Between 1982–4, such reassurances were dealt a great and probably permanent blow.

Reactions varied. Genteel Chinese, who had paid small fortunes to join the Royal Hong Kong Golf Club, could not believe that Britain would ever abandon them or their home. In speaking to a number of these individuals before, and in some cases soon after, the Thatcher visit to Beijing, I was assured that Britain would do a quiet deal under the table with China to perpetuate its links with Hong Kong. Subsequent events showed this point of view to be less and less realistic until, finally, I saw resignation and sadness in their eyes and changes in their lifestyle. No longer were things British to be proudly paraded. Conversations turned to China and its intentions for Hong Kong.

The nationality issue was even more upsetting. Time and time again I sensed that people felt it was explicable and perhaps even excusable to sell out the colony itself, but they could not come to terms with the fact that they had been sold out together with the land. How often have I heard 'where is the justice?' I have yet to find a satisfactory reply. What can be said to a Chinese man in his late sixties who produces a wallet full of photographs of his school and university days in London and of his late Londoner wife, and then runs through a list of his children and grandchildren, some of whom hold full United Kingdom passports and others who will forever be aliens?

The full consequences of Britain's actions were brought home to me at a Christmas party in 1984. Two friends, an ethnic Singhalese who worked for a small import/export firm and a Eurasian who was a senior executive with a hong, told me of their deep dissatisfaction with political developments. Both spoke of the Sino-British agreement as a sell-out. One, indeed, considered Britain could have used the importance of Hong Kong as a source of foreign currency earnings to drive a harder bargain with China. He told me that he had written a letter to the Prime Minister in 1982, putting forward this point of view and urging her government to press hard for a renewal of British administrative rights. His efforts were rewarded with a polite, but negatively worded, answer from what he described as a 'Foreign Office type'.

Both friends were deeply hurt by the nationality legislation. The Singhalese, who had been born in Hong Kong, had acquired British nationality and, in doing so, had sworn allegiance to the Queen. He spoke of his long service with the Hong Kong Volunteer Corps and the free time he had devoted to what must, finally, be seen as a patriotic activity. In telling me his story he frequently stressed that he had acted in good faith, but had received nothing in return. He now referred to the British as 'Brits', the intonation hardly disguising his innermost feelings. His final conclusion was that the lack of interest in, or concern for, his welfare was due to the colour of his skin. And despite the fact that he had married a full United Kingdom citizen well before the 1980s legislation, which entitled him to live in Britain, he felt that permission to reside there should be based on a recognition of his long-standing contribution to Hong Kong and Britain, and on his impeccable loyalty.

The Eurasian was also married to an English woman but had a full British passport in his own right, through what he described as an 'old fluke'. He had converted his Hong Kong passport in London long ago and made a point of renewing it in Britain on every occasion. Others who might have used this loophole had often been dissuaded by senior officials in Hong Kong, who would assure the holders that a British passport issued in Hong Kong was 'just as good . . . why bother going to England?' It was only when these individuals tried to establish residence for themselves or their children that they discovered this was not the case. My friend was bitter that he had achieved his 'superior' status only by chance and that many of his relations were not so lucky. Most of them, including his English grandfathers, were born in India and China, and so the links that might have given his living relatives the status of full British subjects were exceedingly hard to trace.

There are many other such cases. Numerically, of course, they represent a tiny fraction of the entire population of Hong Kong, but their contribution to such a diverse and intricate society is out of all proportion to their numbers. Their situation has been made no easier since 1984 and many are now contemplating moving to other countries. In the meantime, anger and frustration burrows ever deeper into their hearts and shapes their attitude to what they regarded as a distant home. In the process the remarkable glue that has held the colony's society together hardens and fractures.

The unveiling of the Sino-British agreement combined with Britain's attitude to nationality initially provoked panic among the minority groups. The Indian, Pakistani, Singhalese and Portuguese communities and the Eurasians all tried to impress upon the British authorities how few of them there were, what contributions they had made to Hong Kong and why they deserved to be treated as a special case. In doing so, each minority made the grave error of pre-

senting itself as a group of willing residents of Hong Kong, ready to
entertain the thought of sharing in the experiment of 'one country,
two systems' (so long as there was the safety net of asylum in Britain
should things go wrong), but unwilling to be classed together with
Hong Kong's Chinese British nationals. These minorities held the
same devalued British passport that just over three million Chinese
were entitled to, but they felt they should be treated differently; an
attitude that was not lost on the Chinese.

The campaigns run by the individual groups varied, ranging from
the quiet 'word in the ear' approach employed by the Portuguese to
the Indians' more formal assault on the Foreign and Commonwealth Office, a strategy which involved lengthy correspondence,
extensive lobbying and media coverage. With the exception of a few
general assurances and, in deference to the Indians' sustained campaign, a concession making nationality transmittable to children,
little was achieved. British Nationals (Overseas) would be afforded
consular protection overseas and would be able to travel on a British
passport, but their domicile could not be the United Kingdom. As
one Indian pointed out to me, the new nationality was supposed to be
a major concession, but it failed to provide a guarantee of residence
anywhere in the world, even Hong Kong.

Mistrust and recriminations were common, not only *between* the
minority groups, but within them. The Portuguese, who had made
their quiet approaches to the British Government long ago and,
they say, received equally quiet assurances that they would be
looked after, looked on in dismay at what they regarded as the
Indians' wrecking tactics. A leading member of the Portuguese community told me that the Indians had threatened to leave the colony
en masse if they did not receive some sort of assurance, taking their
sizeable share of the economy with them (the Indian community not
only controls about 12 per cent of the economy, but also manages
many of the trading links with Africa). The Portuguese thought this
was a particularly crass ultimatum. He imagined the Foreign Office's
response: 'Well then, there's no problem. Why don't they leave?'

Within the Indian community itself, there was little love lost
between Indian and fellow Indian. I listened to Hari Harilela, the
President of the Council of Hong Kong Indian Associations, present
a neat formula for deciding which members of his community
deserved a superior British passport, and which did not. Out of the
14,000 Hong Kong residents from the Indian sub-continent, 8000

still held Indian passports. They, it seemed, could be discounted automatically because they were 'covered'. Of the remainder, who held British passports, Harilela suggested that the British Government should judge each case on its merits. If someone had had a British passport since before World War II, they should be 'seriously considered'. People's backgrounds should also be investigated. If a man held a British passport but his wife retained an Indian travel document they should be denied superior status.

Similarly, if someone had renounced Indian nationality (India does not recognize dual nationality) after 1975, he or she should be asked why. If the grounds were not good enough, they should be refused. By adopting this approach, Harilela concluded, there would have been no need to group 4500 people so unfairly together (I assume that this figure referred to those who met his minimum criteria).

Harilela is a Sindhi, a member of the Indian caste of shopkeepers and merchants. The majority of Indians in Hong Kong are also Sindhis. This group has come to be associated with a particularly thrusting style of selling that often has shopkeepers darting out of their glistening, incense-doused shops to encourage and pursue potential customers. When recriminations began to fly thick and fast, the Sindhis' reputation was used against them. A friend who was a Parsee – an Indian group traditionally associated with commerce and clerical activity – pulled me aside and earnestly explained how the bad image of 'these Sindhis' had ruined the chances of his own, morally irreproachable caste. Had it not been for the Sindhis, I was told, the Parsees would undoubtedly have been granted preferential status.

The truth is that all these groups have contributed much to Hong Kong. Indian soldiers and a small group of Indian merchants were present at the raising of the Union Jack when Hong Kong Island became the settlement of Victoria. Sikh policemen were a mainstay of the local constabulary for many years and have subsequently become involved in all manner of public activity and commerce. Pakistanis, many of whom fled the disruption of partition, have made their mark on business and security services with an easygoing charm. The Parsees have had a long association with the British and Hong Kong, as the title 'Shroff'* often seen over a till is a con-

---

* Shroff is a well-known Parsee name as well as a synonym for cashier in the former British East.

stant reminder. Among the entrances to the foreign cemeteries across the road from the Happy Valley racecourse is an archway reserved for the Parsees. It was opened in 1852.

The Portuguese too have provided much valuable service to the colony. Macanese families established residence in the new colony at the outset – many of their number having been invited by the British authorities to help form a civil service – and were to account for many a distinguished career in public affairs. Portuguese volunteers fought loyally in World War II alongside British, Indian, Canadian and Eurasian soldiers. Moreover, when British businessmen were interned by the Japanese, their work was taken over by their Portuguese clerks who kept the British hongs and banks ticking over for the duration of the Japanese occupation. The personal cost involved was often very high. During the war the Portuguese were in limbo. They were not European; nor, however, were they Chinese. The Japanese occupying forces treated them appallingly because of this, and because of their allegiance to Britain. Some, in fact, were hacked to pieces for their loyalty. On their return, however, the British authorities suspected the Portuguese of being collaborators, simply because they had not been interned in POW camps.

The sadness that tinges the nationality issue is due not so much to the deep divisions, antipathy and pettiness that it has aroused as to the fact that it arose at all. Members of minorities, like the millions of bona fide Chinese holders of British passports, should not have been forced to squabble and agonize over the use of a key to a firmly shut door; a key that was theirs in the first place.

Fears about the breakdown of racial harmony in Hong Kong were greatly increased by the Braemar Hill murders and their aftermath. Two sixth-formers, Kenneth McBride and Nicola Myers, made their way up a steep, scrub-covered hillside near the young man's home one Saturday in late April 1985. Their bodies were found a few yards apart on a deserted slope the following day. The young woman's body was naked, showing over five hundred wounds. The post-mortem showed that she had been raped and had died as a result of her wounds, brain haemorrhage and cerebral contusions. The young man had suffered over a hundred wounds, but had died of strangulation.

The tragic events and their unravelling shook the community to the core. After an extensive manhunt and much publicized trial, three young Chinese men were convicted of the murders and condemned to death.* With the exception of the bomb disposal expert who had died defusing a bomb during the 1967 disturbances, these were the first known murders of Europeans by Chinese this century.

The gap between Chinese and Western thinking on the murders was readily apparent in the days after the verdict was reached. Westerners displayed a mixture of fear, anger and confusion and at times a dim understanding of the society they lived in. On the morning of the verdict, I listened to *Open Line*, a popular early-morning radio phone-in. One of the earliest calls was from a woman who, in a fruity colonial drawl, at first complained about the long queues in the immigration halls at the Macau ferry pier. Once she had vented her frustration over this perennial topic, she turned her attention to the Braemar Hill verdict. She noted that the three had been sentenced to death, but that the death penalty would be commuted. In principle, she said, she was against the death penalty and thought that most murderers could be rehabilitated. But in this case she would invoke it: 'If someone did it across the border, they would get very short justice . . . they would be summarily executed.'

Another caller said she was confused by the issue. Her immediate reaction had been, she continued: 'How dare these people cross the line and kill *gwailo*† kids?' Although she realized this response was inappropriate she was still in favour of executing the murderers. She would, she added, feel the same if 'local' teenagers had been involved.

'I have always said that Hong Kong was one of the safest places in the world . . . unlike London or Manchester,' she announced, '(but I'm) afraid that it (the murders) will be a turning point unless the death penalty is brought in.' Her train of thought continued along even more pessimistic lines. She said she had always thought that 'Hong Kong people' were not interested in *gwailos*, but that this was no longer the case. She no longer felt it was safe to let her nine-year-old child out on the streets.

The phone-in host seemed to be walking on egg shells as he conducted a disjointed discussion with subsequent callers. Then came a

---

* Hong Kong did not follow Britain's lead in abolishing the death penalty, but by custom it allows all such sentences to be commuted.

† *Gwailo*, often loosely translated as 'foreign devil', is a term which is employed by a remarkably broad spectrum of Hong Kong Chinese when referring to Caucasians and is used quite happily by the foreigners themselves for purposes of identification.

call from a Westerner who thought it significant that there had been equally grisly killings of Chinese which had not had similar coverage. The phone-in host rattled off a series of qualifications which marked out the Braemar Hill murders as being particularly horrifying, more it seemed from nervousness than as an argument against the point being made: 'the sheer brutality, wantonness of the killing . . . 500 blows . . . I can't think of another case in my stay here.'

The caller cut in: 'What about the "Body in the Box"?' He had picked one of the more gruesome murders involving Chinese victims. He could have selected many more, including the case of a murderer who had killed women and then kept their heads in clear glass jars.

'Yes, but this has been very horrific.'

'I would have to go away and read the relevant reports again.'

By this time the caller's point was nearly lost. He then asked what difference there had been between the Chinese and English media's coverage. The host had contacted the station's equivalent Chinese-language programme *On Air*, which had already been transmitting for some time. There had not been one call about the Braemar Hill murders. '(But that) doesn't mean that there won't be tomorrow,' the host added. Locals, he said, liked to go away to think about an issue, sometimes overnight, before making a comment.

Attitudes were hardening in other respects, too. An important underlying consideration in formulating the Joint Declaration was how to convince the growing and independently-minded middle class to stay. Much emphasis was placed by the Chinese, British and Hong Kong Governments on the singular importance of maintaining 'stability and prosperity': so long as the goose continued to lay golden eggs and did so quietly, all would be well. The young professional classes, as was particularly obvious after a decade of prodigious economic growth, were to be regarded as neither complacent nor gullible.

As unsettling as the Sino-British talks were some of MacLehose's proposals for changing the political face of Hong Kong. These came to a head shortly before the initialling of the agreement with the publication of a Green Paper proposing radical changes, including the broadening of the franchise and the introduction of direct elections to the legislature. With the publication of further Green and White Papers in 1987 and 1988 respectively, the issue of direct elections was to become more divisive than the Sino-British talks themselves. A body of opinion felt that the proposed legislation threatened the preservation of the status quo by giving Hong Kong Chinese, and especially the young educated professionals, the chance to 'discover' politics.

In the early months of 1985 young intellectuals, members of pressure groups and politicians showed that battle lines were being drawn up and changes were on the way. Surprisingly, the Joint Declaration held very little interest for those who were looking to a post–1997 world. The attitude of most young professionals was one of brave defiance, a more sophisticated version of the world-view expressed by the remarkable taxi-driver.

A young solicitor, his office a shoe box in a Central high-rise, told me what he saw as the main achievement of the Sino-British agreement. It was, he said, a document that allowed Hong Kong a sense of continuity, not so much for the period after 1997 as for the twelve years leading up to the handover. Similarly, he saw the electoral proposals as no more than a way of seeing the colony through the next three years. Both pieces of paper, he concluded, were deeply flawed, in that they gave no clear framework for a post–1997 Hong Kong. He criticized the agreement for pandering to indigenous landed interests in the New Territories, to the point of providing specific details for home ownership there, and he looked forward to a more rapid transfer of power to the Hong Kong Chinese. When I said that some considered this transfer was occurring too fast, his reply was that top government posts were still occupied by the British and that this had to end well before 1997, not in 1996. Almost as an afterthought, he added that senior expatriates 'should not have any serious worries about their pensions'. Finally, he gave me a detailed breakdown of the existing political picture in Hong Kong and how this would alter. His grasp of the nuances was faultless; his manner assured. As I listened, I pictured him as a senior official in a post-British administration, working efficiently, clinically. Already there seemed to be no place for the British here.

This ebullience and confidence in the future was also shown by an officer of a pressure group known as Meeting Point. This group, and many others like it, had lobbied hard during the talks, sending teams to both Beijing and London. It had tried to impress upon the Chinese authorities how important it was for Hong Kong to maintain an independent character; in London, in May 1984, shortly before the first of the Commons debates (if they can be described as such), attempts were made to convince the British Government that it should speed up the process of democratization. Again, the agreement meant very little to this group. It was what the Hong Kong people could achieve in the transitional period that mattered most. Meeting Point's ideas on the post-British period were based on the view that a successful future for Hong Kong depended on a number of interrelated strands, the most important of which was continued prosperity. If Hong Kong did not thrive, there was no reason for China to let it maintain an independent character. The other crucial factors were democratic government, the fact that a successful takeover in Hong Kong could be used to persuade Taiwan to rejoin the mainland and, in particular, China's sincerity in its dealings with the colony.

The official himself was sure that a successful post-British Hong Kong required fierce dedication, resignation to the colony becoming a Chinese SAR (Special Administrative Region) and unswerving commitment to making a go of it. He saw the sense of nationalism that resided in all Hong Kong Chinese as a particular asset and felt the number of Chinese intellectuals who would remain would dispel myths that they were all about to flee and observe events from abroad. His confidence was unshakeable and our discussion filled with flashes of intellectual arrogance. Whenever I intervened with a cautious note, his response would be: 'that is an outdated observation'. When I remarked that Chinese socialism and Hong Kong capitalism would always be at opposite ends of the spectrum and that, in the long run, there was always a danger that the latter would be swallowed by the former, his answer was: 'that may have been the case a few years ago'.

Such idealism was not exceptional in those early, heady days. These young intellectuals shared a common background. Many had been contemporaries at university and most were lower middle class. They had climbed quickly up the ladders of their professions and now they were blossoming in anticipation of being able to steer Hong Kong into a new era. For a few idyllic months, there were many who thought they were actually in command of their own fate. The next two years were to teach them some harsh political realities: of the cynicism of their joint masters, of the timidity of some from their own ranks and of the durability of an older generation of politicians well-schooled in the art of colonial politics.

A small number of young intellectuals were never convinced by the idea that China could change sufficiently radically or quickly to accommodate comfortably many of Hong Kong's more freewheeling capitalist traits. The problem had been well disguised by the Beijing authorities and their representatives in Hong Kong, who had set out to win over as wide a spread of interest groups as possible: group after group either visited or were invited to visit Beijing to make their own needs and views known. Teachers, trade union officials, medical staff, priests and industrialists were, in so far as was prac-ticable, assured that they would not be ignored or neglected in the run up to 1997. Even the larger Triad gangs were rumoured to have sent a delegation to China to discuss their long-term role in Hong Kong!

Such signs of progress have been taken at face value by those who wish to show that 'one country, two systems' will work. There are some, however, who take a more historical view of the matter. Hong Kong has been extremely fortunate that the talks, and much of the period of transition to date, have taken place against the backdrop of remarkably rapid developments in China; to the point, indeed, of a *near* renunciation of Marxism. But then again, there have been many other attempts to incorporate western techniques in China's social and economic base. All have failed, partly because of China's unwillingness to modernize fully and partly because of the sheer scale of the operation. Taken in such a context, China's present attempt at change is, like some of its nineteenth-century equiv-alents, a half-way house. How successful it will be remains to be seen, but the historical portents are not good.

This in itself worries those who insist on taking a cool, detached look at Hong Kong's future. Willing China to succeed against the odds may be commendable, but it is, given the possible outcome, also potentially foolhardy. There are also nagging doubts about China's frequently-stated intention to refrain from simply taking over the whole show in Hong Kong. One of the more pessimistic commentators on the Hong Kong situation recalled how he had met the editor of *Ta Kung Pao*, a leftist daily, at a party in late 1984. The editor enquired if he was going to stand as a candidate in the colony's first broadly-based elections the following year. No, came the reply, he would not be running for office.

'Why?' asked the left-wing editor.

'Because you will be in control in 1990, so what's the point?'

'No,' ended the newsman with a faint smirk, 'we will be in charge in 1997.'

Such expressions of quiet confidence are hardly inspirational, nor, the commentator assured me, was this an isolated case. An incident of this kind was hardly likely to make him change his mind. On another occasion, a BBC interviewer asked the same man what he would be doing in 1997.

'Packing,' he replied.

Much of the blame for the continuing uncertainty in Hong Kong must be attributed to the absence of any firm leadership in the colony since the debate on its future began in earnest. The most natural source of political leadership was, in principle, the Legislative and Executive Councils, and especially their Unofficial Members, but there was not much scope for a unity of purpose in these bodies, not least because few of the Chinese and English members were bilingual.

When the Sino-British talks were in progress, members of Umelco had occasionally tried to influence their course, but they did so almost always as outsiders. Moreover, these interventions provoked the wrath of either Britain or China. In February 1984, Legco Unofficials announced that the council should be allowed an opportunity to debate the results of the talks before an agreement was signed. Less than a month later, Roger Lobo, the Senior Unofficial Member, tabled a motion to the effect that the chamber should be allowed ample time to review the draft agreement. On this occasion, the Chief Secretary, Sir Philip Haddon-Cave, voiced government support for the motion. The Lobo Motion, as it became known, was passed unanimously.

In subsequent months, Unofficial Members of the council began their own form of shuttle diplomacy, visiting both London and Beijing. Neither capital gave the parties a warm welcome. After the agreement had been signed, the Unofficials made another attempt to show their independence, commissioning their own survey to assess the views of the population in addition to that being carried out by the Assessment Office. In the event, both the official and unofficial surveys produced roughly the same conclusion: that, on the whole, the majority of Hong Kong residents preferred to have an agreement than not to have one. Given the chaos that had reigned in the two years before the agreement, such a conclusion was hardly surprising. But the outcome had clearly been by no means certain as the Unofficials' independent action was regarded as tantamount to sabotage and perhaps even mutiny. A senior British official associated with the exercise spoke at an informal gathering in Oxford in early 1985. When questioned about the Unofficials' action, he described his surprise and considerable irritation at their behaviour: 'These people are supposed to be on our side,' he said, adding, 'How *does* it look. . . ? Luckily the results broadly matched ours.'

In the closing stages of the negotiations over Hong Kong, the Unofficials lost both credibility with the British establishment and favour with China. The latter, particularly, made its views very clear. In June 1984 three senior members of Exco were invited to Beijing, with an itinerary that assured them of an audience with the paramount leader, Deng Xiaoping. It was also stressed that Roger Lobo should not be included in the group. When they reached Beijing, with their own set of proposals in hand, they were dressed down by Deng himself: in Beijing's eyes they did not represent Hong Kong public opinion. On the other hand, according to sources close to Legco, the stand that the Unofficials took did little for them personally at home. The business community, and particularly its captains, had little time for those who rocked political boats.

Nevertheless, the years 1982–5 did more to politicize and embolden the Legislative Council than any other in this century, as is clearly shown by the Unofficials' increasing willingness to take their case to wherever it was likely to make the greatest impact. When nationality legislation was going through Parliament in 1981, the Unofficials made no attempt to make their case known directly at the crucial first and second stages in the House of Commons. As a result, there was only one Unofficial present at either stage, and he was on a private business visit to London. Before the closing stages of the bill the Unofficials made known their intention to make a trip to London to lobby parliamentarians, but were, according to a Senior Unofficial, persuaded not to go. They were told that the majority against giving Hong Kong a special status in the legislation 'would be too large . . . too large to make a difference'. The result was, in fact, very close: Hong Kong's case failed by a margin of one vote at the same time as Gibraltar was recognized as deserving full British status.

The fractures that appeared in the colony's social and political structure at the time of the agreement have not healed since it was signed. If anything, they have widened and become more painful. Growing political polarization left the colonial government in an untenable position. If it were seen to be coming down too far on the side of opening up the political system, there would be a strong reaction from conservative businessmen and established politicians. Moreover, these individuals had influential backing from the most remarkable source: China. Senior Chinese officials had made a point of influencing events by stating quite categorically that their government was opposed to the introduction of direct elections, as this would be breaking the terms of the Joint Declaration. Although this stand was later made less categorical, the damage had been done. Conservative politicians had already begun to use a well-worn argument against reform: 'China wouldn't like it'. On the other hand, if the government were to insist on the *status quo* being maintained in a literal sense, liberals would see this as defeatism in the face of pressure from the colony's establishment and China. If this were to happen, the liberals said, the government would have shown that it was a lame duck administration and, therefore, could not be relied upon to provide the strength and authority that the colony required in the transition to 1997.

And so, for the three years until the 1987 review, the Hong Kong Government sat very squarely on the horns of a dilemma. This did little good for the morale of its own officers. Policy-making became extremely difficult, because each piece of fresh legislation would be scrutinized minutely for evidence of inappropriate radicalism or further concessions to conservatism. Any signs that the government was looking in either direction would be greeted by howls of protest from a hyperactive press and the legislation ritually dragged through the streets until all that was left of it was a fetid corpse.

For a government used, and indeed intended, to rule by consensus, such responses were difficult to absorb, particularly as its senior officials appeared not to have anticipated the tenacious struggle over direct elections. In September 1984, the outgoing Secretary for Home Affairs told me how direct elections were a non-issue. The government, he said, ' had tested the water' some time before on the question of whether there should be one elected representative in the Executive Council, or whether all appointed members should be replaced by elected representatives. He had seen, he said, not one response expressing a view one way or another.

CHAPTER NINE

In Search of an Insurance Policy

W hen Foreign Office officials describe the 'one country, two systems' concept as 'imaginative', this is Whitehall jargon for an excessively bold undertaking. Although the population of Hong Kong was never offered a handbook on how to decipher such elegant and subtle terminology, most have understood its significance. Under the circumstances, it is not unreasonable for those taking part in such an experiment to expect some form of safety mechanism should things go wrong.

Community leaders pressed this very case. They argued that few of those living in Hong Kong would be anxious to leave the colony if they were allowed a choice and would only do so if there was no other option. They also stressed repeatedly that forcing people to make premature decisions about the future would of itself cause great and perhaps ultimately unmanageable destabilization. For many, the heart of the problem was, and is, that 1997 is Stygian. Belief in the Sino-British agreement constitutes an act of faith, not of rationality. Guarantees that 'everything would remain the same' are worth no more than the paper they are written on.

There was little sympathy from the British Government for such fears. The agreement was a good one; the best that could have been obtained. This uncompromising stance was made abundantly clear in the House of Commons debate of 5 December 1984, which had been called to scrutinize and ratify the Joint Declaration. This was generally seen as the last opportunity to bring home what Hong Kong's population could look forward to in the next twelve years. It was not expected that there would be much criticism of the document or its *raison d'être*, and in fact there was not. Apart from an impassioned, critical speech from the Liberal MP Paddy Ashdown and a Conservative MP breaking ranks by asking what had happened to the house's cynics and its anti-Communist talk, the debate was a tame, non-partisan affair.

Attempts by various individuals and groups to convince Parliament and the British Government that some form of safety net had to be created for those who now faced an uncertain future were largely ignored, with the notable exception of an eleventh-hour appeal despatched by a triumvirate of concerned academics to both houses. The appeal urged the government to launch Operation Haven, an international scheme for the creation of resettlement quotas in the countries of the Commonwealth, European Community and NATO for all those with nationality problems who might want to leave Hong Kong after 1997. In addition, the academics urged Britain to review its own immigration policies 'with a view to easing the present restrictions on the right of abode'. The appeal ended with an important observation:

In Hong Kong the search for safety nets for the post-1997 period has already begun, and Britain's formal involvement in this process will be nothing more than a direct response to the general desire for tangible safeguards of . . . freedoms as well as the prevention of panic-stricken preemptive flight.

Operation Haven was proposed by the Shadow Foreign Secretary Denis Healey in the course of the debate on 5 December. In his summing up for the government, Richard Luce made short shrift of the proposal: 'Our aim . . . has been to provide security for the people of Hong Kong in such a way that they would not wish to leave. We have a very good agreement which does just that, and I don't think it is the moment to be taking steps to ask other countries to assist with resettlement of Hong Kong people.'

For good measure, Luce added that other countries would construe such a scheme as an incomprehensible lack of faith on Britain's part, and, furthermore, 'it would inevitably, because it would display a lack of faith, be very unsettling to the very people . . . whose security we are seeking to provide for'. Some months later a former Whitehall mandarin explained how, in his long experience of government and bureaucratic thinking, such options as Operation Haven could not be entertained by any of the countries concerned until a *genuine* political crisis exists, and the problem is 'on the doorstep'.

The feeling of unease, which the British Government glossed over, but which has, nevertheless, resulted in a miniature exodus from Hong Kong, was made apparent to me in a number of ways at the time of the signing of the agreement. A Hong Kong-Chinese government official I spoke to about the outlook suggested that I should observe the behaviour of professional people such as doctors. 'They will soon be charging slightly higher fees and working longer hours to amass capital, just in case. . . .'

Some time later I followed up this observation by talking to a company specializing in accident and medical insurance. They confirmed the general trend. From 1984, they had noticed a sharp and sustained rise in the fees that they settled. Without any prompting from me, the owner of the company said he was sure doctors were building up their own, informal insurance policies. Other indicators, such as the ever-lengthening queue for visa application forms up the steps of the American Consulate, were more immediately visible. The Canadian and Australian High Commissions were also recording increasing numbers of enquiries for migrant visas.

Tragedy and farce intermingled as Britain displayed an inscrutable resolve that neither inspired nor reassured those of a nervous disposition. The harder British politicians attempted to convince sceptics that all would be well, the more convinced the doubters were that they had no choice but to embark on a course of self-help. Streams of assurances were counterbalanced by the appearance of dozens of tiny shops plastered with photographs of properties in Canada and Australia: homes that would serve as sound investments and places of ultimate refuge. A monopoly-like game called *1997* appeared, filled with elements of chance and options. Rarely had Hong Kong enterprise produced a toy with such a limited international market. A shop was opened at the 'Star' Ferry Terminal displaying dimpled, wide-eyed dolls dressed as junior boat people, appealing to passing tourists to take them home. Living 'dolls' began to advertise for husbands: looks were not a great concern, passports were. A growing list of such anecdotal examples made it difficult for outsiders to differentiate between the caricature and the reality of the situation.

Those who wished to search out their own insurance policies had first to consider the difficulty of finding a visa. Quotas at the time, although they have subsequently been raised, dictated that no more than about 7000 individuals would be successful in finding a new domicile every year. At that rate, only about 100,000 could hope to be resettled through official channels. These people would have had to demonstrate some form of sponsorship, skills and, more often than not, the ability and willingness to shift large sums of money (in most cases millions of Hong Kong dollars) to the host country. Having secured a visa, the migrants would have to face the difficulties of setting up their new lives. This would almost certainly take at least two years and would invariably involve being treated as second-class citizens. For those who had already made good in Hong Kong such hurdles would be difficult to contemplate. Most would have wanted to stay, to live out the Chinese maxim that it is better to be the head of the chicken than the tail of the ox.

However, life lived on the basis of such aphorisms has its limitations and ambiguities. Chinese leaders appeared to be heading along a path that would lead to the creation of a mixed economy, essentially socialist but with a large handful of market forces thrown in for good measure. After all, had not Deng Xiaoping himself observed that it did not matter what colour the cat was so long as it caught mice? The problem was whether he and other Chinese officials could be trusted to maintain this course. On the surface, there was little doubt. Deng had even chosen to adopt a time-honoured way of reassuring Hong Kong of his sincerity: at the time of the finalization of the Joint Declaration, he had allowed his jovial son, crippled by a fall from an upper-storey window during an onslaught by Red Guards in the swell of the Cultural Revolution, to visit the colony to pass on his family's goodwill and collect money for China's handicapped. For nearly a month Deng Pufang's wheelchair and broad beaming face were to be seen everywhere, as millionaires stumbled over one another to present huge sums to the fund, which soon grew to HK$50 million. Hong Kong's rich are well acquainted with such traditional ways of securing mutual respect and understanding.

But respect and understanding is not necessarily the same as trust, and here the gulf between Hong Kong and China was enormous. Can a Chinese Government which shoots people for economic crimes just beyond the territory's borders be fully trusted? As a member of the business community put it: 'What are economic crimes? Fraud is comprehensible . . . but crimes against the *economy*? In Hong Kong people are free to prosper. They are free even to commit small "crimes against the economy". Over 10,000 have died in China for such crimes, and they continue to die.'

Another approach that was heard a few years ago would have it

that there is really no point in thinking in terms of trusting or mis-
trusting Communists. What could even the highest-ranking Communist official look forward to? Nothing. They retired from nothing to
nothing. All they lived for was power. How could they begin to
understand Hong Kong, or the wishes of its population? Such officials
could not even be bribed. What was the point, therefore, of thinking
about the promised fifty years of capitalism beyond 1997?

A cruder version of essentially the same argument that is still circulating can best be summed up in two novel medical analogies to
Communism I heard on a recent visit. A gregarious young man,
who had made a modest fortune by juggling a staggering array of
occupations in the decade that he had been in Hong Kong, told me
of his plans for 1997. What did he think of the Communist Chinese,
I asked. Did he trust them to be honourable in observing the agreement? He waved away the question, and the Joint Declaration, as if
it were a fly: 'Communism is like Aids: it may not kill you immediately, but it will get you in the end.'

Did this mean that he would be moving soon? Yes, he replied, he
had applied for Canadian papers. He then complained of the bitter
cold that he would have to contend with there. But this too he
turned into a metaphor: 'It's better to have 'flu,' he said, referring to
the short-term effects of moving to the cold of Canada, 'than to
suffer from a permanent "cold in the head" after 1997.'

Some people, of course, benefited from the mood of uncertainty.
Much corporate and individual effort was expended on formulating
ways in which to help people emigrate – at a cost. Most obviously,
lawyers specialized in helping prospective emigrants find a way out
of Hong Kong. Small island states and Third World countries offered ·
opportunities for wealthier Hong Kong residents to make long-term
investments within their borders in return for the promise of citizenship and passports. Foreign syndicates were set up to look into
the creation of complicated schemes by which personnel skilled in
desirable areas of commerce, industry and technology could be
enticed from Hong Kong in order to work for a number of years as
virtual bonded labour.

One idea for such a scheme was floated by a group of businessmen and financiers with connections in the Bahamas. They proposed
to use these connections to create a company on one of the islands
nearest the North American coast, with the purpose of writing com-
puter software for export to the United States. Well-qualified gradu-

ates between the ages of twenty and forty would be hired in Hong Kong on contracts of two to three years. Salaries were to be of secondary importance. Conditions on the island were to be less than comfortable, with only a tiny population and few social amenities. The great attraction would be a 'clear opportunity for the best and brightest to move to the US . . . and for a small number with leadership skills, the opportunity to remain in the Bahamas'.

Ironically, the venture with the most altruistic motives, a company with the unlikely name of The Hongkong Freedom of Movement and Rights of Abode Ltd, was hampered by the Hong Kong Government. It was founded by T. S. Lo, a Umelco councillor and outspoken critic of the British Government's treatment of British subjects resident in Hong Kong, who resigned in protest from Legco and Exco in early 1985. The company was to be a non-profit-making concern which sought to provide up-to-date information on immigration to Commonwealth and other English-speaking countries for prospective migrants and advice on investment opportunities abroad for those who might want to have 'their eggs in different baskets'. Whereas normal companies require only two weeks to be registered in Hong Kong, Lo's venture, he told me, took months to be given certification, and then only after the threat of legal action and attendant publicity.

For those not searching for an escape hatch, this period was one of considerable excitement. The democratization issue provided two lines of apparent insurance. The introduction of full democracy would act as an important institutional bulwark against any attempt by China to interfere in Hong Kong's internal affairs after 1997. More important still, such an innovation, especially if it came well before the final transition to Chinese sovereignty, would be the seedbed from which might blossom strong, independent-minded leaders who would guide Hong Kong into its new semi-autonomous era and, again, resist Chinese infractions. Ideally, the transitional period would produce a single visionary in the mould of Singapore's Prime Minister Lee Kuan Yew. The appeal of such a leader is understandable. Singapore's post-independence success story is integrally linked with Lee's substantial economic and political skills.

It became the vogue, particularly amongst entrepreneurs in their thirties and forties, to look to the emergence of a political superman such as Lee, who would provide cohesion and instil a common sense of purpose in a population that seemed to be growing increasingly disparate and desperate. Lee appealed to a streak of realism in these young turks: his brand of politics and economics successfully blended vital capitalism with a generally acceptable element of paternalistic welfarism. He also stood for a brand of politics that would sit well with the Chinese leadership, presiding over a single all-powerful political party and suppressing any rival organized opposition.

Britain, too, would be happy for the government of Hong Kong to follow such a course. A strong personality like Lee Kuan Yew, tempered by and reluctantly nurtured in the atmosphere of late colonialism, would ensure that the territory would steer a comparatively even course after the departure of the British. Curiously, however, it was thought that the introduction of democratic politics, and for some British commentators the very signing of the Joint Declaration, would give birth to such a leader. As many sceptics realised, this view was about as rational as waiting for the coming of a new, and in this case purpose-built, Messiah. If a strong personality were to emerge, surely he or she would have done so in the years of debate and crisis between 1982 and 1984, when the situation was at its most fluid and conditions were fertile for a visionary to make his or her mark. As one of these disbelievers put it to me in January 1985: 'Where are these personalities?'

And, indeed, it was difficult at that time to put a finger on any one person who had shown such obviously potent qualities. Later that year, the picture seemed to alter when a QC named Martin Lee was elected to the Legislative Council through the Legal Functional Constituency. A tall, thin man with a mellow voice and scholarly manner, Lee proved to be a staunch advocate for the people of Hong Kong, refusing to give in to official reasoning or pressure, be it from China, Britain or the Hong Kong Government, when this was seen to be against their interests. He threw himself headlong into political life, casting aside any consideration that he might act in a conservative manner more suited to the professional body that gave him his Legco seat.

Less than two years after his election, Lee had already become something of a populist, both echoing and guiding popular opinion on a succession of controversial issues, ranging from the plan to build a nuclear power station at Daya Bay to the democratization question. It was the latter, however, that provided Lee with a true platform. Using arguments that were both fluent and eminently reasonable, Lee was able to weave a spell around all those of a liberal bent. His appeals to democratic instincts and to the idea that Hong Kong should act according to its own conscience rather than bow to external pressure gained him much support, particularly from the young.

When I went to see Lee in early 1987, I had done some background reading on him. It was not difficult: the media seemed to be filled with references to his name and utterances. One columnist, a member of the gung-ho school of colonial journalism, included Lee in his New Year's 'Honours List' for 'telling it like it is'. This accolade played on my mind as I took the lift to his stylish chambers. A great deal of my reading about Lee had emphasized his outspoken nature. Little had been said of his own vision of what a post–1997 Hong Kong should look like. I was no happier on this point when I left some time later. He had spoken eloquently about the need for the early introduction of direct elections, chiding Britain's timorousness in the face of China's anti-democratic offensive. By deferring the issue, Britain was doing Hong Kong a great disfavour: 'you can't lead a population for one hundred years, suppressing all independent thought on politics, and then say one morning, "Right, you're on your own: what do you want us to do?" ' Without the all-important democracy he sought, Lee said, there was little chance of good government. To reinforce the point, he introduced an early statement from Deng Xiaoping on this subject: 'A good system of government can prevent bad leaders from producing harm, but a bad system of government prevents even good leaders from producing good.'

It was difficult, even if I had sought to do so, to find fault with the noble instincts that guided his reasoning. It was equally difficult to fault him for his dedication to speaking his mind. He had been appointed to the Basic Law Drafting Committee, work which he described as 'very tough'. In pursuing the minutiae of Hong Kong's post–1997 constitution, he observed that he spent more time teaching Chinese delegates than negotiating with them. And yet his approach worried me. Particularly so when he chose to support his argument about the urgent need for fundamental changes to the political system with a description of the evolution of his own political consciousness. Two years ago, Lee said, even he was doubtful about the wisdom of giving power to the people. This was because he was unsure how elected councillors and the colonial civil service would coexist. The civil service, he said, acted for the people, whom it also ruled. What would he, or any other elected councillor, say to these administrators? And, in any event, how could he be sure that they would follow his instructions.

These are not the words of a natural democrat. Nor was it clear that his commitment to Hong Kong was as great as I might have expected from a person who was risking all to speak his mind. After he had told me that he was not optimistic about the future, I took this cue to ask what his own family's plans were.

'Frankly, I haven't decided yet.'

His wife, he added, believed that the situation was hopeless. Then there was a five-year-old child to think about. The child would, he conjectured, probably go abroad, as would his wife: 'But then it's difficult for a politician to remain alone here, while his wife and child have resettled.'

These were not the thoughts I would have expected from a Lee Kuan Yew.

The conclusions I had heard were no different to those reached by many other, but less vocal, pessimists who were keeping all options open. In a sense, Lee's argument for constitutional change was based on the premise that only in this way could everything remain the same. This was no blueprint for the future, but simply a more sophisticated rendition of the need to keep the Communists out; a way of creating a 'Fortress Hong Kong'.

Outwardly very little had changed in Hong Kong. The stock market had begun a steady climb and the property market, which had been written off totally by some market experts in 1983 and 1984, showed some signs of life, particularly at its lower end. Smaller flats were again in demand. The joke making the rounds at the time had it that those at the greatest premium were on the lower floors. Chinese lifts were notoriously unreliable, so the climb up the stairs would be bearable after 1997! Luxury accommodation was less sought after. The upper end of the market continued to be depressed for some time after the general recovery of the property sector and was to some extent a more accurate indicator of the mood of the colony. Luxury flats and houses tied up substantial capital and would not be easy to offload if and when conditions in Hong Kong worsened. The reaction of an Indonesian-Chinese multi-millionaire shipping magnate was typical. He and his family had owned and lived in a penthouse flat, which had been made uninhabitable through water damage in 1984. The family moved to a rented luxury flat with a magnificent view of the harbour while their own home was surveyed. Eventually it was decided that a return to the original flat was impossible. And yet, months later, the head of the family seemed to be in no hurry to buy a new flat, despite having to lay out hundreds of thousands of dollars each month in rent, at a time when he could have purchased at a bargain price. Why, I wondered, did he not buy? He replied that the amount of money he would have to sink into such a purchase was too great and the time span of thirteen years was not attractive: he preferred to rent the flat through his company and limit his own capital exposure.

Such cautious behaviour was not unusual. In fact, it could be regarded as the norm. On the surface, Hong Kong's well-oiled cash register was signalling 'business as usual'. Trade had been affected remarkably little during the difficult years. Import, export and manufacturing figures showed nothing of the poison of uncertainty that had eaten into the very bones of the colony. The Joint Declaration had sought to preserve Hong Kong in a state of 'certain uncertainty'. The slender margin of error the drafting teams had to contend with in achieving this precarious balance was emphasized by a comment from one of their number shortly before the document was made public. He expressed a sense of relief at the result of his recent contacts with the more cynical elements in Hong Kong's business community. Before the Foreign Secretary's visit in April 1984 (when he first revealed the essential points in the agreement): 'they couldn't be sure of the next five months. Now they are assured of five years.' A period of five years was important because it was seen as the time that the sceptics would require to make plans and store some money overseas. If they could be induced to stay on for the next five years, my contact added, that would be achievement enough. There was even a chance that they might then be persuaded to stay longer.

These people, probably numbering no more than about 20,000 individuals, hold much of the colony's economic well-being in their hands. What is by no means certain is how they could be induced to remain. Many have proved more slippery than eels. In December 1986 I met a man I had known for many years. He was a Eurasian in his late forties, had built up a glass-fibre business from scratch and was now enjoying some of the fruits of his enterprise. Comfortably bilingual, he had changed little since I first knew him: the clothes were more expensive, the jewellery chunkier and with a 22-carat gleam, the Ford had been superseded by a Jaguar, but his manner was still of the gregarious, classless sort that allowed him to be at ease in company from any point on the social scale. We talked about his business, of the days when he chased government contracts to manufacture new glass-fibre dustbins and of the steady expansion that had encouraged a hong to offer him a tidy sum for a controlling share of his company. He accepted the offer in the late 1970s, initially staying on as a director and effectively running the operation but eventually selling out completely. With the hard-earned profits from his former business safely tucked away, he now works for a company concerned with aircraft engineering.

Turning to the broader picture, he felt that people in the colony's business sector were as quick-witted as ever but that their attitudes had changed because of the need to make money more quickly, and in a safer way. The conversation soon shifted, at his prompting, to nationality, and he pointed to the expertise and skill that Britain would lose by refusing entry to those who held Hong Kong-British passports.

Subsequently I have seen how vigorously the Hong Kong entrepreneurial spirit and accompanying capital have been applied in places that have opened their doors to economic refugees from the colony. In Sydney, Australia, Hong Kong money and vision have regenerated block after block of derelict property, introduced trade and employment and injected a spirit of life and enterprise in suburban areas that have been depressed for decades. In Canada the effects of a positive migration policy have been nothing short of staggering. One project alone, proposed by Li Ka-shing's Cheung Kong Holdings, involves building a high-density mix of offices, shops and housing on the site used for Expo '86 in Vancouver, a development reported as valued at HK$20 billion in March 1988. In British Columbia, a province that is particularly aware of the advantages of taking in Hong Kong migrants, fewer than six hundred immigrants have undertaken to start businesses worth hundreds of millions and destined to create nearly 3000 jobs. In the meantime, city authorities in the north of Britain search for funds for urban regeneration and jobs. And while British trade delegations make their way to China, the glint of a billion-strong market in their eyes, hundreds of potentially vital middlemen are lost to other industries in other countries.

Like the businessman who had moved from glass fibre to aircraft engineering, the more rarified levels of the business community can afford the luxury of delay. The transfer of Jardine Matheson to an offshore base, a plan of action devised by an American banker who has subsequently assumed the 'taipanship', was dismissed as an act of reorganization and rationalization. And, indeed, changes had been initiated between 1979 and 1981 when large amounts of stock had also been purchased in other offshore locations, notably in South Africa, long before the group chairman announced the company's move to Bermuda to an astonished public in 1984. At that time he could quite accurately claim that the move was in title only, although at the time of writing Jardines' cash and credit reserves, amounting to almost HK$4 billion, are not tied to Hong Kong and the policy on acquisitions is one of 'great caution'.

Later in the same year, there were rumours in the Hong Kong media that another hong, Swire Pacific, was intent on selling the airline Cathay Pacific, Hong Kong's flag carrier, to China. By chance I spoke to one of the company's senior managers in Sydney shortly afterwards. When I told him of the talk, he guffawed, suggesting that Swire had cannily removed itself from restraints and risk in Hong Kong, leaving China to deal with the ensuing problems. In January 1987 12.5 per cent of Cathay Pacific was sold to the Chinese, but this deal followed a flotation of part of Swire's holdings in the airline in order to root Cathay Pacific firmly in the colony. In all, the sales have helped reduce the parent company's holding to a controlling 50.23 per cent.

The Hongkong & Shanghai Banking Corporation initiated a strategy of substantial expansion overseas at about the same time. In the autumn of 1980 the bank purchased a controlling interest in Marine Midland, an American Bank, which has now been extended to full ownership. In the spring of 1981, the bank also made an aggressive, unwelcome and ultimately unsuccessful bid for the Royal Bank of Scotland. Again, this may be seen as part of a grander plan for international expansion. But it is also interesting that the Hongkong Bank attempted to persuade the Bank of England of the correctness of its approach by calling itself a British bank, and therefore not to be regarded as a foreign institution angling for one of the country's main clearing houses. The Bank of England viewed the corporation's status differently, helping to highlight the fact that the bank's operating base was very squarely in the colony and that it would be difficult to expand overseas without the appropriate foothold. In November 1987 the Hongkong and Shanghai Banking Corporation tried again, with a bid for the troubled Midland Bank. This time they were more successful. Under the arrangement reached, Hongkong Bank purchased 14.9 per cent of the Midland and promised to refrain from making a full-scale bid for control for three years. At the moment, at least, it has a toehold in Britain.

Although the hongs took the lead in diversification, they were not to remain alone for long. In the wake of the 1984 agreement, most of the big Chinese players in high finance initiated the gradual restructuring of their operations in Hong Kong. There has also been a marked rise in large corporate purchases outside the colony. None of these exercises in diversification has been as spectacular as Jardines' activities, but taken together they reveal the extent to which companies are reducing the exposure of their Hong Kong operations.

In late 1986, not long after he bought a 4.9 per cent share of the Pearson Group, Li Ka-shing sank hundreds of millions of dollars into a raid on Husky, a Canadian oil concern. The following year it was revealed he had built up a 4.9 per cent share in Cable & Wireless too. Then, as we saw earlier, he began to channel billions of dollars into the Canadian property market. But Li is always careful to maintain a show of confidence in Hong Kong. His offer for Husky, for example, was balanced by a timely announcement of his faith in the future in which he stated his intention to plough HK$2.5 billion into the local economy. Like many other super-rich business-men in Hong Kong, Li regularly publicizes what many seasoned observers regard as token investments in the Chinese economy, a procedure that helps to counterbalance the increasing shift to investment abroad.

Sir Y. K. Pao is in a much better position than some of his com-patriots: at least part of his fortune is tied up in his fleet of ships which could, if necessary, be removed or kept away from Hong Kong at a moment's notice. In the immediate post-agreement years his companies continued to concentrate on expanding their prop-erty interests in Hong Kong itself, but recently Pao's organization has revealed that it has a long-term strategy for expansion into hotels and companies abroad. This announcement coincided with the purchase of a large hotel chain in America – with immediate plans for major expansion – for US$135 million in cash.

Remarkably, a lack of reinvestment in Hong Kong and the outflow of capital does not seem to have had any visible effects on the colony. The most plausible explanation is that the Joint Declaration allowed local capital to be 'laundered'. Recent inflows of foreign capital, particularly from the Americans and Japanese, have more than matched the rate at which local capital has been flowing out. Local people have therefore been able to sell off their interests without reducing the overall size of the financial cake. My friend with the glass-fibre business is an example of this phenomenon: although he sold his factory to a hong, he could just as easily have sold it to a foreign investor. And many like him have done precisely that. Often, if alternative residence is assured, such a transition does not result in the actual departure of the former owner of the business, who continues to exercise his or her talents on a salaried basis.

CHAPTER TEN

Return of the Refugee

In the autumn of 1984 I visited a Hong Kong-Chinese civil servant in his office in Central District. It was approaching the end of the working day and he was in a relaxed mood. We discussed the future of the colony. He pointed at the imposing metal and glass form of the new Hongkong Bank building visible from his window. 'Do you know,' he said, 'that such is the sense of suspicion in the territory that people look to it as an indication of uncertainty?'

He explained that the saucer-like helicopter platform on the top of the building – in fact never used because of the dangers of regular landings in such a congested area – had been interpreted by some not just as a quick air link with the airport across the harbour, but as a vehicle for transferring the bank's gold reserves to waiting planes, as quickly as possible, should the need arise. Anecdotes such as these, he said, were symptomatic of a generally unhealthy atmosphere.

Nor was he under any illusions as to how people were reacting to the approach of 1997. The wealthy were continuing to spend, but were keeping their reinvestment to a minimum. The upper middle class were more concerned with accumulating capital for emigration, while the lower middle and working classes, who were unlikely to raise the assets necessary to guarantee a bolt hole abroad, were taking the view that the last few years under old conditions were to be enjoyed to the full.

His diagnosis was remarkably astute. Conspicuous consumption by the rich has made Hong Kong a full partner in the Roaring Eighties. At the same time there are signs of a shifting investment pattern. There are frequent reports of Hong Kong companies selling

169

shares in local concerns to outsiders, often accompanied by statements that such sales should not be viewed as disinvestment, but
rather as illustrating the confidence of foreign investors in the
strength of the Hong Kong economy. Few are convinced by such
statements and gossip soon magnifies the significance of each sale
out of all proportion. While the Swire Group and local financial
pundits were making appropriate noises about the sale of Cathay
Pacific shares forging welcome bonds between Hong Kong and
China, and about China's intent to make good its pledges, most
people thought otherwise. A well-to-do middle-aged physician told
me he saw the sale as a sell-out, even if China had been very anxious
to purchase the shares. He expected another 25 per cent of the airline's shares to go on sale 'soonish'.

As the civil servant had said, it was the 'barely rich' that showed
the most pronounced changes in their lifestyle and this had obvious
repercussions on the retail trade. Almost all the shopkeepers
involved in the sale of luxury goods that I spoke to complained of
tighter trading conditions. Most considered that this trend was
likely to continue. Their customers, they said, were saving steadily
so as to build up reserves for an eventual move. As a result retailers
are not only having to compete in a shrinking market-place, but are
also unable to raise funds for growth or diversification. As a man
involved in the import trade told me, little venture capital was forthcoming from middle-rank Chinese entrepreneurs, as they themselves
now preferred to work using foreign capital.

There are no firm figures available to assess the scale of the problem, but to many of those that I spoke to, figures were in any case
quite unimportant. One retailer, whose shop at a prestigious Chinese
sporting club is aimed at precisely the kind of people who are thinking of emigrating, was quite categorical. All his richer customers are
in the process of moving from the colony. Most will go within four
years. Once they have established residence abroad, he said, some
may return to Hong Kong to pursue business interests, but their
involvement will never be on the scale it was before. Most of their
assets will be stowed away abroad and only 'spare cash' will be used
for further deals in the colony, and even then probably only for a
time before the final departure. He himself was frantically saving sufficient funds to emigrate to Los Angeles, although there was no
guarantee he would get a Green Card (a permit assuring permanent
residence and permission to work).

The shifting patterns in spending habits are quite visible in the streets. The gradual spread of luxury shops, expensive boutiques and prestige dealerships has been visibly stemmed and now seems to be in retreat. Shops devoted to the sale of expensive imports in carpeted, air-conditioned surroundings have been replaced by spartan-looking bazaar-like stores selling up-market factory rejects, catering to the increasingly materialistic lower middle class. Rent rises that retailers once took in their stride by tinkering at the margins are now more often than not met with swift capitulation. The spectre of an unknown future means few are willing to increase their costs. The further one moves from the luxury end of the market, the more alive and resilient seems to be the retail trade. Similar patterns are to be seen in the restaurant trade: cheap set lunches are as much in demand as ever but evening meals in many restaurants are showing alarmingly paltry returns. People, the restaurateurs say, are no longer willing to splurge.

It is impossible to stay in Hong Kong today without hearing some reference to, some enquiry into, some worry about the future. Sitting in a McDonald's in the business district one evening a few days before Christmas, I caught some agitated conversation. Three young men, dressed in crisp white shirts, their company-crested ties askew at an after-office-hours angle, were chatting over their half-finished coffees. The three-way exchange was of the sort that might be expected from people who spend their days catching infinitesimal shifts in forward rates on a VDU. American dollars, Hong Kong dollars flew between them. I listened more closely. This was not business talk: they were holding a round table on future prospects. The figures they were quoting had to do with salaries. They were systematically running through a list of possible options. Should they be looking for a job that paid in American dollars? If so, how much could they expect to earn? They discussed their qualifications, what their friends were doing, what papers they should be looking at for inspiration. Before long the talk ran into a familiar groove. What about visas for Canada? Was there much difficulty in returning? On expatriate terms, perhaps? And off the discussion lurched, exploring the ever-expanding corpus of information on the intricacies of finding an assured future – should they be fortunate – with one foot in Hong Kong and the other elsewhere.

The 'Chuppies' (Chinese yuppies) employed in the financial sector or trained in computing are well placed to find a niche overseas.

Such is the demand for their services and so great has the flow of qualified personnel become that terms of employment can virtually be dictated by the employee. In addition to high salaries, these workers are asking foreign employers, especially American companies, to write the right of residence abroad into their contracts, a request that is frequently granted.

In the course of the 1982–4 crisis much was made of the flight of local capital and the damage this would do to Hong Kong's stability. Today much local capital has already left the territory, but its place has been taken by foreign money. This exchange, a kind of fiscal osmosis, appears to have been relatively painless, but its long-term effects are, of course, still unclear. Under the best of conditions capital is cruelly unsentimental, but at least local money was anchored to indigenous capitalists and small businessmen. The money that has come to play an increasingly important part in the local economy is far more volatile, lacking, as one local observer put it, any 'infrastructural morality'. The involvement of the Australian Alan Bond and the ex-Australian Rupert Murdoch in the local capital market shows this well. The former pursues a high-risk strategy of highly-geared takeovers and property deals, advertising the injection of Australian money when, in fact, much of what he does in the colony appears to be based on minimal investment. The latter, with his eye firmly fixed on an entrée to a potential Chinese media market, has threatened long-established continuities by taking over the colony's premier English-language newspaper, the *South China Morning Post*. The paper has been filled with trusted Murdochites who, unfortunately, have very little understanding of Hong Kong, or faith in the 'old Hong Kong hands' bequeathed to them by the former owners.

What is already making its effect known, however, is the restlessness of the colony's human capital. People of all classes and professions are seizing the chance to move from Hong Kong, should this present itself. This human exodus, of which there is evidence everywhere, threatens to do more irreparable harm to the fabric of Hong Kong society than the flow of liquid assets. Those faced with the most difficult decisions are people with limited finances who are at an age when it is imperative to reach a quick decision about their own and, more importantly, their children's future. Individuals engaged in small businesses are on balance more fortunate than those working in the professions in this respect. The owners of small businesses can spend a few months a year, or a few years, abroad to establish residence, leaving their trade in the hands of trusted employees or, as is often the case, with relations. But civil servants, teachers, accountants, lawyers and members of a host of other professions must think in terms of transplanting their skills. Those who have explored such a move consider that it requires at least a decade to re-establish skills and achieve a lifestyle commensurate with that left behind in Hong Kong, when all factors such as pension rights, housing and schooling are taken into account. Once a decision has been made, there is the time-consuming and by no means certain application procedure for emigration.

The all-pervading uncertainty induced by this situation has had a profound psychological impact, not only on those who have to agonize over their decisions, but also on their marginally more committed colleagues. This was brought home to me in late 1986 when I paid a visit to the school where I had taught some years before, where all the teachers had been local people since the 1970s. It was a highly respected Chinese boys' middle school, with an admirable university entrance record. Competition for senior school places was severe.

Despite my short time at the school, my memories of it were vivid: compulsory assembly listening to bilingual announcements and, twice weekly, words of contemplation and inspiration from foreign priests from the nearby church; the late afternoon history classes with the senior forms, the balmy autumn sun cooled by breezes coming through the wall of open windows; the early afternoon English conversation sessions with eager, lively second formers relishing their imperfect ventures into a strange language.

I returned to the school with an Australian friend who had himself taught mathematics there in the early 1970s. When we entered the staff room, we saw that little had changed from his day or mine. Most of the teachers we knew were still there. But talking to them was deeply depressing. Our former colleagues spoke of the teetering educational system, battered by a series of reforms that were ostensibly intended to streamline it, but were, in the eyes of the teachers themselves, drawing Hong Kong education sharply away from the British system. There was nothing wrong with this, they hastened to add, so long as the changes, which included lengthening tertiary courses in the colony from three years to four (thereby bringing it into line with China and America), were made clear to the schools themselves. Instead, the teachers were being asked to guess at what system might emerge.

A history teacher told me of her dismay at seeing the sharp deterioration in the quality of history, both learned and taught, in the new system. Textbooks, she said, were becoming more elementary, consisting often of copiously illustrated simple documents. The format was intended to interest the children but, unfortunately, it was not having that effect. To facilitate understanding of democratic principles, history had been replaced in the lower forms by 'cultural studies', with an emphasis on civics. In the fourth form, pupils were allowed to choose between history and economics. Over two-thirds opted for economics, not only because of its business applications, but because pupils would then not have to grapple with English.

Indeed, on the question of English most of the teachers were in agreement. A combination of politics and practical problems was playing havoc with the language of instruction. Many teachers were already only using Chinese, often – and particularly in subjects such as history – in a desperate attempt to put concepts across to pupils who would not understand them in English. And yet the textbooks and the exams remained in English. One teacher concluded that the language of instruction had become Chinglish. But the problems did not end here. Many teachers, I was told, felt uneasy shifting to Chinese because the language *they* had been instructed in both at school and in higher education was English. And if they were to change over to Chinese, which dialect were they to use: Cantonese (Hong Kong's main dialect), or Potunghua (the official dialect in China)? If it was to be the latter, many teachers might not have an adequate technical vocabulary with which to teach efficiently.

Of those who look forward to a successful merger between Hong Kong and China, some consider that the most crucial factor is the speed at which the motherland opens up to western thought. This is how those who explain the Hong Kong phenomenon, without suggesting that there is something exceptional about the colony's people *per se*, would argue. The Hong Kong Chinese and China's Chinese are one people. What makes Hong Kong different is, as one young intellectual told me, 'purely the assimilation of Western thought'. An important constituent in this transfer of ideas, one might argue, is the existence of a living English as a *lingua franca*. The problem is how the language is to be perpetuated. Most Hong Kong children will go through kindergarten and primary school with Cantonese. Only when they reach secondary school will they encounter English texts and find themselves having to use the language as their principal tongue. By then, however, the demand on their abilities is very great.

The deep problems that this raises are reflected by the fall in standards of English relative to places such as India, Singapore and Malaysia, where textbooks are written in the native language, studied in the native language, but where there is great attention paid to English as a *secondary* subject. There seem to be no clear-cut solutions. In 1986, for example, a government-subsidized secondary school was offered a choice: English could remain as the medium of instruction, or teaching could be conducted in Chinese with two new members of staff brought in from Britain to teach English. The school chose the first option.

Such broad problems are increasingly accompanied, as I discovered at other schools, with worries about a general decline in discipline, at times involving pupils physically attacking teachers. The popular image of schools filled with diligent, well-mannered pupils has begun to be replaced with a more realistic picture which reflects the inequalities and deficiencies in society as a whole. Some teachers now see their schools as a breeding ground for ill-educated, volatile groups of young people who will eventually cause much trouble.

I could not help feeling that the teachers were bearing the burden of nearly a century and a half of colonial history, and its inevitable contradictions, on their shoulders. Had I been in their position, my conscience and sense of moral obligation might have given way to thoughts of emigration. When my companion and I were invited to sit with two senior masters, one in his early fifties, the other in his mid forties, the subject did indeed turn to more practical matters. The elder of the two began by asking about teaching in Australia, and it rapidly became clear that this was not simply the curiosity of a fellow professional. He asked about conditions of employment there. From time to time he would express doubts about his own qualifications. 'What about language?' he asked no one in particular, and then reassured himself with the observation that there might be some leeway with science teachers. When he was told of rates of pay in Australian secondary schools, he seemed unpleasantly surprised: 'That is not much better than in Hong Kong!'

The younger man laughed at his colleague's discovery, as if, at last, he had firm confirmation of the older man's plans.

175

We went off to lunch with a subject Head. Over plates of *dim sum* (Cantonese brunch) and cups of tea in a smart new restaurant nearby, he spoke of the general conditions in Hong Kong. The uncertain political situation, he said, was most unhealthy. At times there were surges of optimism. Often, however, there was great pessimism. This climate had affected his own thinking, although he seemed to be in no great hurry to leave his comfortable existence in Hong Kong. He and his wife, who is a civil servant, earned over HK$40,000 a month. Her housing allowance and favourable government-backed mortgage had helped them to purchase a two-bedroom flat in Broadcast Drive (so called because it grew around a 'ghetto' of television and radio stations), part of a popular middle-class suburb at the foot of the Kowloon hills. Their young daughter was looked after by a live-in Filipina maid. His wife was eager to emigrate to Canada, where he already had a sister and brother-in-law. Before making such a move, however, he hoped to build up some capital to put into a business.

Changes in the neighbourhood itself were further encouragement to leave. People living in another part of Broadcast Drive told me how they gradually came to know that over half the residents in their block were seeking to move to other countries. Many husbands had become temporary bachelors, forced to look after the household while their wives were notching up the compulsory months of residence in America or Canada. The couple I talked to were a clear demonstration of how infectious the actions of others can be. The husband, a senior executive with a local bank who was approaching a pensionable age, had told me in 1984 that there was no question of the older generation migrating; that it was too late to contemplate such a disruptive move at his age. Two years later he was living alone in Hong Kong. His wife was in America, each month bringing her a step closer to getting a Green Card for herself and permanent residence for them both.

There has always been a steady, but gentle, flow of people from Hong Kong to new lives elsewhere. *Tai tais* (mistresses of the house) met on sleepy afternoons over mahjong or tea to grumble about the deteriorating quality of life, to discuss the stock market and compare notes on property holdings. The conversation at these sessions always included questions about whose children were where in the pursuit of education or careers. Most middle-class families would expect to send at least one child abroad. Today this has become a forced affair. One well-to-do father told me, only partly in jest, that he had provided his eldest son with a large cheque, an assurance of further funds and a place at an American college, and given him strict instructions not to think about returning to Hong Kong until he had permission to reside permanently in the United States. Apparently contradictory statistics that do not support the evidence for increasing numbers of students going abroad – a decline in those obtaining student Certificates of Good Conduct from the police to satisfy American, Canadian and Australian visa requirements – are explained by the fact that young people are seeking to emigrate rather than have temporary residence as students.

Surprisingly, there are no official figures on emigration from Hong Kong; the only statistics available record those leaving and entering through official immigration points. Unfailingly, the annual figures balance out, suggesting that the colony's population remains stable. In fact, until the summer of 1988, the government refused to admit that there was any emigration crisis at all. And yet this was patently not true.* The director of a large office in Central District explained how his operation was being affected. Of a total of seventy employees, five executives had already left permanently and a further twenty-one were making plans to do so soon. Often people's intentions only became clear when, for example, they requested leave to attend a medical examination. One employee had flown to America on holiday when she was eight months pregnant. The director was sure that she would give birth there and then wait for the papers to come through for the baby before returning. His own personal assistant, who was married to a civil servant and was a few years short of retirement, had gone away on three consecutive holidays: one to Britain, another to Canada and the last to Australia. He guessed that her application for residence in Canada was probably already nearing completion. For those with the luxury of choice, I later discovered, Canada was viewed with a trace of suspicion, and especially so by the worldlier 'Chuppies'. One such person, who had visited Vancouver, remarked on the slower pace of life and the many pensioners and newlyweds they had seen there. The settlement was soon dubbed, in young business circles, as 'the city of the

---

*A point emphasized by the numbers leaving government employment. Between 1985 and late 1988 resignations from the civil service (with emigration given as the *official* reason) increased by nearly 175 per cent. Resignations as a whole, moreover, have increased by almost 100 per cent over the same period.

newlywed and nearly dead'.

The exodus is most obvious in central business areas and their middle-class suburbs. Women are told by their hairdressers that most of the salon's regular customers have gone. In some cases the stylists themselves have left. One business woman, who had herself emigrated when her Australian visa came up in 1983, told me how she had returned to her favourite facial shop, buried in the heart of a large office building in Central. The shop consisted of little more than a cubicle with a reclining seat and a small display of cosmetics, sold at prices marginally lower than those shown on the importer's supposedly fixed retail price list. For years it had been run single-handedly by its owner. When the woman walked in for her facial, she was surprised to see an unfamiliar young Chinese woman in charge. On enquiring about the owner, she was told that the latter had gone off to Canada to establish residence, leaving the running of the shop to her sister. Where, then, was the sister, the business woman asked? She too had left for Canada a year later and was now sitting out her term of residence. They had left their niece in charge of the business. She too would have liked to leave. 'But,' she concluded wistfully, 'I don't have money or good English, so I can't.'

Others in apparently similar unpromising situations have routes of escape. A friend and I were looking at some padded jackets in the street when the stall holder asked if we were from Australia. I replied that my companion was. His smile broadened. His daughter, he said, was married to the manager of a Chinese restaurant in Sydney; his son was doing a part-time course at the Institute of Technology. I was struck by the coincidence: my friend taught at the institute. Further conversation revealed that the son had been my friend's student. The man produced a visiting card for his son-in-law's restaurant. It was a luxurious twin-storey establishment in the heart of the city.

Money, language, skills, escape by marriage; all were themes that eddied through the collective consciousness and exposed raw nerves in the political arena. There is a growing tendency to use the existence of a personal bolt hole as an indication of a politician's lack of commitment to the colony. In interviewing a number of the leading personalities in local politics, I could see why this should be so. There have been suggestions that only holders of local travel documents should be eligible for Legco. In December 1986 some members of the council ritually buried a time capsule, to be opened in 1996.

Its contents include a phial of blood from the victims of a controversial industrial accident and the names of all the incumbent councillors. This was not, as it might appear, a resort to superstition and shamanism, but a biting political allusion. I remembered the conservative politician, Maria Tam, telling me that her mother had wanted her to emigrate from Hong Kong and start afresh, but that, after some soul searching, she had decided to stay, whatever the consequences. I would have admired her dedication and self-sacrifice more if she had not also volunteered the information that she had long held permission to reside in Britain, should she wish to. I began to notice that many of those I spoke to were similarly schizophrenic.

The fears and preoccupations of the moneyed classes were so strong that the more resigned and philosophical responses I received from members of less privileged groups came as something of a surprise. I was not alone in this reaction. In late 1986 a friend and I went to see the manager of a tiny branch of a foreign finance company in San Po Kong, a light industrial/commercial district surrounded by a crescent of low-cost housing estates. I had first met him two years earlier when I had asked a number of questions reflecting middle-class anxieties, all of which had been answered with a sense of calm and enlightened resignation.

I had asked him then if he had any worries about the status of his travel document. He had replied that it was not a particular issue as most people had not got the money to leave and it was, in any case, unlikely that Britain would accept many emigrants, although it was desirable that this should happen. A large number of his friends, he had added, held CIs like himself. Under the circumstances, they looked forward to being issued with a Chinese travel document. It would allow them greater freedom of movement than they already had. So the fact that he would be moving from the status of a third-class British citizen to that of a first-class Chinese citizen posed no worries? No, he had replied, none at all: the mainland Chinese had had long experience of coexisting with the Hong Kong-Chinese, and there had been no jealousy. Nor was there likely to be any in future. Nor did it worry him that his children would only have the right to a Chinese travel document. When asked about the agreement itself he had expressed his views remarkably frankly. Although he thought that Britain had done as much as it could to achieve the settlement, he mistrusted its ultimate intentions. Britain, he said, should serve out its remaining time honourably and should not drain Hong

Kong's coffers in a last minute attempt to divert some of the local wealth. He also feared that the Hong Kong Government might become increasingly unresponsive to local needs and wishes.

When I next saw him, his views appeared to have changed only a little. He was still optimistic about relations between Hong Kong and China, still little bothered by the passport issue, although he considered that the new Bn(O) passport was a poor document. Again, he said that he thought the Chinese travel document would be more useful. When our conversation turned to his plans, he was still confident, but there was a trace of reservation that had been absent when we last spoke. He intended to remain in Hong Kong, adding, however, that he had no choice *but* to stay because he did not have enough capital to emigrate. 1997 was not a major consideration for him. His hopes were for a gradual transition beyond that year. Although it was clear that they had had numerous conversations about it, few of his friends were preoccupied with the topic. Again, just a hint of doubt crept in as he concluded that they felt there was little they could do in the short term, but that the 'few years left (before 1997) are now appearing shorter'. Very few of his circle of friends had actually made long-term plans.

While I looked for shades of meaning in his answers, my friend had obviously found the meeting a revelation. On the way back to Central she began to think aloud. She remarked on the fact that many had no chance of leaving and complimented the resolve shown by the interviewee, adding that for people like him it would be the only way of coming to terms with an uncertain future. At the same time she was surprised at the sense of determination that characterized his attitude, 'his willingness to get on with it'.

She proceeded to tell me of her own preoccupations. Before joining the government she had completed a degree and become a secondary school teacher in one of the big New Town developments. There she was asked to take on subject after subject until, finally, she was swamped with work. Her main complaint, however, was about the difficulty of maintaining discipline. Her friends, she said, were sharply divided on the 1997 issue: some were making plans to leave, others had been firm since before the start of negotiations that they would stay. She herself had not made up her mind. She asked me how the British saw Hong Kong, adding that few British tourists seemed to visit their colony. I told her that on the whole perceptions were indistinct.

As if to bring the image into sharper focus, for herself as well as for them, she proceeded to sum up what she saw as the essence of Hong Kong. Her thumb-nail sketch contained all the frustration, pride and fear generated by a colonial society that now stared into an abyss. Hong Kong *is* Chinese in character and spirit, she told me, as our car raced past the mix of new and decaying high-rise buildings on the way to the cross-harbour tunnel, but a benevolent dictatorship had set the territory apart. It had developed its own character, its own way of life, despite the regular contact between Hong Kong and China. Many people in China, probably rightly, viewed their Hong Kong counterparts as skilled, but too shallow. With a sense of the optimism-through-necessity that we had heard at the small office in San Po Kong, she thought the culture which had produced such people might continue to develop. She had even managed to persuade herself of a reconciliation with the colonial heritage. Expatriates in the 1950s and 1960s had been aloof and arrogant and much resented. Now the situation was changing. The expat lifestyle was slowly converging with that of the Hong Kong-Chinese. There was no longer a gnawing feeling of that 'layer at the top'.

In area after area around the periphery of the city, I found an attitude of optimism-in-resignation that strongly resembled the views I had heard in San Po Kong. As one blue-collar worker said to me in Kwun Tong, he could entertain no illusions about escape routes. His financial circumstances were such that he could 'just about walk from day to day'. But even the nerves of people such as this were frayed by the endless series of hitches and delays in negotiations about the future. Always the doubts would be expressed obliquely, usually after a statement of full confidence in the future that was generally based on a belief that the Hong Kong economy would move from strength to strength. A partner in a small printing concern greeted me with a glass of coffee at a traditional working-class café. His business since I had first visited him two years before in 1984 had been good, very good. With contracts from two major international toymakers under their belt, he and his partners had taken over two more floors in their industrial building. I commented on the delays I had encountered on the way to the factory. Laughing, he observed that bumper-to-bumper traffic along the main road indicated a healthy flow of business. When the traffic was free-flowing and light, times were bad.

In the two years since I had last seen him he had not changed his mind about moving out of Hong Kong, even if he could. But he now saw a slight question mark over travel documents. It was not, he assured me, a worry. Rather, it was an irritation, an ambiguity. He had thought that his CI would automatically convert to the new SAR document. There was little clarification, he complained, of the rights of CI holders. Also, all the middle-class talk of emigration was a worry, but he was sure all those leaving would be back. About 30 per cent of his own social circle had left, or were making plans to do so soon, or were placing their families abroad. I asked him how this compared with 1967 (when the last major exodus occurred). About 20–30 per cent of his circle had sold their flats very cheaply then and moved away from Hong Kong; but most of them had subsequently returned. Not many were considering leaving again, he said: most had already made provisions for residence overseas in the wake of the 1967 disturbances.

The most carefree people I met in the course of my travels were the rural inhabitants of the New Territories. As an acquaintance told me, they had every reason to be: whereas the status of their properties before the Joint Declaration was far from certain, it was now firmly established for at least fifty years beyond 1997. On the other hand, people and companies who owned property in the areas ceded to Britain in perpetuity had seen their 75-, 99- and 999-year leases reduced to the same fifty-year span.

But even here the situation was not altogether clear-cut. By early 1987 all the small villages in the New Territories had moved to one side of the political fence, becoming either pro-British or pro-Communist. For these villages the future seemed straightforward, but this was not the case with the larger settlements made up of the bigger extended families in the areas of Saikung, Sha Tau Kok and Taipo. The villages here were in the midst of a great power struggle. Part of the problem was that the indigenous population in the New Territories had been particularly well treated by the British in the early years and, later, by the Hong Kong Government. The villagers felt that they had a special status which they expected to be perpetuated under Chinese sovereignty too. So far, however, China had remained silent, despite frequent representations to Beijing by the Heung Yee Kuk, the principal rural association.

In any event, the rural population seemed to have embarked on a policy of self-help some time ago. A member of a small village that had opted to side with Britain explained that his extended family had done very well from the special relationship they had cultivated over the years. Large numbers of MPs had visited the village, each of them entertained by lavish celebrations and given 'red banners of friendship' to take back to Britain. In return the MPs would frequently leave bottles of whisky and presentation glasses with the villagers. There was enough whisky in the village, he said, to start a bar! Most of the young men had gone to Britain, leaving the village in the charge of the elderly residents. Many of the village elders had themselves lived in Britain, where they had taken advantage of the pension and welfare system and returned to Hong Kong to avoid punitive taxation.

Although there were few breadwinners living in it, the village was well off, and none of the empty houses had to be sold or rented to outsiders. Very few New Territories villages, my informant added, could afford the luxury of keeping themselves populated exclusively by their extended families. When I asked how this had been possible, he replied that it was purely due to remittances from family members in Britain. He had no great worries, in fact no worries at all, about nationality or travel documents. Why should he have? With so many of his family permanently settled in Britain, it would not be difficult for him to join them. When I had last spoken to him in 1984, he had been accompanied by his younger sister. She had subsequently married and moved to Britain. This man was full of optimism for the future, and of faith in the idea of 'one country, two systems'. Indeed, he went so far as to express the hope that there would soon be full and direct elections to the Legislative Council *and* to the post of chief executive (the Governor), wishes that I had not heard expressed by even the most fervent of urban democrats. I marvelled at the optimistic outlook that a little freedom of movement and choice could achieve!

A less happy frame of mind is to be found in the essential services, and especially the police force. At one time, and especially in the 1960s, policemen were among the happiest people in Hong Kong. *Restaurateurs* lucky enough to have establishments near the larger police stations remember those halcyon days with a sense of great nostalgia. Officers came in for a long lunch a few times a week, always starting with dozens of Sydney rock oysters flown in fresh by air. But the government's vigorous actions against corruption in the 1970s had taken a great deal of the sparkle out of the officers' lives. Moreover, the subsequent collapse in morale had affected honest and corrupt alike.

The force never really recovered from those body blows. The

eighties brought with them wave after wave of uncertainty which, for the police, was particularly pointed. Chinese officers who were serving at the time of the 1967 riots feared that the coming of Chinese sovereignty would bring with it the settling of scores by left-wing activists who had been on the receiving end of police action during the riots. Potential recruits had to think twice about entering a service which, more than any other branch of authority, might be seen by the Chinese authorities as being synonymous with the enforcement of colonialism.

The only sure antidote to such worries was for the British Government to issue a blanket assurance of resettlement in Britain, should the need arise. Anxieties had been only partially assuaged by Britain's concession that a limited number of people serving in 'sensitive positions' in the Hong Kong Government would receive entry permits. As a result most Chinese officers are highly nervous. One observer close to the force fears that the consequence will be the emergence of a 'last train syndrome', which will see the police and Triad organizations gradually closing ranks as both attempt to make money out of drugs, prostitution, indeed *anything*, before the popular deadline of 1995. A very senior Chinese superintendent put the point very simply. If he did not get a full passport, or was able to purchase similar rights somewhere by 1995, he said, he would come down to Kai Tak (the airport) with a group of armed police officers and take a plane at gunpoint to Taiwan, considered by most as a sanctuary of last resort.

British officers, on the other hand, were becoming restive about their prospects of promotion and the safety of their pensions. As the uncertainty dragged on, so their spirits declined. Two years after the signing of the Joint Declaration, British officers complained to me that everything was still in the air. Questions such as at what age they would become eligible for a pension and what exchange rate was to be used to calculate the pensions remained unanswered. There was, they said, 'confusion at the top' about these questions. As for promotion, the policy of promoting local people was being pursued avidly 'without rhyme or reason' in their eyes. Fears were expressed about British officers who might be in line for promotion, but would find themselves 'pipped on merit' by Chinese officers of the same rank. Localization here, as in the Civil Service, had already begun to make foreign staff feel isolated and alienated as their numbers shrank day by day. Sitting in a near-deserted officers' mess on the top floor of Police Headquarters, I had a beer with a member of the old guard whom I had first met in the 1960s. We were joined by a former officer who had retired recently and taken up a civilian appointment in government. The barman, having served the beers, returned to his GF200, a form that had to be filled out by all minor government employees, the ex-policeman said. He went on: 'For years people have been working in Police Headquarters without a security check. Now they have to fill in an incredibly detailed form usually used for people applying for government itself.'

The barman seemed exasperated. The form asked him for his primary and secondary schools. His primary 'school' had been a small, cramped place literally thrown together on a hillside, while secondary education consisted of 'a month here, a month there'. As he shook his head ruefully, he said that all the staff were unhappy about the form: other employers only required an identity card number. Here they wanted to know about grandparents, step-parents, relatives abroad, social groups and, if applicable, a list of convictions. I wondered to myself how he felt about the fact that all this detailed information might then be available to the new powers-that-be.

We turned to a postcard view of the city many floors below us. My companions spoke of the development plans that lay in store for the surrounding area. Two new multi-storey structures were planned for Police Headquarters: 'Who will we put in them?' asked the policeman. 'The PLA (China's People's Liberation Army), eventually,' came the response.

Across the street was *HMS Tamar*, the remaining bastion of Britain's naval power in Hong Kong. The officer mentioned that there was much pressure to level the site. Government, he added, had become keen on rehousing its people and selling property. There was an air of futility in these remarks, as if the game had been lost and my companions were only marking time, looking forward to an uneventful retirement. And in many respects these men had been outpaced by events. For all the years the police officer had served in Hong Kong, which included a long stretch in the New Territories, the border between China and the colony had been rigidly enforced. Now, he observed, the situation there was fairly fluid. Chinese officers were seconded for a time in both directions. Hong Kong officers returning from Guangzhou and Shenzhen reported that the police in those two towns 'just can't wait to get their hands on Hong

Kong'. And of the future? 'I hope it will work here,' he said, more in resignation than in hope.

He then returned to the theme of a world we had both lived in at one time, revelling in finding tiny corners that reminded him of the life he had once enjoyed. He pointed along the western seaboard to the 'old world' character of the China Town in Western District where, he said, police inspectors lived in a world of their own. He also looked across the harbour to the old Kowloon Headquarters building, now deserted for new modern premises at the corner of Kowloon Park. The old building, on a tree-lined hillock, had resumed its former slow-moving, comfortable character as the Marine Police Headquarters.

While we spoke, the police were preparing to deal a crippling blow to Hong Kong's organized crime network, the Triad societies, which had, if anything, increased their grip on society since the 1960s. Today they may best be described as a hybrid of Masonic lodge, Cosa Nostra, mutual aid association and multinational corporation. In April 1986 a report was produced on the Triad problem. It described the difficulties of isolating the nature of organized crime and identified a daunting number of loopholes and inadequacies in existing legislation that inhibited effective investigation and prosecution. Proposals were made to tighten up legislation, particularly where the protection of witnesses was concerned, including, for example, the introduction of one-way mirrors on identification parades. Some experienced former policemen viewed even measures such as these as being ultimately ineffective. One of these men put the problem into a personal context: 'What's the use of all this? When I was working to smash an opium ring, a woman that I had just started going out with, who lived in a totally different area from me, very quickly got a visit from some men. They threatened her aged father and promised to smash up her house if I continued to press against the opium people. How did they find out who she was and where she lived?'

It was precisely the all-pervasive multinational character of the Triad operations that appeared, at least partially, to be behind the renewed efforts against the societies by the police. This impression was reinforced by an interview I conducted in late January 1987 with the officer in overall charge of anti-Triad work. I wanted to fathom how the Sino-British agreement on the 1997 issue might affect the Triads, and asked whether he had noticed any differences

in the structure and activities of the Triads since the Joint Declaration. 'There will not be a massive exodus of Triads out of Hong
Kong by 1997, that's for sure,' he replied, barely waiting for me to
finish.

Obviously he had suffered much flack about the much publicized
spillover of Triad operations to the United States, Canada and
Australia. He produced a photocopy of an article from a San
Francisco newspaper about the pernicious effect of the societies on
California. Dismissing the article as being more fable than fact, he
pointed to a number of inaccuracies, suggesting that its author did
not know what he was talking about. The article isolated the United
Bamboo Gang as being particularly active there and stated that it
was Hong Kong based. '(The) Chuk Luen Bong, to put it correctly,'
he said with an air of authority, 'is Taiwanese. . . . That has nothing
to do with us. It's an American responsibility, pure and simple.'

Nor, according to him, did Hong Kong's proximity to the Golden
Triangle make it an automatic centre for the drug trade. Organized
crime and Triads are in every country in Asia. As the officer told me
this, one of his earlier comments about the Triads and 1997 came to
mind: 'On July 1st 1997, we're not going to bring prisoners convicted of murder out of their cells and put a .49 into their brains.' In
most other Asian countries, convicted drug dealers are executed. If
the penalties in Hong Kong remain less severe, would this not suggest that the colony might remain a haven and centre of control for
safety-conscious drug dealers? And would China, with its far
harsher attitude to drugs, do anything to change this situation?
According to the Joint Declaration, Hong Kong's lawmakers will
make up their own minds after 1997. I began to wonder if this would
be a sufficient guarantee to the Triads themselves. If it was not,
1995 – a year which some regard as being as popular with gangsters
as with policemen – might take on greater relevance for them.

In the course of the interview, a sobering, perhaps even frightening image of the nature of the Triads' influence in the colony
emerged. The Triad organization is very fluid. It demands no day-
by-day duties of its members, who are free to do what they like.
Only when they are required to fight are they summoned by the
leaders. Some of the more structured organizations have local managers to co-ordinate the mustering of ranks. Also, there is no strict
geographical distribution of Triads. If they are not feuding, a number
of organizations can share the running of a building, a business,

even a single nightclub. In the case of the nightspots, this is often done through shift work: the bouncer working during the day can be from one society, the evening shift bouncer from another. The man outside selling overpriced flowers 'for the lady' can be from a third. In addition, organizations frequently co-operate on individual ventures. This makes it impossible for the police to concentrate on a particular district in their efforts to knock out a Triad gang.

Nor is there a preserve of Triad activity. Triads are the 'muscle behind drugs' the policeman told me, but are not the only ones who deal in them. With the growing tendency for drug shipments to arrive in smaller quantities, he said, so the funds required to back them financially become smaller too. Triad money is in fact found connected with the most unlikely projects. For some years the government gave aid on housing by providing the framework for a one-storey building and also the funds for the occupant to complete the work. Seeing an opportunity for profit, the Triads began to make bulk purchases of building materials and then sold them to the occupants at a hefty profit. Although the police told the government of their suspicions, no action was taken until the police put up a couple to purchase the materials at inflated prices. Only then, with the evidence in their hands, did the authorities change their policy.

Triad finances, it is clear, is another grey area. Money is sometimes shifted quickly from bank account to bank account, with between HK$20–30 million residing in each of these for only a few weeks. The overall picture of each account is that it is empty. Alternatively, the money might find its way into a front operation such as a restaurant, which is not seen as being suspicious, and then be used to finance drugs. The Inland Revenue Department makes the tracing of these funds more difficult still by discouraging access to bank accounts and tax returns, unless the police can produce a suitable reason for such an investigation to take place. Nor is it likely that the police will be able to achieve the necessary changes. America has long been upset by the fact that Hong Kong allows people to bring in suitcases of money and deposit them on bank counters with no questions asked. There are, the policeman pointed out, practical – and with the signing of the Joint Declaration, political – reasons why the government is not keen on acting to limit the freedom of movement of money. Also, he said, the banks enjoy the profits on money deposited in this way.

Triad gangs are quick to make full use of modern technology in increasing the efficiency of their illegal pursuits. When radio pagers became widely available in the early 1980s, the police pressed the government for control of their issue and, in particular, permission to prevent known Triads from using them. The request was, to quote the policeman, 'laughed out of court'. Yet the pager became the single most potent device for rallying up to 150 'soldiers' for battles with rival gangs. The uphill struggle was to continue with the arrival of small, wireless telephones!

The Triads represented just one of many daunting obstacles faced by the police, yet the officer was sure that they would be dealt a body blow in the next few years. How was this to happen? A number of his detectives had infiltrated the 14K Society, leading to a test case in which the success of prosecution was due to the testimony of these 'plants'. The overall goal was, he concluded, to 'aim at the very top of the more established organized groups', while conserving on manpower by dealing with the smaller societies in a conventional way. Why, I asked, had this process not been initiated sooner? The answer was a classic example of colonial one-upmanship: 'We don't have a point system here. Unlike the UK, there isn't a "Richter Scale", the bottom of which is "record only". . . . Here, whether it is one dollar that is stolen or a million, we investigate it.'

I was able to savour the irony of this answer a few hours later. In the morning paper, which I had not had time to read before the interview, was an item warning that another Triad war was brewing. A gang of men had entered a bathhouse at noon, smashing it up with axes and terrorizing staff and customers. The bathhouse was located a few yards down the road from Police Headquarters.

With fractures and fissures developing in Hong Kong society, it was striking that the Shanghainese and Shanghailanders seemed to be taking all this in their stride, as if they had seen it all before. With good reason. Through the cracks that appeared in everyday life rose spectres of the disintegration of Shanghai, with memories of the Chinese Communists' attempts to inspire confidence and gain wide support in the city. There had been diverse, and often confused, interpretations of what the future held: some thought there was no choice but to leave; others that they could bribe their way out of difficulties, as they had done so often in the past, and perhaps even establish a working relationship with their new masters; many felt increasingly confused and frustrated as conditions deteriorated.

In Shanghai the Communists had spoken of their government's

wish that capitalism and socialism co-exist, assuring worried capitalists that their property and businesses were safe, guaranteed by the administration's need of taxes derived from capitalist endeavour. Two years later, punitive taxation, forced transfer of title deeds to the government and the confiscation of suburban property – classified as 'semi-rural' after the introduction of wide-scale land reform – had ensured that western-style business was squeezed out of existence.

In the case of Hong Kong, the Joint Declaration provides extensive written guarantees of non-interference in these essential areas for at least half a century after 1997. It is also frequently stated that the Chinese cadres themselves are more sophisticated, more responsive to the delicate nature of a capitalist enclave than were their predecessors in Shanghai. No doubt this is right. But business people point to other ways in which the Chinese cadres may do irreparable damage. Hong Kong companies involved with mainland Chinese agencies worry about senior Chinese officials brought to the colony for wining and dining. These officials will often stay for a fortnight rather than just a few days. Mainland Chinese middle managers, when visiting Hong Kong, normally require first-class hotel rooms and expect to be presented with television sets (often of a particular make), and with large numbers of tickets to popular variety shows. This leads to a rise of 10 per cent in the projected costs of a contract. Such 'indirect taxation' threatens the competitiveness of the firms concerned just as much as rises in formal taxation would.

And the gulf between the lifestyles of prosperous people in Hong Kong and Chinese officials is enormous. Although the distinctive cotton boiler suits in blue, black or grey which the Communists sported in Shanghai, and the blue cotton drill trousers and severe white shirts adopted by the Maoists during the 1967 disturbances have been replaced by western-style dress designed to suggest dramatic changes in attitude, what ranks as well-dressed in Beijing is seen as cheap in Hong Kong. By comparison with Hong Kong civil servants, senior Chinese personnel appear to be paupers. In a typically Hong Kong frame of reference, a high-ranking Chinese official 'can't afford to gamble at the racecourse or buy silk stockings for his girlfriend, if he has one'.

While senior officials at China's 'consular' offices exist on paltry Beijing salaries, their locally appointed juniors are on 'reverse expat terms', being paid competitive salaries in Hong Kong dollars. Both groups are comparatively better off than the rank and file in China itself, the result being a three-tier scale of affluence which many regard as an insuperable obstacle to successful integration.

There is also a hint of the fear which began to take hold of Shanghai's Chinese middle classes within months of liberation. There, Chinese who had at one time subscribed to foreign magazines stopped doing so. Information about the outside world was obtained from quiet conversations with foreign acquaintances. Gradually even this practice became inadvisable.

Soon after the Sino-British agreement had been initialled, I was invited by some Chinese friends to a meal in Tsim Sha Tsui East, a recently-developed area of hotels and shopping malls. The restaurant was elegantly decorated in red and gold, with tables covered by snow-white cloths and laid with fine porcelain, ornate silver-plated utensils and ivory chopsticks. We were led to our table by a slim female maître d'hôtel in a long silky *cheong saam*, with a slit on either side that seemed to reach to her waist. It was a picture of Hong Kong gastronomic chic. Dish after dish was immaculately presented and served by a waiter who seemed never to leave our side, each course being brought to him by assistant waiters and waitresses in humbler coloured garb. As we ate, conversation turned, as it invariably did and does, to 1997. I made a funny but mildly critical comment about Deng Xiaoping, raising my voice as I did so. A tiny warning signal was triggered in my mind: was anyone around us listening? I needed no further proof of what Hong Kong had lost in being transferred to Chinese sovereignty. Freedom of speech can be written into legislation and guaranteed over and over again, but exercising this right is a far more delicate task.

Since then, the chances of someone overhearing a conversation, a careless remark, have increased. As more and more mainland Chinese use Hong Kong as a business centre, holiday camp and duty-free shop, so it becomes more important to maintain tact and discretion in discussing sensitive political matters. Moreover, some have already noticed that the mainland Chinese presence is changing in character. By early 1986 there were comments that the structure of the New China News Agency organization was beginning to resemble a shadow cabinet. At a lower level, an inhabitant told me of transformations taking place in the running of the many mainland-Chinese emporia throughout the colony. As senior management retires, it is being replaced by Party members from China itself.

This trend, my informant said, was causing much distress. The waterfront in Western District, the area my policeman friend described as Chinatown, is taking on the appearance of being just that: mainland-Chinese terrain, where groups of Chinese hungry for consumer goods move wide-eyed and acquisitively from shop to shop before boarding vessels bound for Guangzhou at a nearby pier.

The presence of these 'northern neighbours', as they are known, already inhibits free speech in some quarters. The more timid are now reluctant to voice criticisms of the powers that be in Hong Kong lest their views block some future avenue of escape. One such man, active in local politics and well-known in smarter circles, cautiously enquired about some criticisms I had made publicly about Margaret Thatcher and the British Government's nationality legislation: 'Your point concerning a full passport being given to everyone that needs or wants one is good. Do you think it is too idealistic?' I said that it was not so much a matter of idealism as principle. He then continued: 'What you have said (about Thatcher): do you think there will be any repercussions?'

From the tone of his voice it was clear that he meant that he was thinking of effects on me personally. I laughed the question off, but understood the frame of mind that encouraged such fears. For the next hour or two, he spoke quite freely about what he saw as British shortcomings, of a close relation's move to Australia, which he regarded as 'too parochial, slow', and the lack of faith in the future amongst *all* professional classes. Paradoxically, however, he also said that people believe China is sincere when it says that it wishes to maintain stability and prosperity in the colony. Nearing the end of our chat, he made an impassioned plea: 'Please don't quote me! I may decide to emigrate at some stage.'

The conversation brought to mind an observation from a former civil servant, now dividing his time between Hong Kong and London. There is much anxiety, much suffering, he said. Most people, however, will not say anything about the difficult decisions they are making, or their innermost fears.

A further facet of this undercurrent of disquiet was revealed by the experiences of The Hong Kong Freedom of Movement and Rights of Abode Ltd. Located next to the offices of GEC on the fifteenth floor of a modern building on the east side of Hong Kong Island, the company has seen a long stream of humanity seeking advice and help on emigration. The young man who runs the office described the heartaches and pitfalls encountered by people who were searching for safety nets, often with incomplete information and the risk of being cheated by unscrupulous lawyers and the many immigration 'experts' that have set up shop to take advantage of the demand for visas. Although most of those who approach these agents and agencies stand little chance of getting a visa, they will none the less proceed with an application, having been assured that they will get their money back if the effort fails. The hapless clients will often pay out a first instalment of 2500 American or Canadian dollars for the initial 'application and investigation', and then a further $2500 when their applications are submitted. A further $2500 is payable for a medical examination, the balance, making up a total of $10,000, once the visa is received. If the application is unsuccessful, there is no refund. The would-be emigrants are told 'But you haven't failed yet. There is still the appeal.'

Thus, unscrupulous individuals who have already pocketed $7500 force their clients onto the treadmill of fresh applications and appeals. In other cases, lawyers insist that their clients purchase houses, businesses and furnishings in the country of resettlement in advance of their applications. It is not uncommon for the lawyers to have acted as proxy buyers or brokers in the transaction, and they will often be the guardians of the assets. If the purchasers are lucky, the businesses they buy into are viable. If they are unlucky, they may find themselves with concerns that have 'one-and-a-half feet in the grave', or become minority shareholders in ventures where the majority shareholder has built up a shell and left that to his 'junior partner', pocketing the profit in the process.

Most of those who approach Freedom of Movement are from the prosperous professional classes. Some poorer people approach the company too, but they are told that their chances of emigration are slim unless they have family resident overseas or their circumstances change. For a fee of HK$500, they are promised that their case will be investigated and the file will be kept open for a year. After that, their application will not be renewed. At times, the manager of Freedom of Movement told me, circumstances do change, as in the case of a 'no-hoper' who won first prize in a popular lottery and immediately emigrated. There are also examples of those who emigrate returning because they are unsuccessful overseas. One such man, a building contractor who did very well before the collapse in property prices in 1982, went to America to resettle. There he

193

bought an ineffective supermarket. Because it was making no money, he decided to dilute his losses by buying another, and another. Finally, he bought an entire chain of supermarkets. And still he failed to realize a profit. Dejected, he returned to Hong Kong: 'I can't afford to live there', he said grimly.

The people who approach Freedom of Movement are worried and nervous. Many of them search for microphones in the manager's room and have to be reassured that everything said is in strict confidence. They have, the manager said, 'no faith in anything'. Often there is also a fear of the 'loss of face' they would suffer if they were rejected at the interview for the visa; applicants have to be convinced that it will be a one-to-one situation and that they would lose face only to their own family. And there are many who come to Freedom of Movement as a last resort, having already done the rounds of immigration lawyers without making any headway: 'What they often come in for is to hear what they want to hear. . . . If they don't, they frequently get upset.' The work is not without its humorous side. The manager recalled a man who limped into the main office. When he entered the 'inner sanctum' of the interview room, he angrily took off an artificial leg and slammed it down on the desk: 'There, that is what the Communists have done to me! I want to leave!'

With Freedom of Movement, and in general, the emphasis of emigration has changed. Between 1983 and 1985 people sought passports and visas with the intention of escaping quickly and then coming back in due course. In 1985 people began to be interested in staying abroad and waiting to see what would happen after 1997 before deciding how to proceed. Mini-crises help to spur the faint-hearted into precipitate action. In 1985, when the democratization issue first became a major concern, Xu Jiatun, the Chinese representative in Hong Kong – and a former mayor of Shanghai – waved a copy of the Joint Declaration in the presence of a group of reporters, saying that Britain was in danger of breaking the agreement. Freedom of Movement immediately had a rash of enquiries from people who said they wanted to leave straight away. Equally, the controversy over the Daya Bay nuclear power plant precipitated another series of telephone enquiries. Of these, one was particularly memorable. A man called to say that he did not want to wake up one morning with an atomic bomb beside him: 'I don't want to be carried up by an atomic cloud.' 'But this project is to be completed only in 1992, even if there is a danger of an explosion.' 'Yes, but papers take time to get. Before you know it, it is already 1990. And then there are only two years to prepare!'

There seem to be few efforts to foster a spirit of understanding and co-operation. The preoccupations of the mainland Chinese are largely a closed book to the people of Hong Kong and the Communists in their turn are still far from appreciating the innermost sentiments of the Hong Kong Chinese. This yawning cultural gap is beautifully illustrated by an anecdote that I heard from a Chinese banker friend in Hong Kong. A Communist Chinese climbs into a taxi and makes light conversation with the driver: 'Do you think that China will be better than Hong Kong one day?' 'Sure', replies the driver, 'when the people of Hong Kong start swimming over to China.' Here, in a nutshell, is the same dilemma that faced Shanghai forty years earlier. Then the Communist Chinese were anxious to bolster the confidence of their captive Shanghai capitalists as they saw mutually beneficial coexistence as a way of helping the motherland with the task of national reconstruction. Hard-nosed capitalists, on the other hand, cynically scrutinized the Communist cadres for evidence of human weakness and perfidy. What was missing then – as it is now – was any sign of genuine co-operation.

Despite the remarkable advances that China has made in adapting to reformist ideas since the downfall of Maoist ideology, the situation in Hong Kong is still a curious blend of socialist idealism and uncompromising capitalist realism. Some might say that blending oil and water would be no more difficult. And yet China has made unprecedented efforts to defuse people's anxieties, with the detailed guarantees written into the Joint Declaration, increased investment in the local economy, and frequent reassurances by all levels of the Chinese leadership that all will be well after 1997. In all of this China has gone well beyond anything it offered Shanghai capitalists in 1949. None the less, much to China's consternation, far too many people in Hong Kong consider these efforts insufficient or, more goading still, almost irrelevant. The Communists are both irritated and confused: it is as if the people they are dealing with are Chinese and, at the same time, not Chinese.

For the people of the colony there is no cause for optimism. The abstract concept of 'one country, two systems' has no place in the concrete vision of a person such as the Shanghainese Mr Y, who considers Hong Kong in its present form would survive a maximum of three years under Chinese control. Deng Xiaoping and his Communists might be interested in Hong Kong. They may speak about Hong Kong issues. They may shake hands with Hong Kong's representatives, 'with genuine intentions, perhaps'. But they have no time for Hong Kong. Even if the leadership issues directives like Mao did, these will only be translated into effective policy if they are closely followed up. And how much time does the Chinese leadership have to devote to Hong Kong every day?

For Mr Y, the future looks bleak, and he feels that the status and dignity of his family are being threatened. His children are already overseas: one studying in Australia, the other working as a nanny in America. She works, he said, for $700 a week, but this could be seen as nothing but a diversion. What if this had to be a permanent job? What sort of profession would that be? His children, his friends' children would have to start as dishwashers in Chinese restaurants, with no self-respect, no pride in their work. It would be just a living. Whether they needed it or not, he gave his children a lump sum to bank, to give them the reassurance of *something* in reserve. Without this money, he thought, the children may feel 'cold'. Far from looking forward optimistically to a prosperous future under the new arrangements with China, Mr Y daily faces a choice: whether to move with insufficient capital to guarantee a dignified life in a calm, friendly environment or to stay and 'risk losing everything . . . worked for since 1949'. Neither the latest balm from China nor the most promising of local economic forecasts are likely to break through such a wall of doubt. This is the impregnable heart of 'Fortress Hong Kong'.

CHAPTER ELEVEN

Mouldering Pearl

O n the eve of the last decade of British rule, Hong Kong was deep in a crisis of confidence. On the night of 4 December 1986, the Governor, Sir Edward Youde, died of a massive heart attack at the British Embassy in Beijing. Although he had a history of heart complaint, Youde had latterly operated as a roving ambassador of trade in addition to his gruelling work with the Sino-British negotiations. His trip to Beijing had been associated with a Trade Development Council event, as well as with political matters.

The news of his sudden death shocked the colony to its core. In his short but very full time in office, Youde had earned considerable respect and trust from a wide cross-section of the population. But the circumstances surrounding his untimely end were extremely unfortunate. To a highly superstitious population, Youde's death was associated with the worst of omens. A young woman explained to me why this should have been so. To those who believe in omens, his death in a hospital bed in Hong Kong would have been bad enough; to have died away from home territory was a terrible sign, and to have died in Beijing suggested the ascendance and longevity of the Chinese leadership. For people who interpreted Margaret Thatcher's unfortunate tumble in Beijing in 1982 as indicating weakness, Youde's death was a disaster. The young woman told me that she had had no intention of emigrating, but that the bad omens had caused her to change her mind and she had decided to apply for American papers.

In the days and weeks that followed, the Chinese press relentlessly sifted the information concerning the Governor's death. It became known that Youde had met Premier Zhao Ziyang the day before he died. The Chinese leader had kept him waiting outside in the chill Beijing winter air well after the designated time of the appointment. That evening there had been further talks and an official dinner. According to reporters milling around, waiting for a quote, the sessions had not gone well. They had asked the Governor about the meetings and received only a faint smile in response. Some of their number had composed a rhyme: 'The Governor said nothing. We lose face, because we can send back nothing.'

The Governor's death, it was reported, had been conspicuous by the associated confusion. A foreign doctor had been summoned by the embassy. Later, a Chinese doctor was brought in and it was he who pronounced Youde dead. There had been, it was said, no careful examination or autopsy. The Chinese press talked of white 'death spots' on the Governor's body, which implied that he had died much earlier than reported. Conjecture was heightened by the fact that the body was brought back to Hong Kong in a HK$21,000 coffin, built as a 'spontaneous gesture' by the Chinese authorities. The casket, contrary to Chinese custom, was not kept open for senior government officials to pay their last respects. One Chinese friend said that this implied that the Governor 'must have died a horrible death'.

The tension extended to Hong Kong's officialdom. In addition to the eulogies on the day the sad news broke, there was also a stream of reassurances. A senior government man said that he thought that the Governor had not been under particular strain 'because he never looked as being under stress. . . . He was a fast worker.' Ronald Li, the head of the unified stock market, suggested that Youde's death would not affect the political situation unduly because everything had been done and the system leading to 1997 was 'in action'.

The stock market supremo, who is now awaiting trial on a number of allegations of corruption, was not quite on the mark. The Hong Kong Government had embarked upon the formulation of an eagerly awaited new Green Paper on electoral reform, a document which had already become the focus of considerable controversy, both between liberal and conservative elements in the colony itself and between the Chinese leadership and its representatives in Hong Kong. Untimely outbursts by senior Chinese officials about the unsuitability of a western style of democracy, together with equally unfortunate hints from British parliamentarians that they were in favour of substantially broadening Hong Kong's democratic base, had left the Hong Kong authorities in an untenable situation.

Youde had a crucial role to play in reaching a generally acceptable compromise that would not leave the Hong Kong Government appearing a 'lame duck' administration. During his time in office, the Governor had gained respect and had also become adept at knowing how far each side could be pushed in finding a credible position. Unlike some of his predecessors, Youde was known for his democratic instincts and was regarded by some highly placed politicians I talked to as having been the major driving force behind the efforts to bring greater democracy to the colony, even if this conflicted with Chinese ideas. Paradoxically, such instincts often reduced Youde's standing in the eyes of the person on the street, many of whom still cling to the traditional Chinese notion that the person at the top should be all-powerful, and seen to be so.

To such people, MacLehose was the ideal benign authoritarian, a view which probably came closer to the truth than they will ever know. A retired senior civil servant told me he was once telephoned by MacLehose when he was working at district level. The Governor said that it was important that there should be some grassroots representation within Legco and that the government should appear to be encouraging such participation. The civil servant was instructed, quite simply, to 'get some'. A suitable person was finally produced: well-intentioned, capable, but with little grasp of English. As a result, this grassroots representative had to be briefed on all the council's reports and proposals, as at that time there was no provision for translation into Chinese.

In contrast to MacLehose, although Youde was regarded as being an essentially good man, whose knowledge of the Chinese language and informal contacts with Chinese representatives were invaluable, he was also seen by many of those I spoke to as 'weak'. A middle-aged blue-collar worker told me he had formed this view at the stormy Legco session on the proposed Daya Bay project. One councillor, he said, had referred to the government as having 'licked the boots' (literally 'shined the shoes') of the Chinese authorities, a piece of contempt which should have been severely reprimanded: '(He should have been) sent out immediately . . . it was within his (the Governor's) powers'. When the Governor comes into the Legco Chamber, all the members rise to their feet to show their respect to the chief executive. How could a councillor be allowed to take such a liberty? Surely it clearly demonstrated the Governor's weakness.

A few weeks after Youde's death, an official involved in drawing up the Green Paper told me that his absence would leave a major gap, as there was no one with similar knowledge or expertise who would be able to steer the document along its treacherous course. Even within the confines of the office where we spoke, I could sense the depths to which the government's morale had sunk. The present Green Paper had to a large degree been dictated by its predecessor, which contained many ideas which were now too radical. The problem was how to produce legislation which was both generally acceptable and could be seen to give some 'teeth' to the Hong Kong Government.

I heard this point again from a member of a pressure group: if the legislation's wording was not strong enough, this would prove that the government was lame, folding under the pressure of Chinese wishes. People would then feel that the sell-out was continuing, and that they were right to be pessimistic about the future. But because China had raised the issue of the Joint Declaration and its reference to elections, it had become impossible to institute electoral change which was not specifically provided for in that document. At the same time, the Joint Declaration had also promised that the government would institute steps to open up the electoral process. The matter had been further complicated, in so far as this was possible, by the fact that any legislation produced had to 'converge' with the drafting of the Basic Law, which was China's responsibility. Moreover, the first draft of the Basic Law was not due to be completed until well after the deadline for the Green Paper.

There was also the difficulty of testing public opinion about the proposed options. A recent poll conducted by an English-language newspaper had announced that elections and politics were well below items such as housing on the population's list of priorities. Newspapers and journals, however, were dominated by radical editorials and articles about the issue, suggesting a much greater level of concern than was apparent from the poll. There was even a clear split between the attitudes of the Chinese and English-language press, with some of the former being against direct elections and a proportion reserving judgement so as, the government official said, to be able to slot into the correct line under the future SAR. Because of these cautious views English-language newspapers seemed to be more sensational in their approach. The government official's fear was that a fierce debate would be conducted at a rarified level, making the question of elections a raging political issue without their being any bona fide popular political platform.

It was clear from what had been said that those drafting the Green Paper faced an impossible dilemma. There was also little doubt that the democratic lobby's battle had already been lost. I volunteered my view that the first significant step towards the introduction of direct elections should have been taken before the signing of the Joint Declaration, when the Chinese authorities were trying to muster maximum support in the colony and were propagating the slogan of 'Hong Kong people ruling Hong Kong'. At that time a move to direct elections could have been proposed at face value, as a natural adjunct to China's own proposals. The official nodded, agreeing with my reflections.

The situation had been further complicated a few weeks after Youde's death, when China found itself in the grip of scenes of protest on a scale not seen since the Cultural Revolution. Thousands of students took to the streets in major cities, demanding greater democracy, human rights and an end to bureaucratism. Although the marches were in support of Deng Xiaoping, they soon caused a conservative backlash, in the form of a campaign against 'bourgeois liberalism', so insistent that in January it brought down the Party General Secretary Hu Yaobang, one of Deng's main reformists. His fall had a profound effect on Hong Kong: despite his over-exuberant ways, he had become an important symbol of China's adaptation to the West. He was the first of the Chinese leaders to openly wear western business suits and had even advocated the use of western cutlery in preference to 'unhygienic' chopsticks. More than that, however, this episode reminded Hong Kong of the unstable nature of Chinese politics and of the vulnerability – and mortality – of the Grand Reformer himself.

At the height of the December demonstrations, an analyst of Chinese and Hong Kong affairs postulated the effects of a change of leadership in China. If it was peaceful, there would be a temporary fall of 300 points on the stock market. If Deng died in his sleep or was shot, the market would fall by over 500 points. The situation in Hong Kong then might or might not be salvaged by the British Prime Minister contacting the Chinese Foreign Minister and asking him to reaffirm the Joint Declaration. If there was no clear outcome to the situation in China and it turned into a protracted conflict, perhaps even a civil war, *then* the 'Three Runs' would take place: people would run across the border into Hong Kong, people would run out of Hong Kong and the dollar would run. The result would be disaster.

Although the situation in China stabilized quite rapidly, with the favoured Zhao Ziyang taking over from Hu, Hong Kong continued to be worried by its northern neighbour. That summer there was a sustained campaign in the press and by a number of Legco members against a government plan to enact legislation that would allow it to ban films considered 'seriously prejudicial to good relations with territories outside Hongkong'. Hong Kong censors had for many years excluded films that might upset China. Nevertheless, formal censorship by government decree was regarded as the thin end of a wedge that might eventually be used in other media too. Indeed, a revised public order ordinance that allowed the authorities to prosecute publications that transmitted 'false news' was used by some critics as evidence that further controls were on the way.

The Green Paper appeared in May 1987. In its content and presentation, the document suggested that it was an exercise in damage limitation, presenting the public with a long, detailed list of often subtle options on which to make a decision. As with the Joint Declaration, the population was invited to submit opinions to a Survey Office overseen by two independent monitors. Similarly, as with the Joint Declaration, the assessment seemed destined to be an exercise in 'guided democracy', as the following telling anecdote shows. A now very senior government official was speaking to a Legislative Councillor about testing popular opinion on direct elections and about how the government would 'balance' opposing views. 'What if 50 per cent of the people,' the councillor asked the official, 'are in favour of elections and only a handful of industrialists and businessmen are against? Whose view would you accept for striking this "balance"?' 'It depends on *which* industrialists and businessmen were in the minority,' came the reply.

To ensure that the exercise sampled as large a body of opinion as possible, a private company was commissioned to conduct two independent surveys. The official survey produced a very large response: over 131,000 opinions were recorded by the Survey Office, as opposed to a mere 364 for the 1984 Green Paper and 2727 for the Joint Declaration. The results, however, were acrimoniously contested. The government concluded that opinion on the principle of direct elections was profoundly divided and that, in any event, a large number of those who favoured their introduction preferred that this should not be done in 1988 (a year favoured by the democracy lobby in order that the population might get used to the democratic process).

The democrats complained bitterly that the survey had been manipulated to achieve the desired result. First, while the Survey Office had accepted identical letters as proper written submissions, it had refused a petition signed by some 230,000 names, accompanied by identity card numbers, in support of direct elections. Second, the company carrying out its own surveys was said to have used unusually complicated and ambiguous questions that confused respondents. Three other market research companies had carried out their own polls and these, they said, had shown three to four times as many in favour of direct elections. There were comments too on the fact that the Survey Office's report was first seen by the Chinese Government, before being presented to Legco or the population. The row refused to die away, making an already troubled year more difficult.

Given the level of vehemence and bitter recrimination that the seemingly diluted nature of the Green Paper and the subsequent survey brought, it was inevitable that whatever positive proposals might derive from the exercise would be trampled under foot. They were. In the fury over direct elections an important, indeed historic, point was lost: the 1988 White Paper, while it delayed the introduction of direct elections until 1991, transformed Hong Kong from a colony into a 'non-sovereign territory'. The obscure Colonial Validities Act of 1865, the instrument by which Britain maintained its colonial legislative powers, required that the number of elected members in the Hong Kong legislature should be less than 50 per cent (and there is no differentiation between councillors brought in by direct or indirect election). Once that number was reached, however, Legco would be automatically transformed from a colonial to a representative legislature and would assume 'full power to make laws respecting the constitution, powers, and procedure of such legislature'. In essence, this meant that Legco would be empowered to make all laws with the exception of fiscal policy. Even that, however, could be brought within their ambit if enough elected members had a mind to do so.

The 1984 legislation, which provided for indirect elections by electoral colleges and functional constituencies comprised of professional bodies, had already raised the number of elected members in Legco to 42 per cent. The 1988 review had only to add two elected and remove two appointed places for the balance to shift to 50 per cent. This was quietly done. For the first time in their history, Legco members, who until then had served a purely consultative function, were provided with genuine powers. As important, however, the 1988 review fulfilled the promise made by the 1984 White Paper that the reforms should 'develop . . . a system of government the authority for which is firmly rooted in Hong Kong'. No official pronouncement had done more than hint at the possibility of direct elections in 1988. What was consistently promised was the further development of representative, but not democratic, government. Had Youde survived, he might have been able to force through the early introduction of a limited number of directly elected seats *in addition to* the institutional changes that were such a vital corollary to them: without a change in the balance of elected versus appointed seats, even a comparatively large number of directly elected councillors would have sat powerless in a colonial legislature. Indeed, it may well have been Youde's tenacity in pursuing a twin-pronged development that had provoked the annoyance displayed by the Chinese leadership on the eve of the Governor's death. Equally, it now seemed clear that what China feared most was not a genuinely Hong Kong-based legislature, but the premature appearance of political parties in the territory.

It is difficult to know if outspoken democrats knew of the direction in which the legislation was taking the colony's political system. When I spoke to Martin Lee in early 1987 he showed no knowledge of it. This had left me troubled at the time: his stirring talk of democratic rights was appealing, but ignored the question of what good the growing democratic voices in Legco would do if the actual mechanism of government, i.e. the relations between Legco and the bureaucracy, did not alter significantly. What advance would louder voices bring, especially as the Joint Declaration dictated that the essential system of government should remain the same? His answer was that of an idealist: that when the voices get loud enough they will be the basis, might be the basis, for institutional change. How was this to occur, I asked him. His answer was nothing more than a shrug of the shoulders.

Lee remained true to his principles when the matter of elections was debated in the House of Commons in February 1988 and then the White Paper itself was debated in Legco in mid March. With little chance of altering the proposed changes, Lee and his fellow demo-crats made last-ditch attempts to sway the British Government's thinking. In the course of his quixotic mission, Lee frequently employed a lurid image to convey what he saw as a betrayal: 'The sun will set . . . in Hong Kong on the 30th June 1997 with shame because of what has been done to us by the British Government.'

On the first of his two visits to London, Lee and the delegation he came with spoke in the crypt of St Martin-in-the-Fields. The session was packed with predominantly young, idealistic Hong Kong people who had come from all over Britain, many of them having to sit in an adjoining corridor and listen to the speeches through a crackling improvised public address system. Outside the church angry banners denounced Britain for selling out Hong Kong. How heartening it was to see such common purpose, and how sad that it was focused on such now-or-never defeatism!

In Hong Kong, the drama and agitation continued. During the two-day Legco debate, crowds of demonstrators sat in front of the council building cheering and chanting and taunting arriving and departing councillors. In the chamber, the divisiveness that had by now characterized its activities and, by extension, the city's life, was reflected in barely disguised invective. Szeto Wah, elected to the council by the teachers' union, expressed his view of the govern-ment in a stinging analogy: 'If you had noticed,' he said, 'I haven't called the government a lame duck – for charitable reasons. Now I am warning you that an animal will come: a short-sighted furless rat in a woollen coat.'

In their attempts to find increasingly more colourful terms to describe the White Paper, the democrats failed to notice that their staunchly conservative colleagues were equally unhappy with the document. Helmut Sohmen, Y.K. Pao's son-in-law, summed up the views of big business as a whole when he portrayed the White Paper as a step sideways into a blind alley, not The Way Forward, as it was subtitled. Moderates such as Professor C.K. Poon who tried to urge the chamber to take a broader view were largely ignored.

The debate ended with Martin Lee calling for and getting a division – itself an unprecedented development in the history of the Council – on his amendment 'regret(ting) the government's decision to introduce partial direct elections to the Legislative Council in 1988'. It was defeated by a vote of forty-two to eight. Ten councillors had walked out. As for the government's main motion, of the forty-three councillors who spoke, thirty-five had supported it. On the Sunday following the debate, Lee ritually burnt a copy of the White Paper and, together with 500 demonstrators, marched on Government House to lodge a list of demands. Among these was the insistence that the elections to the Legislative Council scheduled for the autumn of 1988 should be carried out by direct ballot.

Since then, attention and fears have shifted inexorably from the question of electoral reform to the formulation of the Basic Law, the first draft of which was published in late April 1988. But the points of concern are largely the same. Those who had advocated direct elections in order that Hong Kong might maintain its quasi-independence were amongst the first to highlight section after section of the draft that might violate this semi-autonomy. In their rush to look for loopholes and inconsistencies, they help to fuel the doubts and misgivings that already plague the population and encourage the spread of a siege mentality: the concerns raised by the draft of the Basic Law are the same as those prompted by the Joint Declaration nearly four years earlier. Can a British system of common law be preserved? Will Hong Kong people be allowed to rule themselves? Will there be a clear enough division between China's socialism and the Hong Kong SAR's capitalism? In one form or another these questions have been repeated *ad nauseam* ever since.

The restatement of such fears has a demoralizing and alienating effect which encourages comparatively small concerns to snowball into major crises. The difficulties the present Governor, Sir David Wilson, has had in stamping his authority on the post he assumed in April 1987 stem from distrust of Britain's motives in the Sino-British negotiations, a distrust that has been compounded by the pall of secrecy hanging over the talks. Before his appointment to replace the late Sir Edward Youde, Wilson had been a key member of the negotiating team and, most recently, head of the British component of the Joint Liaison Group. The delay in announcing his appointment had in itself generated a sense of unease in the colony. Margaret Thatcher and her administration, it was said, had 'pressing business' to take care of before turning their attention to the governorship.

'What could be more pressing than the fate of five and a half million people?' one disgruntled Hong Kong resident asked me at the time. As soon as the decision to appoint Wilson was reached, he held a televised press conference in London with a selection of Hong Kong's press corps by way of a satellite link-up. His pale, inscrutable half-smiling image shone down upon the congregated reporters, answering questions as a practised diplomat might, speaking eloquently while saying very little. In the course of the interview he was asked the question that was on many lips: if there was a conflict of interest between Hong Kong and the British Government, which side could count on his loyalty? Wilson's answer, which neatly side-stepped the issue by referring to his overriding loyalty to the Queen, was in a sense immaterial. For many of those who were watching, the question was a way of telling the new Governor his actions would be carefully scrutinized.

A year later, his achievements and failures were assessed by the *South China Morning Post*. The crumpled white ceremonial uniform he wore on arrival in April 1987, the article said, summed up his 'image problem': 'he always seemed to be more a diplomat than a Governor'. During his year in office, it went on, there had been growing loss of faith in the government and thousands of people had chosen to show their doubts by emigrating, producing an alarming brain drain. This had created tensions in a society that 'does not know where to turn for leadership'. The Governor himself had done little in the way of establishing a sense of direction: 'During his highly publicised walkabouts to the factories, housing estates and schools around the territory. . . , he has still not shaken the image of an interested tourist who just happened to drop in.'

To Wilson's credit, Sino-British relations had never been better, but this in itself was viewed with deep suspicion. After all, had not Lord MacLehose made a point of charting the increasingly amicable relations between China and Britain in his yearly 'state of the colony' reports? The Joint Liaison Group, too, was progressing with 'work-manlike efficiency', but here again the wall of confidentiality which effectively screened their work did nothing to reassure the population.

Wilson's failures were rather more tangible. The Governor had achieved little in the haggling over Hong Kong's share of its defence costs. Equally, Wilson was regarded as having been unable to do anything about Britain's weakness in the face of Chinese pressure over direct elections. Even more serious than these two criticisms was Wilson's handling of the Vietnamese boat people. He is seen as having failed to persuade the United Kingdom to increase its quota of Vietnamese refugees, thus minimizing the chances that other host countries will raise theirs and saddling Hong Kong with a hard core of stranded and unwanted people, whose housing, feeding and administrative costs must be borne by the Hong Kong taxpayer.

Ironically, Wilson also played an important part in making Hong Kong a magnet for these refugees. From the fall of South Vietnam in 1975 to the end of 1977, the number of boat people had increased from about 400 to over 21,000. By 1978 there were well over 100,000. Malaysia, Singapore and other Asian states that were popular destinations for the fleeing Vietnamese began to take a hard line on these illegal immigrants, particularly as it became clear that syndicates had begun to exploit the situation by ferrying thousands at a time in large steamers. Hong Kong was confronted with its first test case involving mass transportation in late December 1978, when the *Huey Fong*, with over 3000 refugees on board, anchored just outside the colony's waters. The ship's captain had contacted the Hong Kong Marine Department a few days earlier with the news that he had rescued boatloads of refugees off the South Vietnamese coast. But senior government officials felt strongly that the refugees should not be allowed in, lest this create a precedent and open the door wide to more such arrivals. According to one of the officials involved, the government even went to the lengths of suggesting that these refugees were, in fact, nothing more than opportunists with 'suitcases full of money', denizens of Saigon life. The consensus view was that the ship should be kept outside Hong Kong waters, but visited regularly to check on conditions on board. Once these had become very bad, the authorities would agree to let the refugees in on humanitarian grounds.

After less than a month of this treatment, the *Huey Fong* was allowed into territorial waters. The exclusion policy had been reversed, largely as a result of intervention by Dr David Wilson, then recently appointed as the Governor's adviser. At a meeting of the officials concerned – according to one of those present – Wilson had used 'strong logic and superlative argument' to undermine the government's by then well-established position on the question. In the process he made a mockery of the reasoning of two of its strongest advocates. Consensus crumbled and the amendment he proposed was passed. As the media observed, when the *Huey Fong* disgorged its passengers, most emerged with suitcases in hand looking nothing like the pitiful wretches the public had been led to expect. As a result, there was a massive backlash against the government for weakening on its earlier stance. 'The way Wilson acted,' my informant concluded, 'it wouldn't have been surprising if he had received a 'phone call from London the night before (the meeting) and been told: "this is a potentially embarrassing issue. See that it does not remain so." '

In the first seven months of 1979, over 70,000 refugees arrived in Hong Kong. In 1985 more than 30 per cent of all boat people in south-east Asia were held by Hong Kong, and by the following year over 112,000 Vietnamese had made their way to the colony. It is an unkind twist of fate that a small territory which is increasingly regarding itself as a refugee settlement should be saddled with thousands of refugees, a constant and unwelcome reminder of what Communist rule and its associated material scarcity might bring.

The nature of the Vietnamese presence has changed considerably since I first heard about these people through Indo-Chinese friends, many of whom were themselves illegal immigrants in the late 1970s. The overwhelming majority of refugees then were from South Vietnam, using Hong Kong as a stepping stone on their way to a better life elsewhere. These people stayed in improvised transit camps, from where they had access to the city and an opportunity to do piece-work in nearby factories. In many cases they were positively welcomed by industrialists with an eye to a fresh pool of cheap labour. Refugee agencies, in particular the Intergovernmental Committee for Migration (formerly known as UNHCR, the agency that dealt with the Chinese, Indonesian-Chinese and Russian refugees in the post-war years), worked with commendable efficiency to move their self-appointed charges on to over twenty-five host countries. There was a sense of urgency and vitality then. My Indo-Chinese friends told me excitedly of new arrivals and collected old clothes to pass on to them for their short stay. Some had been old army friends who had fought to the bitter but inevitable end in Vietnam. Stories circulated about some of those waiting to be shifted from the boulevards of Saigon to those of Los Angeles: men who, if these tales were to be believed, had grown accustomed to, and indeed relished, life on the edge.

A hundred thousand souls later, the stragglers now serving their time in the last of the open camps or, for those unlucky enough to arrive after 2 July 1982, in the isolation of closed camps, have neither a colourful life to look back upon nor a promising future to look forward to. Most are from North Vietnam. Many are provincial people without education, marketable skills or knowledge of a European language. The flow of visas to favoured countries such as America, Canada and Australia has become a trickle. A host of reasons why these people cannot be granted speedy resettlement – saturation; worries about national security; that these are 'economic' rather than 'political' refugees; fears about Vietnamese-run crime rings – hide a simple, horrible truth. These human 'dregs' are unwanted because they have nothing to offer except the desperate will to be resettled. Many of those I saw in the camps had been there for three years or more and were still eager to impress visitors and consular officials alike with their threadbare tales of political and religious persecution. Few listen to these tales. When I told my Vietnamese friends that I had visited the camps, their glazed expressions announced that they did not want to hear.

The plight of the boat people is filled with bitter irony for people in Hong Kong appraising their own situation. Each block of the closed camp on the island of Hei Ling Chau (formerly a leper colony) houses about 180 people in curtained-off plywood living areas bunked three high. Beyond the wire fences that surround the concrete compound are rolling green hills, tranquil bays and a brilliant blue sky. There is little to do in the compound itself apart from attending daily language classes, watching generally unintelligible television and wandering about. The meals provided are well balanced but institutionally cooked and regimentally served. The closed camps were intended to serve as a deterrent, to encourage inmates to discourage their family and friends from following them. They were regarded as interim measures, but, much to the frustration and anger of inmates and Hong Kong people alike, they have become what seem to be permanent fixtures. Even so, the refugees refuse to consider Hong Kong as anything but a transit camp; most would rather stay in their temporary purgatory than think seriously of making the territory their home if, as has been hinted from time to time, they were allowed to do so: 'If China takes Hong Kong, that will be the same as living in Vietnam,' a refugee said to my government companion at the Hei Ling Chau camp. 'I would prefer to move on to other countries.'

The certainty of the answer ignored the official's earlier reminder that repatriation might eventually be the only solution to the Vietnamese problem.* Later, the official, an indigenous Chinese, spoke in hurt tones of the adverse publicity that Hong Kong had been subjected to over conditions in the closed camps. Her people, she told me, were deeply conscious of social problems: 'Perhaps we do not see solutions, but we are very aware of the problems. We are willing to face them, to discuss them.'

There were many questions in Hong Kong in those days, but very few answers. Not even the territory's normally sparkling young people seemed immune to the mood of self-doubt. In the run-up to Chinese New Year in 1987, posters began to appear everywhere advertising the film *Legend of Wisely*, an expensive production set in exotic locations and filled with high-tech, glamour and fight scenes. These features, as well as the presence of superstar Samuel Hui, should have been enough to shatter box-office records, but the film was only moderately well received. *Legend of Wisely*'s downfall was that it could be seen as an allegory of transitional Hong Kong. In it, Hui portrays a suave adventurer, explorer and popular writer, completely at home in foreign settings and with foreign ways. He is, in short, the consummate image of modern Hong Kong Man. The plot revolves around a frantic and improbable chase through Nepal, Hong Kong and Egypt for a magical 'dragon pearl' (itself a twin image of Hong Kong).

The film is loaded with the imagery of diaspora. Almost all the action occurs outside Hong Kong and, when the territory does appear, it is presented as a ghost town. Even the inevitable panorama of Hong Kong Island, past which the adventurer sails in his yacht en route to Egypt, is not the typically brightly-lit, bustling image that usually appears in films. The peaks are shrouded in cloud; the neon lights of the city barely break through the blue-grey dusk. Like the film, Hong Kong continues to chase after its own 'dragon pearl'. This is a search that neither Britain nor China can fully appreciate, for it is filled with paradoxes and conundrums that the people of Hong Kong themselves are not able to resolve. In the meantime, the queues at the doors of the consulates grow longer, nurturing seeds of doubt in the minds of those who had earlier committed themselves to stay. The result is a society working frantically toward a future that it also fears and cannot comprehend.

This endemic wariness of the future has made the task of administering Hong Kong more difficult. One reason has already been high-

*As the book goes to print repatriation has, indeed, become a reality.

lighted: the routine modernization of laws and regulations is no longer viewed simply in its own terms, but in terms of how the revisions might be used a decade later. There is also the broader problem of how the administration is going to adapt itself to the post-1997 period. Some, if not most, senior British officials in Hong Kong see this as occurring in a purely mechanical way: once the Basic Law has been formulated, and this is scheduled for 1990, the territory's administration will *de facto* begin operating by it. One very senior civil servant considered that this process might even begin with the publication of the draft version of the Basic Law. On the other hand it is enshrined in the Joint Declaration that the governing of Hong Kong is to be a strictly British preserve until the end of June 1997.

This has led to a distancing of Hong Kong officialdom from its Chinese counterpart. At a higher level, communication has been seriously hindered by the controversy over direct elections. For over a year after the publication of the Green and White Papers, the Hong Kong Government had stood firm on the issue of electoral reform in the face of Chinese opposition. In accordance with the spirit of the Joint Declaration, the colony's administration insisted that the reform was an internal matter not open to interference. As a result, there were no channels for informal talks between the Hong Kong authorities and the Chinese Government's local represen- tation. The Chinese authorities made tentative attempts to initiate regular informal discussions at a high level in Hong Kong – some- thing that the British Government had been encouraging for some time – only after an intemperate display by Xu Jiatun in December 1985 over the proposed reforms, and the predictable panic this created in the business sector.

At a lower level, however, the only contact is through formal channels, with links in most departments confined to short recipro- cal visits and, in some cases, seminars. A police inspector told me that such visits in his division had been taking place since 1981, with Chinese officers coming to Hong Kong for five days at a time at six-monthly intervals: 'In ten years that will total over nine months *solid* . . . that's a great deal!'

Many of the 'last train' officers who view 1997 with morbid apprehension would probably not agree. Although such visits may be constructive in a formal sense, they do little to foster relations between individuals and the kind of face to face discussions between civil servants that will give Hong Kong officials the opportunity to reassure *themselves* of their future prospects, working methods and pensions. A delay in initiating such an exercise on a wide scale will attack the very foundations of the civil service. There is already a shortage of competent personnel and the situation will get worse in the next few years. If the younger, more promising officers have no opportunity to establish informal links with their opposite numbers in China, they are likely to draw their own conclusions about the future and take their talents elsewhere. Those who believe that the British always intended to hand over Hong Kong suggest such a desertion is what the government wants. According to this view, the depletion and, more importantly, the weakening of the civil service will continue to produce a shift in power to Legco.

It is from the ranks of the more cynical, those who strongly believe that Britain has 'sold Hong Kong down the river', that a New Realism is gradually emerging. Ironically, this may become the source of real strength in Hong Kong's transitional politics. At the heart of this approach is the renunciation of the defeatist mentality that has already caused so much damage, and a determination to face reality. The New Realists argue that Hong Kong has worked very well for over 140 years of British colonial rule, and could con-tinue largely as it is as a Chinese colony, with a Chinese appointee, preferably one trusted by Beijing, as Chief Executive. Once he is in place, this 'Governor' can be influenced locally and brought around to the territory's way of thinking.

Such a pattern, the New Realists say, has been the way with all former British Governors. And, indeed, it is an approach that is far more in harmony with the ways of China than either a crude form of 'one country, two systems' or a Westminster-style democracy. As an example of mutual accommodation, this school of thought points to Beijing's chief representative in Hong Kong and the changes that he has gone through since he first arrived. When Xu Jiatun first set foot in Hong Kong, he was very insecure, going on demonstrative walkabouts and hiding behind dark glasses. He has subsequently changed greatly. He still lacks refinement, but none the less he has become genuinely aware of local needs and exigencies. The New Realists believe that other officials could also be brought around to Hong Kong's way of thinking, but that this has to be done on the spot, not by sending endless delegations to Beijing to 'educate' its leadership, or by building castles out of scattered Legco bricks. In the past year particularly, this reasoning has become quite persuasive. In an interview in a Chinese journal in early 1988, Xu gave his most polished performance so far in demonstrating his understanding of the capitalist economy and, more importantly, conditions in Hong Kong. When commenting on 'comrades' who had advised China to intervene to stem the alarming slide of the Hong Kong stock market in the October crash, Xu said: 'This illustrates that some of our comrades do not have sufficient knowledge of modern capitalism. One cannot interfere in stock markets and our financial resources cannot support the markets.' His observation that 'capitalism is a great creation of human civilization' and still had room for further development was also likely to warm the heart of many a Hong Kong entrepreneur.

But if the Chinese officials have learned in this period, so too have the New Realists. An important part of their approach involves getting to know Chinese officials as people, learning their ways and weaknesses. A New Realist of considerable wealth and influence told me how he had introduced himself bluntly on his first trip to China as a wealthy capitalist who could leave the colony, but had none the less made it clear that he wanted to find common ground with the Chinese. On subsequent trips he was accompanied by his family and became friendly with some very senior officials. Since then his daughter has become very friendly with a favoured granddaughter of an even more senior official. In the course of his familiarization, this New Realist has come to feel at ease in Beijing, where he hosts parties and, on occasion, stays at some important guesthouses, including the one that Margaret Thatcher stayed in on her trips to Beijing.

Whether such a rational approach can take root in Hong Kong and, more importantly, recreate the consensus rule that characterized the British period is uncertain. Hong Kong society, and especially the middle classes, may already be too divided for that. Also, although they enjoy much quiet support, the New Realists are suspected by some of having gone soft on Communism, or of intending to perpetrate a sell-out of their own.

Hong Kong's survival as a city is not at stake. The departure of both Chinese and foreign capitalists and entrepreneurs from Shanghai did not result in the collapse of that city either. In drawing the Hong Kong/Shanghai parallel, it is worth bearing in mind that Shanghai is *still* the most important, most productive centre of trade and commerce in China. And it is still as crowded and bustling as it was when it was dominated by capitalists. At the same time, its tall elegant buildings suggest that it has been frozen in its heyday, as if it has become a shell. There is no longer that intangible feeling of a productive intermingling of East and West. Hong Kong too may find itself inheriting this twilight status: changed from a window on the world to just another Chinese city.

Further Reading

A book such as this that relies so heavily on personal reminiscences and anecdote must ultimately do so at the expense of political and historical detail and analysis. For the reader who wants to go more deeply into the subject of Hong Kong, I would recommend a number of books. On the early history of the colony, the reader should refer to E.J. Eitel's *Europe in China*, first published by Kelly and Walsh in 1895, and reprinted, with an introduction by Henry Lethbridge, by Oxford University Press in 1983. Also recommended are the two volumes by Geoffrey Robley Sayer, *Hong Kong: Birth, Adolescence, and Coming of Age* (London: Oxford University Press, 1937) and *Hong Kong, 1862-1919* (Hong Kong: Hong Kong University Press, 1975). For its later history, the reader might look to G.B. Endacott and A. Hinton, *Fragrant Harbour: A Short History of Hong Kong* (Hong Kong: Oxford University Press, 1962) and Endacott's *A History of Hong Kong* (Hong Kong: Oxford University Press, 1973). John Luff's *The Hidden Years: Hong Kong 1941-1945* (Hong Kong: South China Morning Post Ltd, 1967) and Endacott's *Hong Kong Eclipse*, edited and with additional material by Alan Birch (Hong Kong: Oxford University Press, 1978) should be consulted for Hong Kong during World War II.

Further reading on Hong Kong's society and politics includes the excellent *Hong Kong: A Society in Transition* (London: Routledge & Kegan Paul, 1969), a collection of essays edited by I.C. Jarvie and Joseph Agassi, and Joseph Y.S. Cheng, ed., *Hong Kong in Transition* (Hong Kong: Oxford University Press, 1986). Henry Lethbridge's *Hong Kong: Stability and Change* provides a collection of essays on a diversity of sociological and historical themes. Endacott's *Government and People in Hong Kong, 1841-1962* (Hong Kong: Hong Kong University Press, 1964) is a useful volume on the territory's constitutional history, as is Norman Miner's *The Government and Politics of Hong Kong* (Hong Kong: Oxford University Press, 1975) on the nuts and bolts of its government. For the Sino-British talks, the late David Bonavia's *Hong Kong 1997: The Final Settlement* (Hong Kong: South China Morning Post, 1985), is the best and clearest study. It also contains the full text of the September 1984 Draft Agreement between Great Britain and the People's Republic of China, and the November 1984 White Paper on electoral reform. An interesting set of readings may also be found in Cheng's *Hong Kong: In Search of a Future* (Hong Kong: Oxford University Press, 1984). Peter Wesley-Smith, *Unequal Treaty, 1898–1997: China, Great Britain and Hong Kong's New Territories* (Hong Kong: Oxford University Press, 1980) provides a thorough exploration of the lease question. For a concise study of Hong Kong's economy, the reader should look at A.J. Youngson, *Hong Kong: Economic Growth and Policy* (Hong Kong: Oxford University Press, 1982).

For the broad spectrum of radical approaches, be they right or left, to the Hong Kong question, see the Hong Kong Research Project's study *Hong Kong: A Case to Answer* (Nottingham: Spokesman Books, 1974). There is also Gregor Benton's *The Hongkong Crisis* (London: 1983). A right-wing interpretation may be found in the Tory MP Robert Adley's book, *All Change Hong Kong* (Poole: Blandford Press, 1984). For a local perspective on Hong Kong's society and politics there is the pressure group Hong Kong Observers' book, *Pressure Points: A Social Critique by the Hong Kong* (Hong Kong: Summerson Eastern Publishers, second edition, 1983). There is also an enlightening set of six studies written by John Walden, a former senior civil servant, entitled: *Excellency, Your Gap is Showing!* (Hong Kong: Corporate Communication Ltd, 1983).

Index